Violent Inheritance

Violent Inheritance

*Sexuality, Land, and Energy in Making
the North American West*

E Cram

UNIVERSITY OF CALIFORNIA PRESS

University of California Press
Oakland, California

© 2022 by E Cram

Library of Congress Cataloging-in-Publication Data
    Names: Cram, E (Emily), author.
    Title: Violent inheritance : sexuality, land, and ener gy in making
the North American West / E Cram.
    Other titles: Environmental communication, power, and culture ; 3.
    Identifiers: LCCN 2021048511 (print) I LCCN 2021048512 (ebook)
I ISBN 9780520379466 (cloth) I ISBN 9780520379473 (paperback) I
ISBN 9780520976757 (epub)
    Subjects: LCSH: Queer theory—Rocky Mountains. I Violence—
Environmental aspects—Rocky Mountains. I Sex—Rocky Moun-
tains—Environmental aspects. I Colonists—Sexual behavior—Rocky
Mountains. I Landscape archaeology. I Sexual minority community—
Rocky Mountains.
    Classification: LCC HQ75.16.U6 C725 2022 (print) I LCC
HQ75.16.U6 (ebook) I DDC 306.76010978—dc23/eng/20211109
    LC record available at https://lccn.loc.gov/2021048511
    LC ebook record available at https://lccn.loc.gov/2021048512

31 30 29 28 27 26 25 24 23 22
10 9 8 7 6 5 4 3 2 1

To those who, despite all odds,
work toward a more environmentally just world

In memory of
Daniel C. Brouwer and
John Frederick Cram

Contents

Figures

Preface

Rooted Kinship

Some inheritances feel like unwelcome debts. As my father and I tumbled along dusty Wyoming highways in the summer of 2010, I began to consider how a sense of place could be challenged by relationships to the land and the environment that supposedly root cultural belonging. Land and *feeling* attached to that land as westerners pervade most stories throughout the West, from travelogues to memoir to headline news. On the road, our automobility afforded by fossil fuel infrastructure, we followed the imprints of military expeditions, the names of settler victors inscribed into the land with concrete markers. All these infrastructures and technologies produced spaciousness as an orientation, a map, a feeling. We were at the start of a regional memory tour, getting lost in the grip the land took on our bodies: howling wind, the passage of an imminent thunderstorm on the horizon through our nostrils, the steady hum and vibration of tires meeting the friction of highway asphalt or dirt roads. Although the distance of decades separated me from these queer childhood archives, the urgency of returning to these roadways seemed clear. To question the production of that affective attachment to "openness" is to ground spaciousness as a feeling rooted in violence. Moreover, it opened the possibility of rooting stories and memory within the vast infrastructure that made normative inheritance feel so natural.

As we moved along Interstate 80 in southeastern Wyoming, the prairie flew by my body while I sat docile in the passenger side of that silver

Ford Ranger, holding my gaze outside the window. The prairie spun into circles when the speedometer reached seventy-five miles per hour, and, beneath Johnny Cash's guitar on the radio, I could hear my father's low fading voice murmur, "You know, they say if you really love this place, you have to bury your nose down deep and smell the blood in the soil." My father died seven years later, and in a sense this book is an attempt to work through the various stories I have inherited of the region, simultaneously intimately personal and globally connected.

In retrospect there are multiple registers to make sense of my father's words, so emblematic of the way old-timer wisdom has a habit of boiling down words into a single phrase. The invoked "they say," an unknown body of speakers or writers, tapped into a regional consciousness and feeling of living amid a residual past, time pulled through soil and roots by claims to inheritance. In this moment "they say" offered a reflection about attachments to place, an allegory transferred between father and grown child. Knowing my father, who came of age somewhere between the oil patch, a small family farm, and a one-bedroom lean-to in Riverton on the border of the Wind River Reservation, the "blood in the soil" he referenced was an ocean of unmarked graves from the centuries of nationalist expansion, forced relocation, and settler land grabs. He did not talk in the vocabulary of settler colonialism, or culture or structures for that matter, but his life and mine were articulated through them, most of all through structures of settler familial kinship in the Rocky Mountain American West.

Settler violence embodied by military and corporate expansion (that "blood in the soil") constitute my roots, including the conditions of possibility for a homestead under patents 545866 and 101881 from the General Land Office, in the names of Frederick and Nancy Cram, my great-grandparents.[1] Their homestead in Neble, Wyoming, tethered state and family formation, inscribing violence into both land and kinship. Kim TallBear (Sisseton Oyate), Scott Morgensen, Mark Rifkin, and others argue that settler sexuality systems such as reproductive heterosexual marriage have been central to land-based nation building, settler encroachment, and coercion of Indigenous peoples across North America.[2] When Frederick passed from heart failure, his son John (my grandfather) left school in the eighth grade to manage the homestead. As time passed, his interests turned to the oil and gas boom in Sand Draw: constructing the Northern Utilities pipeline, working in the Sand Draw gas plant, and building a life with Frances, my grandmother.[3] Bisected by draws and washes, Sand Draw is expansive sagebrush desert, supported by higher rims packed by juniper and cedar. Temperatures know only the extremes. Water feels scarce. Many miscarriages later an explosion at the gas plant violently rattled the bones of the small house as they both crouched beneath the oak breakfast table for shelter. Frances declared, "I'm not raising kids in an oil camp." Her defiance moved them to a small farm outside of Riverton, where they farmed, and John Senior supposedly continued prospecting uranium for the Lucky Mac mining project. Frances continued to have miscarriages and stillbirths, the source of her anguish a matter of family disagreement between environmental factors and a so-called incompetent cervix.

Perhaps my father was referencing the most intimate experience of violence in his young life: the trauma of losing a parent. On May 23, 1955, a dull thud of a twelve-gauge shotgun pierced the air, emanating from the washroom at the back of a farmhouse on West Prison Farm Road. A little over half a century later, my father and I passed the family's old farm, stopping at the grand cottonwood tree nestled between that dirt road and barbed wire. Sitting next to him in that silver pickup truck, I could feel his body tense, his voice quiver. That place and the memory of his father's suicide haunted him, but it also seeped into the family tree. His death an open secret, I recall now an assortment of stories that tried to fill a reservoir of the unknown. These included claims to an accident requiring the curative properties of a full body cast, the possibility of debilitating chronic exposure to DDT, or maybe even radioactive exposure from uranium mining.

Stories my father inherited or believed as the deep truths behind an explosive resolution of psychic and physical pain continue to shape my sense of self and of the region. Supposedly, letters were kept but ultimately destroyed before they were read. Be it from the state or from others, I imagine the stories he was told functioned to assuage the stigma associated with incapacitating pain and white rural manhood. The state's "official" cause of death: self-inflicted gunshot wound, due to a five- to six-month span of "mental depression" from "male menopause." We always want something from the archive of evidence, don't we?

Even still, the possibility of extractive industries writing the life and death of my grandfather didn't change the later fact that my father, too, would live a life adjacent to the energy industry. Because of his decision to continue a life enmeshed in regulatory structures, the formative places of my queer and trans life were consequences of my father's path through fossil fuels and governing bodies, a life cycle of booms, busts, and fast exits. This book also is an attempt to grapple with those contradictions: remembering not just systems of violence that are part of my inheritance but also how the atmospheres of this region generate affects of longing, desire, and healing.

Tracing the rooted kinship of my own family of origin brings me to a space of reckoning in the interstices of state and family, routed through the reproducing structures of settler colonialism. It would be impossible to think about my relationship to the Rocky Mountain region without considering the force of "the family" as an immediate domain of sexual governance in U.S. settler culture. Beyond the obvious spatialities of the homestead or, later, the private domestic home, this relational form stretches into space through settler practices such as "family vacation," the "family car," and "family camping." It is its own kind of inheritance that queer studies has challenged as an object of both abolition and re-invention.[4] The form of the heterononormative white settler family unit is a consequence of and a violent legacy enmeshed in making a national landscape.

At the center of this familial form was an obsession with the optimism wrought by bodily energy, a critical dimension of the racialization of sexualities in the turn of the twentieth century. From stories about the electrifying atmospheres of nineteenth-century Colorado to the invention of tall tales fetishizing the vital energy of white settlers, narratives of sexuality and the western region illuminate an environmental theory of modern sexuality as partly enmeshed in the capacity building conditions of western climates. Simultaneously, the region as it exists today was made through weaponizing that land for conditions of forced confinement, under the eugenic auspices that particular environments and spatial design would sever familial ties and that exposure to remote environments would facilitate assimilation into the national body.

Even now I'll never know exactly whose blood occupied my father's sentiment. Maybe he meant military violence. Maybe it was from stories he still felt he couldn't share. I don't remember exactly when I started to filter these experiences and question through my childhood queerness, but doing so rattled me, as I feigned interest at every new encounter with monuments to victors of war. Here too I learned a steady art of disassociation, of dwelling within my mind's frenetic energy to learn to be with the clouds, the aspen, and worlds beyond the horizon. As I would realize in the final weeks of writing this book, the land and sky, the water and dry breezes, took care of me as I moved through depths of despair and so many other queer feelings I did not have a language for at the time.

So, in rethinking energy through sexuality, this book is an intellectual reckoning with queer decolonial ecologies guiding the way. Queer decolonial ecologies make space for imagining modes of living that fundamentally challenge the reproductive time of infrastructural whiteness and settler futurity. Memory cultures of violence so often are responsible for the flourishing of settler life; still, what worlds become possible by sitting with that beckoning "to bury your nose down deep and smell the blood in the soil" and then to ask the enduring question that remains: What can be done with violent inheritances?

Acknowledgments

This book has been profoundly shaped and nourished by the geographies, kinships, and intellectual communities I've inhabited throughout my life. Writing in a moment of planetary duress, I am most grateful to the lands and waters surrounding the Rocky Mountains, for holding breath, memory, eros, kin, heartache, healing, questions, and struggle. This book also would not be possible without the interlocutors who trusted me to witness with them and hear their stories. I give sincere thanks to Friends of Minidoka and many elders who remain anonymous. A thank you goes to so many unnamed queer and trans folks who invited me to listen to their stories. A most special thank you goes to Pinar and So of Queer Nature. All royalties from this book will be redistributed on a rotating basis to Friends of Minidoka and, on request of Pinar and So, the All Nations Gathering Center, Ancestral Lands Project, and Native Women's Wilderness, in addition to mutual aid for Indigenous water and land defenders. If this book moves you, I hope you will do the same.

I formally started this project about a decade ago in Bloomington, Indiana, though its seeds were planted much earlier. Researching and writing this book, originally imagined as a deep dive into geographies of feeling and violence, have deepened and stretched my own difficult relationship to the place that raised me. Though the process was difficult at times, I have also been guided by past and present energies of environmental justice work and all of those audacious to dream of a just transition and more livable future.

At the University of Iowa, my department homes in Communication Studies and in Gender, Women's, and Sexuality Studies provide intellectual support and nourishment. I can't imagine my professional life here without the administrative brilliance of Jacquie Albrecht in Communication and Laura Kastens in GWSS. My department chairs, Tim Havens, Kembrew McLeod, Leslie Schwalm, and Rachel Williams, have each served a pivotal mentoring role. I am extraordinarily lucky to share intellectual space with my rhetoric colleagues Natalie Fixmer-Oraiz, Ji-yeon Kang, and David Supp-Montgomerie, whose meals, friendship, mentorship, and listening labor have pushed and grounded me in the best of ways. Prior to his departure Darrel Wanzer-Serrano was a hallway interlocutor, an endless resource of dad jokes and unsolicited tech advice. Conversations about infrastructure with Jenna Supp-Montgomerie reminded me of the deep joy that comes with collaboration. In the project's early stages, Tyler Snelling provided helpful research assistance. Morgan DiCesare was invaluable in her support and research assistance in the book's final stages.

My GWSS colleagues inspire me every day. Naomi Greyser in particular has given so much brilliant labor to this project—from its earliest and roughest edges to my four-hour Book Ends workshop and to the almost weekly writing solidarity at the tables of Prairie Lights and the writing closely at a distance during a global pandemic. My colleagues in GWSS have provided mentorship, deep solidarity, and reminders of the brilliance of feminist community. A thank you goes to Corey Creekmur, Meenakshi Gigi Durham, Aniruddha Dutta, Brady G'Sell, Lisa Heineman, Meena Khandelwal, Teresa Mangum, Lina-Maria Murillo, Kristy Nabhan-Warren, Leslie Schwalm, and Rachel Williams.

Teresa Mangum and the Obermann Center for Advanced Studies have provided substantial support for the research and writing of this book. In the winter of 2017, I workshopped an early version of the introduction with POROI. In the summer of 2019, the Obermann's newly imagined Book Ends workshop afforded a four-hour book workshop with four senior scholars, a truly pivotal experience. The staff at the Obermann, Erin Hackathorn and Jennifer New, deserve special recognition for making the coordination of this experience feel seamless. In the fall of 2020, I gathered virtually with a group of Obermann residential fellows to support ongoing revisions to the manuscript.

For environmental humanities scholarship to thrive, institutional support is vital. The Graduate College at Indiana University supported parts of my fieldwork through small grants, as did small research funds for visiting assistant professors at Saint Lawrence University. At the University of Iowa, I was afforded a pretenure leave to complete final revisions, and a Dean's Micro-Grant helped me adjust to the context of the 2020 pandemic. In addition to the Book Ends program, the Obermann Center's residential fellows program provided funds for final editing.

My earliest mentors at Indiana University generously supported my research and fostered an incomparable intellectual environment. I am grateful for the time and energy of Alex Doty (rest in power), Ilana Gershon, Mary Gray, Robert Ivie, and Robert Terrill. John Louis Lucaites saw potential in this project from its roughest edges, supporting me in my effort to take on an ambitious challenge while asking me the most difficult questions and listening while I tried to find my footing. Phaedra C. Pezzullo's brilliance and early encouragement pushed me to fall down rabbit holes and chase otherwise inarticulate connections between sexuality and environment and guided me toward intellectual communities whose perspective has been life changing. She has worn many hats since we first met, and her commitment to this work has been a true gift. Ted Striphas introduced me to the work of Raymond Williams, passing on in turn his generosity and excitement for the value of cultural studies more broadly. Through Indiana's Department of Gender Studies, I met Colin Johnson. So much of my thinking has been shaped by our simply delightful conversations about environment and sexuality. I am most grateful for his generosity and wit. Indiana University's Queering the Countryside workshop, organized by Mary and Colin in 2010, nourished my thinking and planted seeds for this project. Finally, Susan Stryker revolutionized my thinking about somatechnics.

Over the course of my career, I have met so many brilliant people whose encouragement and support has come through conversations in conference lobbies, dinner tables, and more formal spaces. CMCLers have stayed together despite it all: Jeff Bennett, Lisa Braverman, Byron Craig, Suzanne Enck, Eric Harvey, Melanie Loehwing, Jeff Motter, Rudo Mudiwa, Norma Musih, James Paasche, Justin Rawlins, Claire Sisco King, and Darrel Wanzer-Serrano. In particular I deeply value the mentorship of Isaac West, who has been a source of damning wit and honesty since my earliest days as a PhD student. Isaac's friendship has supported me through the frustration of shifting this project from a

dissertation to a book, always in a spirit of frankness and generosity. At
Saint Lawrence University, Erik Johnson encouraged me to write when
I was overwhelmed by my first academic position.

In addition to those mentioned earlier, within the world of rhetoric,
I have found an intellectual community who has embraced my weird-
ness, including Rob Asen, Dan Brouwer, Caitlin Bruce, Karma Chávez,
Catalina de Onís, Cara Finnegan, Lisa Flores, Constance Gordon, An-
nie Hill, Maine Writing Group (Jean Bassette, Peter Campbell, David
Cisneros, Diane Keeling, Tom Nakayama, and Nathan Stormer), Chuck
Morris, Tiara Na'puti, Catherine Palczewski, Erin Rand, K.J. Rawson,
Mary Stuckey, and Armond Towns. In particular Chuck Morris is a
steadfast interlocutor and a model of generosity to which I aspire. In the
summer of 2021, we lost Dan Brouwer. He was a wellspring of so much
guidance, support, listening, laughter, electric charm, and ease. I still
cannot fathom the field and world without him. Catherine Palczewski
is responsible for much of this book, in that as my MA adviser she encouraged me to pursue a PhD in rhetorical studies. Always an avid mentor and confidant, she has become a wonderful friend. Finally, though
not in NCA proper (gasp), ongoing conversations with Greg Seigworth
have sustained me, calling me home to cultural studies and reminding
me what intellectual home feels like.

A number of people read early drafts of this manuscript at key mo-
ments. With Book Ends I was afforded four wonderful hours of at-
tention and conversation with the incomparable Naomi Greyser, Dana
Luciano, Kembrew McLeod, and Greg Seigworth. Constance Gordon,
Colin Johnson, and Tom Nakayama each provided critical suggestions.
At Indiana a gender studies writing group graciously moved through
emerging ideas. A thank you goes to Jae Basiliere, Nick Clarkson, Susan
Eckelmann, Katie Schweighofer, and Dillon Vrana. In Iowa a Friday
Writing Party group gathered amid crowded tables and caffeinated am-
biance at Prairie Lights Café, always emanating solidarity on days good
and bad. Thanks go to Natalie Fixmer-Oraiz, Naomi Greyser, Andy
High, Jiyeon Kang, Rachel McLaren, David Supp-Montgomerie, and
Jenna Supp-Montgomerie.

Although I completed nearly all of the fieldwork during my dissertation research, much of the archival work and thinking of the project
is new. An earlier version of chapter 2 appears in "Archival Ambience
and Sensory Memory: Generating Queer Intimacies in the Settler Colonial Archive," *Communication and Critical/Cultural Studies* 13, no. 2
(2016): 109–29.

At the University of California Press, Stacy Eisenstark saw this book through all the challenges of academic life during COVID-19, moving it to its successful publication. Naja Pulliam Collins facilitated this book's move toward production and has my endless gratitude. Lyn Uhl stewarded this project in its very early stages and was an avid mentor. I thank Susan Silver for her work copyediting the final manuscript. Cathy Hannabach and Ideas on Fire provided both editing and indexing support. I am also indebted to the anonymous reviewers who supported this project and pushed me to make this book the best version of itself. I am beyond grateful for the interdisciplinary vision Phaedra C. Pezzullo and Salma Monani have given this series and their commitment to an environmental cultural studies that values race, sexuality, and disability as truly indispensable. This work and the community generated by this book series provide deep sustenance at a profoundly difficult time for those who care about climate, energy, and environmental justice.

My dear friend, Tiffany St. Bunny, very generously provided the photograph for the book cover, capturing a mood of white, western spaces that she and I talked about at length when our paths crossed in Bloomington, Indiana.

My care web, friends, and families, given and chosen, have tended for me amid illness and change over the years and across the miles. Their care made writing this possible, especially amid the all too many devastating losses we have sustained individually and collectively. I send much gratitude to Leah Allen, M Barclay, Anna Blaedel, Jorge Castillo, Kyle Cheesewright, Chris Crowe, Bunny, Kat, Natalie and V Fixmer-Oraiz, Constance Gordon, Jiyeon Kang, Renee McGarry, Leila Walker, Tiara Na'puti, Risa Puleo, Brian and Hena Shah-DeLong, and Jess Waggoneer. In particular Tiara's long friendship provides a constant source of humor; her long-distance support through the everyday to career changes to the heaviest losses has truly been a profound gift. During the intensity of COVID semesters, Zoom writing with Constance was life changing and clarifying. She is a vital comrade and interlocutor, and my gratitude for our friendship is deep and profound. I would like to thank my family of origin, who helped me fill in what I could not remember: Rob Cram, Sherry Cram, Travis Cram, and Amy Cram Helwich. My four-legged babies embody queer kinship everyday: Bowie, Finn, Rilo (rest in power), and Sappho (rest in power). I wrote parts of this book in the early mornings at my parents' home in Cheyenne, sitting at the kitchen table before long days spent in hospice with my father, John Cram. I wish he could read this so that he knew I was listening, in my own way.

Introduction

Land Lines of Violent Inheritance

Exact knowledge of the causes and conditions of development of sexual aberrations, and of the influence on them of
heredity constitution, education, the impressions of every-day
life, and modern refined civilization, is the prerequisite for a
rational prophylaxis of sexual aberrations, and for a correct
sexual education.

—Charles Gilbert Chaddock, translator of *Psychopathia Sexualis*, 1893

But not alone to these suffering with pulmonary affections
has the climate of Colorado proven a blessing. It is coming to
be recognized more and more that nearly all chronic diseases
do far better in the high, dry altitude of the Rocky Mountain
region than in the lower and more humid atmosphere of the
east and south. This is particularly true with those whose
vital energies are at a low ebb. There is an exhilaration in the
climate which awakens to new life the dormant powers.

—*Colorado Sanitarium Bulletin*, November 1902

What does it mean to route "sexuality" through modernity's relationship to energy? For John Harvey Kellogg, a medical doctor and eugeni-
cist who fervently believed in the combined forces of nature and science
for enlivening hereditary constitution, energy was something to be har-
nessed from climate and transferred somatically. Similar to many reformers of his time, Kellogg believed poor climate and vice contributed
to a rapid rise of degenerate behavior, threatening bodily stores of vital
energy presumed in his time to be a key component of racial hierarchy.
To those gathered in the parlor of his Battle Creek Michigan Sanitarium
in early January 1897, he delivered his lecture, "Why We Are Cripples,"
repeating his philosophy of individual hygiene while clarifying the role

of "nature" and "climate" in producing white racial deterioration. He boisterously declared, "Man has more natural endurance...more real constitutional vigor...than any other animal that lives, and it is because of this wonderful toughness of constitution that a human being is able to live. It is not because of the bad conditions of life over which we have no control...that we deteriorate, but by reason of our evil habits."[1] Although Kellogg announced his affinity for many of the key ideas of dominant evolution theorists, he repeatedly affirmed a predominantly spiritual orientation to the energetic force of nature. Distinguishing himself from the British sociologist and Darwinist Herbert Spencer, whom he believed left "little room for faith in science," Kellogg emphasized divine intelligence as the central driver of natural and racial order. Kellogg believed he could work to harness energy of the divine as it traveled through a series of converter chains: emanating from the original point of the sun downward to plant material and later converted into food. Kellogg believed that herbage, like some kind of solar monument, would deliver energy to humans, making brains, thoughts, and bodies.[2] In his speech Kellogg charts a racial theory of vital energy: a desire for hereditary-based acquisition made possible through the command of elaborate chains of production and consumption. In short, his theory routed race through *nature* as energetic value.

Just two years prior to these series of sanitarium lectures, Kellogg's health philosophies and treatment regimens migrated westward to a Rocky Mountain settlement of fifteen thousand at the urging of John Fulton, a member of the Seventh Day Adventist Church.[3] Located at the base of a mountain range, the Colorado Sanitarium in Boulder provided many of the marvel technologies and nutritional guidance lauded by its institutional origin in south Michigan. But what made this resort different was its proximity to the idealized climate often romanticized by Kellogg. At the crux of his plea, Fulton tapped into the location's supposedly unique therapeutic capacities for restoring bodily vigor, especially those claims circulated by Denver Boosters and medical climatologists who promised access to stimulating air, abundant sun, and pure water from lakes and streams surrounding scattered settlements in the Front Range. Written for prospective health seekers, the sanitarium bulletin marveled of the air as an "invigorating life-giving elixir," declaring that "the very atmosphere seems charged with electricity."[4] The promise of innervation, or the invigoration of vital capacity, through the generative qualities of remarkable water, air, altitude, and dramatic vistas created a powerful image for boosters longing to draw health seekers to western climates.

For white elites western climates also offered an "electric" answer to the energetic problem of sexual degeneracy, a catchall for the "crimes against nature" believed to emanate from the social milieu of urban infrastructures and tropical climates. The snapshot of Kellogg offers one of many examples of how moral reformers, cultural producers, political actors, and members of the scientific class were keen to understand the linkages of climate and sexual degeneracy. Careful anthropological study of climate's influence, many believed, promised to unlock the so-called laws of nature so central to racial theories of vitality. In the opening epigraph, from one of the principal texts of sexology, Charles Gilbert Chaddock implores careful study of "exact knowledge" and "conditions" generating sexual aberration that throw the sexual reproduction of racial order into crisis. Reflecting on queer theory's discomfort with the power of environmental thinking in sexological texts, Benjamin Kahan forwards these kinds of climatic frameworks as critical to a "historical etiology" of sexuality. In this way sexuality is less about subjectivity and more about the intellectual systems, historical processes, and spaces that contribute to *making* a theory of sexuality.[5] We can understand this climatic theory from Chaddock, Kellogg, and others as a critical moment wherein anxieties about climate and energy infused the "patterns, models, and categories of sexuality," as Kahan argues, without aligning our own allegiance to etiology as a matter of truth.[6]

While recovering the intellectual systems that rendered climate and environment a critical dimension in the production of theories of sexuality, queer studies must also take up dimensions of *energy*, perhaps *the* dominant relationship between humans and the environment. How culture shapes desires for and the acquisition of energy is a sweeping one, largely taken up by the environmental humanities. Energy cultures linger in elaborate chains of acquisition, production, conversion, and consumption. These windows into the world of the sanitarium illuminate not just energetic metaphors enlivening desire for the region but a picture of "health" constituted by technologies of vital capacity and the ability to generate raced energy, enhanced and invigorated through elemental exposure: sun, water, and air as resources for individual absorption.[7] This story is in turn one of a somatic energy system premised on already existing extractive relationships, values, and structures. The story of the Colorado Sanitarium helps to highlight how those ideas of environmental degeneracy migrated to the western region, wherein climate itself was imagined as a *technology* of racial and sexual vitality production.

We might tell any number of stories about sexuality's entanglement with energy, though I start with Kellogg and the Colorado Sanitarium because it so clearly brings into relief a chain of consumption and production wherein calls for racial and sexual vitality converge with extractivism. Whereas the sun, water, and air operate as elements with powers to *extract* and convert into bodily vitality, *extractivism* refers to the "cultural and ideological rationale that either motivates extraction or is the consequence of it."[8] Both the practice and rationale help discern how value in different historical moments is generated for shifting conditions of racial capitalism. So we might interpret health seeking in the region at the turn of the twentieth century as shaped by particular logics of extractivism: the energy optimism that maps the West for endless capitalist value, the need to *enclose* that energy through regimes of property, and the sexual and racialized theories of energy shaping discourses of vitality from political elites and the scientific class. Speaking solely in terms of periodization, the emergence of "sexuality" as a modern regime of subjectivation accompanied another formative shift on the planet: the making of "petromodernity," an age accelerating the extraction, refinement, and consumption of fossil fuels.[9] All these together make up logics, systems, and environmental traces of residual violence to compose a profoundly violent inheritance for the planet today.

Returning to the opening question, then, this book's goal is to think broadly across these two unwieldy shifts and their ecological inheritance to, first, reimagine the place of racialized sexualities in contemporary conversations about environment, energy, and systems of violence. Second, I anchor these questions in contested memory cultures of the North American West—a region so central to the development of North American energy extraction, racial capitalism, and imaginations of vitality. Drawing from four places in the region, I trace the evolution of extractivism from the turn of the twentieth century, to show how its "inheritance" is not inert or uncontested but alive and ongoing. Amid a region at the forefront of what just environmental futures might become possible, encounters with the social archives of violence can contest the reproduction of extractivism as a modern mode of living. This is what me might call a struggle over what we inherit, specifically the relationships between culture, energy, and, yes, even sexuality. But to apprehend these connections, we have to denaturalize myths of the region and the stories we tell about sexuality.

Violent Inheritance: Sexuality, Land, and Energy in Making the

North American West contends that patterns of administratively assigning racial and sexual value to the production of *innervation* and *enervation*—revitalization and exhaustion—necessitates another story of sexual modernity. Long provoking sexuality and queer studies, "sexual modernity" generally speaks to a historical conjuncture that facilitated the dissemination and proliferation of discourses of sex and the body, largely responsible for making a possessive and "modern" sexual subject. Self-disciplined, singular, and oriented toward progress, the modern subject supposedly marshaled interior capacities to adhere to a matrix of power dispersed through the proliferation of classifications of perversion. For Michel Foucault, "sexual modernity" also enabled mapping particular logics of sexuality: "to ensure population, to reproduce *labor capacity,* to perpetuate the form of social relations: in short, to constitute *a sexuality that is economically useful* and politically conservative."[10] Foucault's speculative question here offers a stunning revelation of implicit logics of energy in his account of "sexuality" as one dimension of biopower and biopolitics. If we take energy to mean the transformation of matter into its *usefulness,* then what he calls "sexual modernity" could be helpful to trace environmental and energetic domains of sexuality. The challenge here is rooting capacity as an environmental term. Otherwise, the stories lost in our account of sexual modernity are distributed forms of racialized labor and environmental resources produced to fashion this vision of autonomous white settler self making. In other words, what we lose is an understanding of sexual modernity's place in making contemporary *extractivism.*

As a whole, I argue for an energetic and ecological theory of "sexual modernity," tarried between the intimate scale of the body to global energy regimes. In doing so I confront the relative absence of energy analytics in queer studies more broadly. One exception includes *vitality,* that multivalent word I've used to reference discourses of race and sexual degeneracy so important to Foucault's conceptualization of biopower and biopolitics. Vitality also shimmers across queer intrigue of the lively capacities of matter so often maligned as "dull" or "unlively" by human-centrism or sometimes may challenge hierarchies of life and death altogether.[11] And though it is accurate that we will not find in Foucault's oeuvre a reference to fossil fuels or energy systems as we imagine them in contemporary terms, his preoccupation with vitality as a dimension of sexuality presents a much needed opportunity to reexamine vitality's environmental making.[12] Consequentially, this book develops a set of vocabularies for mapping sexuality within extractivist energy regimes and draws on their contemporary mediation in contested memory cultures of the West's inheritance as a region wrought with contestation.

To think sexuality through an energy regime means grappling with the historical, social, technological, and economic relationships that structure value regimes of capacity.[13] By "energy regime," I'm referencing a term from the energy humanities that helps us think through various "ages" of energy, such as "the age of fossil fuels" or its shorthand, petromodernity. Regimes are made in part through abundant interconnections of specific *resources* (say, the sun, horses, coal, petroleum, wind, and water, among others), their respective technologies of acquisition and materialization, and elaborate delivery systems.[14] But this technical vocabulary can quickly shift into unwieldy territory, so the specific *social* dimensions of energy matters most for my own engagement.[15] By *social* I reference energy humanities' well-treaded ground of the values, stories, and ideologies that make *possible or desirable* the transformation of matter into capitalist value, to meet the needs for the so-called good life.[16] But this book makes clear how queer studies, in addition to the energy and environmental humanities, cannot leave behind energy's intersection with structures of settler sexual modernity. I discuss this term with greater depth later in this introduction, but it refers to interlocking though contested political processes by which settler states regulate indigeneity to produce "elimination" of "Native as Native," through laws regarding marriage, gender, and reprosexual kinship.[17] Far from race neutral, the linkage of energy regime, sexuality, and land offers maps to communicate relationships scattered, emplaced, or forgotten across time and space. This book thus considers the multitude of ways one might dwell, inhabit, and feel through the violent inheritance of this energy's periods of renewal, adaptation, and contestation. Inheritance bears recursive layers of residual violence.

From the standpoint of the contemporary present, *Violent Inheritance* dwells in the nonlinear traces of this regime's enduring materiality and sedimentation: the ecological, energetic, and affective inheritance of what I call "land lines." As a concept that grasps the connections between the regime, sexual modernity, and the affective and material conditions in making the North American West, land lines function as this work's primary key term and method. As a key term, it points to key sites of racialization and state violence wherein political and economic actions *tether,* or forge connections, between domains of sexuality and land use in settler colonial North America, inclusive of enclosures, appropriation, sacrifice zones, and labor. Conceptually, land lines communicate how this nexus of the biopolitical and land forge a different understanding of the relations of energy and power in the region and the continent more broadly. What we find, then, is a concept that names the aggregation of layers of cultural sediment or the violent inheritance of any given place. Land lines evoke a temporal trace that mediates settler whiteness and ecological affect. As a method, to *trace* land lines asks in earnest how places of memory and memorialization mediate these relationships, what kind of attachments they foster, and, fundamentally, how in situ encounters might invite grappling with what one can do with archives of violence in the present to collaboratively foster more just environmental futures.

Inheritance offers a communicative dimension of accessing and moving through this energy regime through a knot of ecological feeling, archived or curated stories, and the mnemonic power of the environment. The environmental and energy humanities have well established how regimes tend toward imperceptibility in their totalities and live within social relationships, cultural imaginations, and modes of historical preservation.[18] By tending to sites of memory contestation throughout the region, land lines become perceptible within the social life of the archive, a communicative process of preserving, archiving, circulating, and remediating remains. In the context of the North American West, then, land lines name the sexual and racialized logics of possession and land appropriation that continue to govern life, to exhaust racialized populations, and to forestall necessary transformations in how we imagine value. Their domains include physical land (land forms and their surrounding ecosystems), layers of contested legal geographies (such as federal acts and later appropriations), and infrastructure (transportation, water, energy, agriculture), alongside entrenched social beliefs about how to *make* and *convert* energy for proper, productive use.

Transfusing ecocultural rhetorics of environmental memory with decolonial queer ecologies, cultural geography, and affect studies, I walk alongside formal spaces of cultural memory so central to the reproduction of self and nation to ask these questions: first, how does sexual modernity intersect with historical and ongoing contests over land, accumulating into land lines; second, how do land lines move from the imperceptible to the felt; third, how do ecocultural critics account for how encounters with these memory spaces uphold, contest, or offer conditions for more just ecological relationships; and, finally, under what conditions of imagination might these spaces shift to open possibilities for regenerative thought and feeling? *Violent Inheritance: Sexuality, Land, and Energy in Making the North American West* makes two openings at the confluence of queer studies and the environmental and energy humanities. First, I illustrate the centrality of land and infrastructure to the bodily production of vitality and capacity, fundamentally rooting sexuality within environmental processes. In situating the production of sexuality through modern infrastructure such as rail and commodity production chains that link regions and the movement of people, animals, and ideas, the object of so-called modernizing sexuality functions akin to the production of a commodity, or the eugenic alteration of so-called nature.[19] In this way we might think of the creation of a normative sexual subject as possessing a particular kind of bodily vitality that simultaneously necessitates ongoing environmental privilege to sustain energy's actualization.[20] Second, this book bridges grounded knowledge production with queer ecology, underscoring sensation, mediation, and affective atmospheres in denaturalizing normative regimes of energy that ground relationships to "environment" or "nature," both historically monopolized by eugenic settler whiteness. Struggle over these terms and their roots in making race, sexuality, and disability too is an inheritance.[21]

Sifting through durable sediment throughout archives, museums, historical sites, and the tempos of everyday living, I trace and denaturalize an environmental and energetic theory of sexual modernity, challenging the assumptions North American settlers make about sexuality, land, and relationships between life, time, and violence. Rather than offer a totalistic history of the region, the book's arc turns to key sites of racialized sexual subject formation grounded in the ecologies of the North American West. Between 2010 and 2018 I gathered archival sources and conducted interviews, attended community gatherings and pilgrimages, and toured museums, all the while crossing state and national borders in automobiles, airplanes, buses, and the legs of a body itself in a state of transition of gender and capacity, moving between rural, urban, and seemingly nowhere. During the course of traveling, I passed through airports in metropolitan hubs; went through border checkpoints with relative ease afforded by my U.S. passport and whiteness that compensated for my body's gender nonconformity; gazed out the window of moving vehicles into spinning prairies amid dry, hot summers; and walked along sidewalks and past railroad tracks hardened by the brisk chills of the transition between winter and early spring. Although I draw from movements across and through the span of twenty-some years from my own experiences and knowledge of living in the suburbs of Colorado in the 1980s, rural Oklahoma in the early 1990s, the more populous Wyoming state capital of Cheyenne, and the college bubble of Laramie in southeastern Wyoming at the turn of the twenty-first century, this book is not autotheory nor what some would call an "ethnography." Rather, I ground embodied queer ecological criticism with an array of interpretive methods in archives, participant observation, and personal interviews to understand how the lingering of sexual modernity through layers of land appropriation shapes what it feels like to be situated in relation to landscapes of violence, memory, and potential regenerative futures. Throughout the remainder of this introduction, I detail with greater depth the book's primary key terms: *sexual modernities, land lines,* and *regeneration.* But, first, I need to pull back from the bad romance of regional myth to more fully grapple with a region of sacrifice and environmental privilege.

WHY THE NORTH AMERICAN WEST?

The geologically splendiferous North American West is a region easily defined by capacity, if we root that word in the capitalist fantasies of seemingly exponential value mined from cracks in the earth. Long before the consolidation of fossil fuel infrastructures in the twentieth century, militaristic and settler desires for land and minerals would in many ways deplete and exhaust a landscape forged through a period of dispossession. Enacting a "manifest destiny" to expand national empires, the consequence of military campaigns, infrastructures, extractive industries, laws, maps, and divisions of knowledge all leave a toxic legacy on western lands. The use of the region as such makes this place a "sacrifice zone," sumps for disposing of unwanted people, energy experimentation, and wastelanding.[22] As environmental historians and justice advocates have long argued, the logic underlying this process of sacrifice includes the financial calculus of risk against reward. This is the primary context for how I consider the relationship between *innervation* (individual expansion of capacity) and *enervation* (exhaustion of "population" capacity). Within contexts of environmental violence, we have to understand these as intertwined: capacity is a critical dimension of what Lisa Sun-Hee Park and David Naguib Pellow call "environmental privilege," or the entrenchment of ongoing, generationally reproduced access to the planetary infrastructures necessary to support life. Park and Pellow underscore how the enclosure of the environment is itself an environmental injustice, afforded by the "siphoning" of life from populations rendered as "energy reserves" for the biopolitical state.[23] The aspiration of Anglo-American settler modernity to accumulate and extract life simultaneously exhausts. The question we must ask here is what kinds of selective traditions enable the retrenchment of environmental privilege through the cyclical reproduction of inheritance as a land-based logic.

As both a bioregion and historical regime, the North American West partly refers to unique land and water ecosystems that also exceed political boundaries. This way of framing the region as a regime helps understand that what we often call "nature" functions as *part* of capitalist processes rather than as some passive layer stamped with the imprint of "culture."[24] The precision of this definition matters because it forces a different understanding of the "western myth," long (and I mean *long*) traced by American studies and New Western scholars. Here the scenarios and internal contradictions of this myth have been well established: it encompasses the dispossession of Indigenous land base; the enclosure of private property through the taming of so-called virgin land; the pioneer as embodiment of national mission; individual over community; domination and extraction of nature; individual resilience against pain and obstacles; nostalgia for a rural past; settlement as refuge from corrupt and emasculating institutions; and seemingly limitless prosperity.[25] At its core the western myth is a symbolic resource of nature-based nationalism and illuminates values and archetypes of vitality as they generate relationships between land, body, and nation.

Those myths are also *regenerated*: adapting to contemporary conditions that renew their foundational archetypes, an observation documented across a broad range of cultural production. Still, racialized sexualities remain eclipsed in much of this work, with rare exception.[26] As feminist and queer scholars of color carefully note, sexuality, disability, and race do not operate as discrete categories; they work to produce one another in often contradictory ways. I present four case studies where contests of inheritance figure in the foreground, be it in scenes of the archive, museum, historical site, or ambient places of environmental memory. To begin to trace sexual modernity's entanglement with energy requires first a deeper engagement with the scale of the body, a porous form whose capacity necessitated energy *actualization*.

SEXUAL MODERNITIES: ENERGY
AND ENVIRONMENTAL CAPACITY

How we answer the question of sexuality's convergence with modernity's relationship to energy depends largely on two dimensions: *where* we root this question and what we mean by sexuality, sexual modernity, and energy. In the opening anecdote of the Colorado Sanitarium, even the atmosphere conjured an electric pulse presumed to enliven those poor in vital energy. By the end of the nineteenth century, vitality and energy enveloped a range of anxieties of bodily and mental capacity: to work, to accumulate, to sexually reproduce, and, for Kellogg and western myth makers, to prevent racial degeneration.[27] But those imaginations of environmental vitality were also forged by conditions of dispossession and the unlawful seizure and occupation of sovereign Indigenous lands across North America. For example, decades prior to the opening of the sanitarium in Boulder, both the United States and Canada adopted official policies to kidnap hundreds of thousands of Indigenous children from their homelands and families to place them in state- and church-run institutions. These spaces, called "industrial schools" or "residential schools," facilitated the expansion of empire through increasing access to land. Many decades later and into the twentieth century, many of the departments responsible for the oversight of these policies in the United States would also oversee during wartime the forced removal of Japanese Americans from the West Coast into government incarceration centers. I detail these accounts in chapters 3 and 4, respectively, but for now I need to emphasize how their administrative overlaps have much to do with what Karma Chávez calls the "alienizing nation" and the intersection of expropriated land, labor, and racialized energy, or the rendering of a racialized population as bodies to *exhaust*.[28]

One of my primary goals in this book is to remember how the "sexually modern" body was an ecological one, tarried between contradictions of energy's latency and actualization. Under the auspices of *energy*, sexuality functions as a technique of transforming the biopolitical body into an economically useful form. The contemporary world often roots cognizance of sexuality as a fully entrenched property of the self and personhood, where mutable desires, drives, or even libido vitality transform as testimonials of personal virtue. More colloquially, the energy politics of sexuality might register as the emittance of "big dick energy" that wafts with swagger. But historians of sexuality remind us this linkage between self-hood and sexuality is historically contingent: one wherein the authority of the science of sex would ascend with eugenics. In the context of North American eugenics and sexology, the drive for "physical vigor and the moral cleanliness of the social body" became in part a vision of vitality that cleaved so-called aberration from the web of life, to expand the bodily capacity of a natal ethnonationalism. Competing for cultural, moral, and scientific authority, these discourses of sexuality prized elimination and disposability of "defect" and "degenerate," justifying the "racisms of the state on the horizon."[29] This story of bodily capture by scientific knowledge, the naming of aberrations as "crimes against nature," and the dissemination of technologies to produce a subject adherent to logics of human difference is what Foucault describes as one modality of biopower, and what I've referenced as "sexual modernity." Sexuality's historical specificity thus helps us remember the proliferation of cultures of sex—love, intimacy, kinship—that long precede this moment, as many critics of Foucault and the modernity thesis have argued. However, in Foucault's account, we also find a story of sexuality as one vector encompassing the modulation and regulation of life, making nature and energy two largely unrealized dimensions for queer and sexuality studies more broadly.[30] Biopower and biopolitics offer a critical entry point into understanding sexual modernity's extractivist nature.

Energy is a scalar problem and facilitates connections between concerns of bodily vitality and the global cultures and systems of energy extraction. My point here is not to quibble with legitimate critiques of substance, nor is it to offer a deep dive into the archive of the sexual sciences to suggest a new periodization for the history of sexuality. Rather, my affinity for Foucault's vocabulary comes from wanting to stretch "mosaic," the metaphor he deploys to observe a milieu.[31] When read in the context of making the North American West into a mythic place of vitality production, I see mosaic *environmentally* and as an infrastructural imagination. To start, why should sexuality studies scholars take for granted that the notion of "possessive sexuality" emerged precisely in an age of modernizing infrastructure that governed how individuals were encouraged to imagine and feel movement?[32] Take, for instance, the Chicago World's Fair of 1893, rendered as a monument to Columbus's "discovery" of the Americas, but also the white, electrified, forward-looking, technocratic imagination of Anglo-American modernity. The question matters because it shifts away from origin stories to stories of layering, a space-time so vital to mapping the Capitalocene.[33]

Mosaics want *moorings* and necessitate stories of *sedimentation*. Origin stories fundamentally miss how infrastructural time lives in *layering*, through the development and appropriation of systems and networks of energy actualization. When we speak of *modernities*, the fetishization of progress, speed, and rationality indeed come to the foreground, but the term also speaks to confluences: urbanization and its moral panics, emerging consumer capitalism, the rise of technocratic administrative governing, architectural aspiration, agricultural practice, forestry management, and more.[34] Modernity also marks a particular relationship to energy through its capacities for optimization: for making and exploiting racialized labor, transforming cultures of work, fetishizing efficiencies, streamlining through design, and experiencing new sensations afforded by new forms of movement made possible by modern infrastructure and attendant energy systems. Each of these relationships were made possible through an even longer history of racialized capital accumulation in the form of slavery, settler colonialism, and empire.[35] I work with sexuality's entanglement with dominant infrastructures and energy systems so central to capitalist geographies and the social production of nature: inclusive of transportation, communication, and water, among others. Still, how understanding of these intersections take shape depends on *where they materialize,* making ecology, or the connections between place and systems of interdependence, vital in confronting the fundamental disconnect of sexuality from colonial energy systems, making sexuality a multiscalar, environmental problem.

Temporally and spatially, sedimentation attunes us to deposits left behind—the land lines—and their slow build up, weathering, erosion, overlap, friction, and pressure. As an interdisciplinary problem, sedimentation envelops cultural and ecological processes, making it possible to understand the long life of sexual modernity's environmental imprint as an inheritance conjured and passed generationally. That passage enables the ongoing replication of a codified and concretized selective tradition. I do not want to suggest that energy cultures are static nor outside political struggle, as scholars and activists of energy justice have argued time and again. For that reason, for the remainder of this section, I want to take a multiscalar approach in more clearly delineating how *heredity* came to matter as a subject of territorial and energy expansion efforts in the late nineteenth century in addition to its lingering throughout much of the early twentieth century.

To the scientific class the optimization of whiteness necessitated securitizing sex from *enervation*, or slow devitalization mapped through biological, neurological, and nervous systems. As I detail in chapter 1, the nineteenth-century crisis of enervation encompassed domains of life from work to sex to broader atmospheres of urban environments believed to cultivate degeneracy. Overwork and overstimulation thus became a whiteness problem to be sorted, studied, and classified. Neurologists, physicians, and moral reformers echoed warnings against new rituals of labor, transportation, and consumption. Medical missionaries excoriated foods and sexual habits of the racialized poor inhabiting salacious urban centers, warning against dangers of excess and contagion. At the core of these anxieties was a fear that depleted energy would mean a loss of vitality, threatening the reproduction of whiteness.[36] That "energy" indexed a range of relationships of individuated mental and physical capacity and the potentiality to adhere to reprosexual norms in addition to racial hierarchies. These energy cultures grounded race as malleable matter and forwarded the optimization of heredity through *innervation* (energy expansion) as the crux of eugenic ideals of racial management.[37] This obsession with heredity and its malleability given external forces made an *etiological* argument about sex and race.[38] The classification, analysis, specification, and causal study of climate's etiology in degeneracy would promise—for some—disciplinary intervention. For sexologists the search for order through classification could discern the origins and influences of sexual (and thus racial) degeneracy, so to cultivate therapeutic cultures of management, discipline, and self-cultivation.

The cultural milieu of the scientific class largely defined "civilization" as a "perfect race," encoding white supremacist taxonomies of race and sex into everything from medical climatology to sexual science, agriculture, urbanism, criminology, and early conservationism. One of their primary modes includes constructs of "heredity," a marker of population and a core vocabulary in turn of the twentieth-century classificatory systems of race.[39] I'm drawing from Stuart Hall, who described race as a set of historically constituted vocabularies "that organize the great classificatory systems of difference that operate in human societies. Race...is the centerpiece of a hierarchal system that produces differences."[40] One of those profound differences includes the difference between techniques of *innervation* and *enervation*.

For state administrators and elites, the logic of heredity served contradictory ends: to *innervate* (or optimize and expand bodily capacity) and to *enervate* (to exhaust), and, through extractive knowledge practices, their belief in an optimizable heredity inscribed racial hierarchy into western lands. For example, in chapter 2 I trace one of the shifts in heredity from belief in its interior malleability to the grounds of "heritage," specifically romanticized stories of the vitality actualizing "frontier." Tall tales of brawny horses commanded by enterprising pioneers spatialized national nostalgia, at a time when arguments of heredity and vitality again surged to the forefront of national and nativist conversations about immigration.[41] In the course of her career, Grace Raymond Hebard, a professor of political economy at the University of Wyoming, took up the task of collecting Wyoming and western ephemera. She would compose regional histories, engage in suffrage activism, and teach courses to aid in the naturalization of immigrants. Hebard was guided by a "romance" of western "heritage." For example, her pamphlet, *The History and Romance of Wyoming,* includes a bibliographic guide linking settler maps to books and authors, the pamphlet borders marked with phrases such as "From the beginning of things the setting sun has always been the magnet" and "Here in the West the dreams of the east come true." The landscape, now named and a romantic attachment, is a political possession transferred to a new generation. I offer this extended example as one way inheritance moves through moments of reinvention; heritage is an imagined relation to the past that *also* invites particular action in the present. As someone who lived in worlds of nonreprosexual kinship, Hebard became an ideal subject of sexual modernity through her commitment to the settler state in addition to her later assurances to naturalization efforts, both securitizing energetic whiteness through claims to land possession.

But, in contrast, *enervation,* the exhaustion of populations to create energy reserves, is a relation of state violence that imagines settler futurity through the extraction of racialized labor and energy. Chapters 3 and 4, respectively, grapple with state projects of forced relocation in Canada and the United States in the context of Canada's industrial schools and the United States executive branch and War Department's wartime incarceration of Japanese Americans. In both cases administrators made different, though related, arguments about *racial* malleability, a word I use with caution. In the case of residential schools, race was an operative logic of state governance to *racialize* First Nation peoples through law and language to disavow nation-to-nation relationships and invoke a paternal relationship of setter state and "Native child."[42] In the case of the wartime incarceration of Japanese Americans, state administers in the Department of the Interior and War Relocation Authority made arguments appealing to heredity logics for containment *and* the utility of remote environments for producing their fantasy of assimilation. Both of these biopolitical histories overlap, Jodi Byrd (Chickasaw) emphasizes.[43] I build on these insights by emphasizing how enervation functions as a proxy for a "population" as latent energy reserves to produce value for the settler colonial state. As much as arguments about the hereditary basis for potential assimilation shaped these different administrations, the surrounding environment of confinement functioned as an extension of state control.

One way to map the structural and communicative dimensions of energy (as vitality and as a logic of resource extraction) includes their connection to particular dimensions of North American settler colonial modernity. I understand settler colonialism as an enduring but variable attempt to *structurally* disappear indigeneity, a term I use to reference a particular sovereign relation to land.[44] One of the mechanisms in doing so is through articulating gender and sexuality with a propertied sense of personhood, reproduced through conjugal romance, following Mark Rifkin, Scott Morgensen, and Kim TallBear (Sisseton Oyate). One of the key takeaways of settler colonial studies includes a need to trace specific modes of its reproduction over time, its contestation, and at times the moving transit of "Native."[45] Settler colonialism, writes Byrd, "depends on reproducing the propertied relations through which dispossession itself occurs and then reenacting those relations subsequently upon settlers and arrivants over time as a generative process that ensures the original colonization of Indigenous lands remains unassailable, natural, rational, and necessary as the condition of possibility for all other dispossessions to come."[46] Within these generative processes I am particularly interested in the role of inheritance as a structure of meaning making, feeling, and, moreover, an imprint on land itself. As a communication scholar, I am also attentive to settler colonialism as a reservoir of political imagination, an affect generator, and a power network of naturalizing particular relationships of energy.

When it comes to thinking through the biopolitics of vitality, queer ecologists have been after some of these questions for some time but have had less to say about the problem of energy extraction or settler sexual modernity as a form of extractivism. Queer ecologist Catriona Sandilands has long argued for a cultural ecocriticism accounting for the queer potential of life, historically and as a mode of ongoing pressure on racialized and heteronormative imaginations of sex, generativity, kinship, and relationality.[47] Sandilands and Bruce Erickson define the task of queer ecology as the ability to "probe the intersections of sex and nature with an eye to developing a sexual politics that more clearly includes considerations of the natural world and its biosocial constitution, and an environmental politics that demonstrates an understanding of the ways in which sexual relations organize and influence both the material world of nature and our perceptions, experiences, and constitutions of that world."[48] One of the challenges of this work I confront herein includes energy as one of the ways normative sexuality deeply impoverishes relationships to the ecological world.

This book extends and deepens these commitments by, first, elaborating a distributed imagination of sex that cannot be contained by reprosexual practices.[49] Reframing sexual modernities past solely thinking about subjectivity or desire opens the field of the sexual to include atmospheric relationships to the land. I redefine sex as not just about desire and identity with a thinking-feeling body but also about orientation and land, *denaturalizing* the body and its relationships to space. Second, queer ecology can better do this work by bridging its analysis with critiques of settler colonialism. I do so by engaging encounters with inheritance that enact conditions for regenerative intimacies against "nature" within a eugenic, settler colonial enclosure.

LAND LINES AND UNSETTLING THE BIOPOLITICS OF INFRASTRUCTURE

This project conceptualizes land lines to name particular cultural and ecological inheritances made perceptible in spaces dedicated to national and regional memory. The human agencies of western expansion have always been entwined with the more than human, shifting and constituting modes of affecting and being affected. In worlds that imagine the body as a latent reservoir of energy, broader infrastructures provide another converter chain to *actualize* that energy into usable matter. One of the implications of my environmental account of settler sexual modernity is that such a formation requires land and energy to support and forward nationalist projects of expansion, movement, and extraction of value. Access to extractive regimes is bound up in the promise of mobility, meaning it makes little sense to extract its subjects from the infrastructures that *actualize* their capacity for the rightful alignments of desire. As such, taking seriously underlying networks of movement and land restructuring matters to any account of North American sexual history precisely because they are *constitutive* of the distributed making of sex. In this section I clarify the concept of land lines: the relations it holds and encompasses, its agencies of energy actualization and, finally, how they break.

Land Lines: A Hold, a Tether

First, land lines conceive land as an infrastructure that interweaves the right to make life through territorial occupation, what Rifkin calls the entanglement of "biopower and geopower."[50] In the environmental humanities, "infrastructure" typically engenders underlying physical networks and sociotechnical systems that organize modern life worlds and enable the movement of bodies, resources, and information.[51] *Infra-* means "below," "under," or "beneath," a disappearing act central to ways of knowing land in settler societies. In a settler common sense, land might be described as the passive base that underlies all these systems. Yet nineteenth-century legal geographies illuminate how excluding land from the definitional domain of infrastructure depends on regimes of value. Infrastructure and sexuality enliven each other, mapping unexpected sites and practices under the auspices of the organization and management of life; in Ara Wilson's words, infrastructures "embed intimate relations in fields of power."[52] By thinking of land as an infrastructure of sexuality and of sexual modernity as extractivism, I make queer ecologies more deeply accountable to critiques of settler colonialism and racial ecologies.[53] By challenging infrastructure's definitional domain through the concept, land and energy occupy a more central place in the infrastructures of sexual modernity.

When I first started thinking about this project over a decade ago, I imagined a study of queer regionalism, an approach that never truly gained traction because it assumed so much about queerness relative to how the region has been used as a space for extraction and sacrifice. As I thought more carefully, I realized what was necessary was to go *deeper* into the land's structuring over time as a basis for building settler kinship claims. Kinship, especially of the reprosexual variety, underwrites the naturalization of settler entitlements to land, a foundational claim from queer critiques of settler colonialism. For example, Rifkin points to lineaments constituting heteronormativity through a nexus of kinship, land tenure, and state-sanctioned policies that instantiated a land-based national identity.[54] Who has access to and sovereignty of land are at the center of producing extractive social formations over time. More important, moving through the depths of land appropriation, sacrifice zones, and labor became vital to my ability to think about frames of meaning making around "violent inheritance" in different spaces.

The land isn't just infrastructure—legally and politically—but also supports and forwards transportation as a nationalist commodity and infrastructure of its own, to the point of becoming radically inseparable from the concrete, rails, bridges, and pavers that traverse its surface. Richard White contends that for many in nineteenth-century North America, rail defined the age of modernity, powered through coal-based energy regimes. Despite popular western myths of roughneck individuals settling the unruly West with horse power, the technologies and labor of the institution of rail in Canada, the United States, and Mexico were endeavors of state and finance capitalism restructuring the continent. A quintessential modern infrastructure, rail collapsed perceptions of distance, made space legible to distant bureaucrats, and fashioned a physical infrastructure that maximized revenue through the control of space.[55] Though the nineteenth century was the age of rail, the twentieth century became the age of the automobile, deepening the reorganization of space and commodification of resources that powered individual movement. Built in the shadow of rail in the age of petroleum, the development of roads and, particularly, interstate travel would build another layer of landscape and technical ecosystem producing attachments to automobiles and individual mobility.[56] This is what infrastructure thinkers call "path dependency." For settlers each of these layered infrastructural lives are engineered to seem "natural" and hidden away. Yet the affective promise of mobility underscores its hold on the body through the "poetics of infrastructure."[57] Land lines are rife with aliveness and bring into focus the transition from the biopolitics of heredity to the diffusion of biopower throughout landscape.

If inheritance marks temporalities, then land lines provide a spatial orientation for the sexual body, one whose perennial attachment to possession affixes a tether between land, life, and body. As a noun, *tether* is a connective or confinement device whose reach underwrites conditions of (im)mobility. But, as a verb, *tether* also implies multivalent action that moves between scales of power and everyday intimacies. In the context of this book, tether can operate as a colonial process, forcing elements and life into relational dominance; tether also provides an optic to trace a network of convergences in the production of land and the extraction of energy. "Line" explicates connection, but its history of usage often conflates relationality for linearity or straightness. Lines also share etymology with electrical currents and patterns of *generation,* an engendering process delivering matter to life. Throughout the North American West, and the Rockies in particular, lines deviating from straightness are present in the spired hoodoos and cragged edges of granite, winnowed by the force of millions of years of wind gusts, edges of tree roots coming upward to the surface of the ground, or sediment traipsing across asphalt highways.

Land and Infrastructural Violence

Across the chapters I think about land, energy, and land lines through relationships to infrastructural violence. In particular, the property logic of *tether* underscores a racial regime of mobility and confinement. The militarization of landscapes to confine, to sacrifice peoples and ecological interdependencies, necessitates grounding infrastructural violence and movement within the politics of mobility. The first two chapters respectively consider the expansion of vitality through innervating movement or romanticized and secured domesticity. To contrast, chapters 3 and 4 both engage the weaponization of land and the transformation of population into capacitating potential through the site of Indian residential schools and the World War II–era confinement of Japanese Americans. Although I map the politics of residential school memory in Canada and the localization of U.S. administrative policies of the incarceration of Japanese Americans, both countries share these techniques of confinement, going so far as layering on each other. I am not the first to read these historical landscapes against one another; indeed, as I referenced in the previous section, Byrd maps the evolution of the settler nation-state to identify perceived threats to capital and to transform surplus land into places of confinement and labor extraction.[58] Byrd underscores how war-era incarceration in the United States grows out of the administrative apparatus of the Bureau of Indian Affairs. Building on Byrd in chapter 4 in particular, I read these transits as land lines, explicitly rooting transits as structures embedded in the land through layers of appropriation and sacrifice. What we need, I argue, is an account of how those forces impress on the land as an ecological and cultural inheritance.

Grounded accounts of these property regimes add a crucial dimension to environmental humanities' ability to describe resistance to infrastructural violence, especially as enactments of racism. Infrastructure is something of a trademark of modernity. For instance, Paul Edwards has argued "to construct infrastructures is simultaneously to construct a particular kind of nature," one that seemingly splits nature from culture, constituting perceptions of "raw materials" for human appropriation and use.[59] This definitional domain matters because it, in part, delineates the ontological basis on which infrastructure depends on subjugation to build life.[60] Ruth Wilson Gilmore's work has long highlighted these dualisms of life and death embedded in infrastructure and environment, and both structure her account of racism. She defines racism as "the state-sanctioned or extralegal production and exploitation of group-differentiated vulnerability to premature death." Following Gilmore, infrastructures to confine and control life (including land-based relationships) build on previously existing forms of state-defined crisis.[61] Infrastructural violence is a biopolitics of the capacity to debilitate *and* produce life, embedded within the logics, construction, aesthetics, and use of infrastructures of modernity.[62] As dimensions of sexual modernity, sex, race, and capacity are produced *through* and *in* the extant infrastructures that ground what it feels like to be situated in the memory atmospheres of the region.

Feeling, Contesting, Breaking Land Lines

Not only can land lines be traced through the production of infrastructural violence, but they also have an aesthetic and sensorial quality—an accumulated structure of feeling—operating through registers that have also become important sites of contestation. Land lines attune various audiences moving in or through spaces of memory to space as a meeting up of histories: atmospheres and layers of matter that permeate one another but may nonetheless become separable under critical pressure.[63] Here is where I want to stress the entanglement of biopower and geopower through the term *lineament,* connecting how white settler futurity dwells in the diffusion of land lines over time. As Mishuana Goeman (Tonawanda Seneca) explains, land is material and a meaning-making medium and process.[64] Goeman's reclassification of land short-circuits settler orders of life; her orientation of land as a life force opens "lines" as a spatial-temporal event laced with competing modernities. Restructuring of space over time produces excesses that challenge any sense of a unified past. North American sexual modernity has restructured land for various usages: extraction of value, ethnonationalist containment, mastery of nonhuman reproduction through agriculture and ranching, land grant universities, military bases, and the diffusion of intimate colonialisms, amid broader divisions between regimes of private property

and public lands.[65] All endemic to the social organization of capital—
land, extraction, finance, and commerce—these layer on and imbibition
one another. Layers in turn produce surplus, whose presence remains.
Those excesses, grounded in the atmospherics of land lines, shape and
energize situated modes of contestation.

My reading method throughout each site is to trace imperceptible
tethers that affix and hold sentiments to sediment. Moving deeply into
the past and outward into landscapes of the contemporary present, this
method enables me to better grasp what I call "infrastructures of feeling," a concept I take up in the book's conclusion. As infrastructures
take on a poetic and aesthetic life in cultural memory, they elucidate
what it feels like to be located in time and space, even more specifically
between the recorded culture of the past and lived culture of the present.
Raymond Williams's "structure of feeling" continues to evade specificity as it gets deployed across contemporary work on affect, emotion,
and feeling. In *Marxism and Literature* Williams defines the term as
"characteristic elements of impulse, restraint, and tone; specifically affective elements of consciousness and relationships: not feeling against
thought, but thought as felt and feeling as thought: practical consciousness of a present kind, in a living and interrelating continuity."[66] Later,
in *The Long Revolution* he clarifies, "It is as firm and definite as 'structure' suggests, yet it operates in the most delicate and least tangible
parts of our activity. In one sense, this structure of feeling is the *culture
of a period:* it is the particular living result of all the elements in the
general organization." Here Williams attributes structures of feeling to
something akin to prosthetic or postmemory that define an emplaced
generation—a feeling amid a culture constituted by "recorded communication that outlives its bearers."[67] Structures of feeling are collectiv-
izing, an undercurrent of communication, and thus provide a source for
social transformation. In my read their potential is *regenerative.* Further
demystifying the term, Lawrence Grossberg argues that Williams and
Richard Hoggart, respectively, used the concept to address the question
of "'what it feels to be alive' at a *certain time and place.*"[68] Generative
as the term may be, I want to tread carefully alongside some of the tensions embedded within Williams's capacious limits. Possessive geographies live in his attempt to map feeling of the world through situated
experiences.

Though Williams believes a structure of feeling was a "very deep
and very wide possession," mapping the relationships between violent
inheritance, environmental memory, and the grounds of feeling all call

situatedness into question as a relation to possession. Sexual modernity subsumes feeling and sensation such that the ideal subject possesses sentiment for the nation and takes pride in ongoing extractive projects, often justified as "good work." These each underscore how feeling becomes a project of possession and incorporation into a national body, as argued by affective biopolitics critics such as Dana Luciano, Mel Chen, and Kyla Schuller.[69] I confront the limits of "structure of feeling" for understanding the complexities of race and sexuality and revisit Williams's concept to argue that the residual offers political potential of regeneration, creating the conditions of possibility for an elsewhere.[70] Stretching the term to the infrastructural, the conclusion meditates on the question of "infrastructures of feeling" for collaborative stewardship. These highlight the relationship between infrastructures and affective, incorporative practices, like the feelings of release one might experience going for an aimless drive to burn off steam as a tactic of navigating violence. These geographies nonetheless offer political possibility of imagination and eroticism that might cultivate more just relationships between humans and their nonhuman kin.

REGENERATION BEYOND EXTRACTIVISM
AND THE SOCIAL LIFE OF THE ARCHIVE

The pernicious, but necessary, challenge of sexual modernity's violent inheritance is how to move against and beyond extractive world making. Informed by Indigenous scholars and queer ethics, I turn to regeneration as one orientation to the rhetorical process and practice of contested memory. Above all, regeneration questions the practice of extractivism as a relentless cycle of exhaustion and, more broadly, the incessant production of *value*. As I understand it, regeneration, as carefully defined through a queer ethic and critical orientation that affirms life and eroticism in all of their creative abundance, functions as a counterpoint to extractive dominance. I contend regeneration breaks the tethers composing land lines, so this book offers an interpretive and writing practice attentive to excess, creative archival practice, and collaboration. I engage with archives that unspool the human-centered story of sexual modernity to address how its ecological inheritance initiates a condition of struggle over a whole way of life always-already in a cultural process of renewal and contestation. For American studies scholars the renewal of violence through myth predominates and limits the capacity of regeneration as a critical orientation and vocabulary for cultural transformation.[71] My approach differs because it holds the density and tension of inheritance as a lived hegemony: a communicative force that maintains or challenges the gross vitality of biopolitical whiteness.[72] As I detail later in this section, my horizon of regeneration builds on existing queer and decolonial imaginations, wherein the settler relinquishing emotional attachments to land that was never any of ours becomes necessary for a more affirmative, reciprocal imagination of life and the grammars necessary for its constitution.

First, regenerative practice necessitates a confrontation with modes of memory acquisition that amass as the body archive, what Julietta Singh describes as the "assembly of history's traces deposited in me."[73] Too often cultural memory is conflated with some kind of content about historical events, neatly packaged into discrete episodes. Instead, cultural memory is a communicative process: of bodily incorporation and of inscriptive practices such as recording observations, choices of preservation, and later archival processes that render "the past" intelligible to future generations.[74] Cultural memory is not the content of what may have happened in the past but a textured process shaped by the technologies and media that circulate, mediate, or contextualize a public's relationship to collective experience.[75] When I first started researching this book, I was drawn toward what felt like the confluence of bodily incorporation and "the archive," a split that has long vexed scholars in the humanities. How could environmental cultural studies account for how claims to extractive or regenerative genres of inheritance *feel* so *bodily?*

I can't help but dwell on Singh's invocation of "deposit," a metaphor that tarries between the infrastructural and intimate and between the inscribed and incorporated. Historical residue lingers, incorporated into the body through movement ritual, bodily practice, and sedimented habit. Deposit also conjures the assignment of value, becoming something of the dead weight of past generations that Karl Marx believed weighed like a nightmare for the living. But the assembly of history's traces in Singh's account poses a contrast to the accumulative power of value that grounds the environmental and sexual body at the heart of chapters 1 and 2. As elaborated earlier in this introduction, these deposits substantively and metaphorically live as land lines, creating atmospheres through infrastructures of feeling. Tracing historical deposits across land, skin, air, and water generates a "way of thinking-feeling the body's unbounded relation to other bodies," human and nonhuman.[76] I want to believe this is a kind of eroticism made possible through decolonial sexualities, something I take up in the second half of chapter 5 and the book's conclusion.

North American institutions of memory powerfully shape some of our earliest concrete encounters with the ongoing replication of the selective tradition. I myself find perhaps hundreds of childhood photographs of my queer body reluctantly propped near military monuments on family vacations. Collective remembrance is a well-documented technique of state craft, and cultural industries, archives, museums, and historical sites constitute spaces for the constitution of national subjects through adherence to a partial historical narrative.[77] As this book brings readers into public archives, museums, historical sites, and more ambient locations within the region, I trace how differential relations to inheritance offer pathways for both the renewal of extractive regimes in addition to potentialities for remaking. That tension—between four domains of sexual modernity—and the communicative conditions of "inheritance" speaks to the generative power of structures of meaning making for enacting a *different* kind of futurity. Though always grounded in historically and culturally specific moments, institutional motives, and localized struggle, I contend *inheritance* in each of these emplaced genres of memory move through the social life of the archive, a term I use to account for uneven practices of preservation and generational circulation. If dominant forms of inheritance such as possession, extraction, and ongoing dispossession *depend* on their ongoing replication as a "lived system of values and meanings," we need a vocabulary that accounts for that complexity. I want to tend closely to the possibilities of living otherwise, of what it might mean to be *untethered* to the intimate and infrastructural forms of sexual modernity's violent inheritance.

Untethering may become regenerative assembly: a creative practice and critical orientation. In queer and Indigenous thought, regeneration points to potentiality and horizons. For Leanne Betasamosake Simpson (Mississauga Nishnaabeg), regeneration functions as value of systems that affirm life in multiple forms, species, and relationalities.[78] Drawn from the vantage point of Michi Saagiig Nishnaabeg political systems, Simpson's regeneration is antithetical to settler colonialism. Naomi Klein offers a western view, also meditating on the possibilities of regeneration beyond extractive regimes, a "worldview that must take place if we are to move beyond extractivism. A worldview based on regeneration and renewal rather than domination and depletion."[79] As a critic of environmental and queer cultural studies, both of these conceptualizations of regeneration invite wrestling with structures of affect in attachments to land and energy. I am particularly moved that regeneration challenges how critics make sense of inheritance, and how expressive cultures (art, visualization, memory making) can interface with these political challenges.

Moving within and beyond discrete texts, my modes of observation and feeling have been habituated to grasp historical traces and paths of circulation, follow their lifespan, and remediate differences. The remainder of this book engages with voices living and dead who tried to make worlds—extractive and regenerative—relative to what they *felt* was their inheritance. And often that renewal restructured relations of slow and acute violence as much as they adapted to conditions of the present. I first began this project with an interest in residual culture, particularly creative practices that reanimated seemingly dead matter. These projects can potentially foster more just futures by offering sites of imagination for publics to contemplate ongoing struggles over land.

My interpretive contribution reads archives of memory not for their *restorative* or recuperative potential, in effect suturing the gap of a marginalized past. Instead, I read the excesses of memory for their possibilities in speculative fabulation. This mode of storytelling, drawing from Donna Haraway, "is the patterning of possible worlds and possible times, material-semiotic worlds, gone, here, and yet to come."[80] In thinking through the western landscape itself as an object of desire in the making of modern sexuality, I offer no promises of restoration to make whole, as if any project could fulfill such a fantasy. Instead, I toggle with the desire to grasp hold of and possess the past, to become entangled in matter and earth and blood, and to move with them in a different direction. The directive—"you have to smell the blood in the soil"—is an invitation to make belonging conditional on relinquishment of the possessive.

UNTETHERING LAND LINES, A CHAPTER MAP

Rather than deliver a comprehensive history of the region, the arc of my chapters untethers key sites of state violence that underwrite the relationality of sex, energy, and environment. Each chapter respectively draws from different domains of sexual modernity: vitality, intimacies, childhood, and state racism. My purpose in doing so is twofold: first, to elaborate the longevity of sexual modernity's trace on the region and, second, to locate moments of contest in which that longevity is communicatively challenged across institutions of memory. Those institutions—archives, museums, historical sites, and ambient locations—reproduce the selective tradition through frames of possession. Chapter 1, "Cartographies of Sexual Modernity," turns to the energetic philosophies of sex, race, and disability that predominated late nineteenth-century beliefs in the sexual body's *capacity*. The chapter as a whole traces networks of capacity building tethered between the West, the Northeast, and Chicago. Juxtaposing medical writings about neurasthenia with city planning and the Chicago World's Fair of 1893, the first chapter maps how, amid anxieties of heredity and racial vigor, neurologists, urbanists, sociologists, historians, architects, and planners constituted "capacity" through an environmental, electric, and biologically engineered body. Owen Wister, a then reformed neurasthenic (a catchall term for nervous energy), traveled to the fair to reflect that he was "deluged by splendor," recovering only when he sauntered to Wooded Island, joining Theodore Roosevelt and his company in the pioneer ambiance of Hunter's Cabin. The chapter draws from Wister's journals of his therapeutic travels west in addition to the Chicago fair, medical writings of neurasthenia diagnostic criteria and causal explanation, and stories of depravity and degeneration in Chicago more broadly. As a whole, I argue that climate and environment were central to the production of the "modern sexual subject," defined by a porous white body who maximizes capacity. This chapter underscores sexual modernity as an inheritance to be denaturalized and as a capacity-building formation that links extractive subjects to land, energy forms, and infrastructure.

The goal of the remainder of the book is to trace with field methods how regional publics manage, interpret, and act with the emotional, spatial, and corporeal legacies of sexual modernity.[81] Chapter 2, "Settler Intimacies and the Social Life of the Archive," turns to the *grounds* of sexual modernity as a perceived place of heritage and domesticization. Here I encounter and engage the archival holdings of Grace Raymond Hebard, a Wyoming suffrage activist, university professor, and historian of western settlement. This chapter draws connections between her *sentimental* West and how her materials have been archived at the American Heritage Center. By sentimental, I mean a feeling cartography that, in Naomi Greyser's words, maps "interior emotions in externalizing, spatial terms"…and describes "geophysical space in intimate, emotional terms."[82] Inscribing a western romance into her cartographic mapping and land surveys, teaching Americanization courses for the Department of the Interior, and relentlessly chasing the memory of Sacajawea, Hebard's affect generates the grounds of sexual modernity and emplaces the proper subject of civilized sexuality. Given her "intimate friendship" with Norwegian poet and professor Agnes Wergeland, her memory *could* be recuperated as a "queer place" in the Rockies. Yet, moving against this want, I instead ask how toggling with the desire to grasp hold of Hebard and Wergeland's relationship might instead force us to grapple with the social life of the archive in reproducing the violence of eugenic whiteness. Rather than recuperate a lost figure of state craft, I ask instead how archival imaginations might regenerate relationships: to the past, the land, and queer and feminist politics.

Chapter 3, "Childhood and Settler Aesthetics of Violence," maps how sexual modernity's property logics square directly with Canada's residential school system. In particular, I map inheritance through colonial paternal authority and the lineaments between the figure of the child and abstraction of *childhood*. This chapter focuses on two exhibits related to residential schools at the Canadian Museum for Human Rights, a national human rights museum in the heart of Manitoba. Both Canada and the United States aggressively pursued policies that for the state promised the elimination of Indigenous peoples and "Native *as* Native." One such policy included the vast network of residential schools scattered throughout the territories. These policies, as Philip Deloria argues, instantiate relationships of state paternalism.[83] This chapter maps how the Canadian Museum for Human Rights reproduces the colonial relationship through design, aesthetics, and infrastructural violence and dwells more intimately with two starkly contrasted exhibits. I read the museum's own exhibit dedicated to residential schools, *Childhood Denied,* against Carey Newman's (Kwakwaka'wakw, Coast Salish) *Witness Blanket,* temporarily installed in early 2016. By contrasting the two, I evaluate how inheritance as a structure of meaning making may be negotiated through different invitations to witnessing: one of the state-sponsored "reconciliation" and one of anticolonial regeneration and collaborative stewardship.

Chapter 4, "Affected Persons, Sexual Transits, and Contested Public Memories," maps how sexual transits over time interface with landscapes of confinement, particularly as they intersect with labor in the region. This chapter recollects a pilgrimage to the site of a former Japanese American incarceration center in Idaho, named Minidoka. I draw from a pilgrimage to the site amid an ongoing controversy about the permitting of a Concentrated Animal Feeding Operation, colloquially known as "factory farms." In 2012 the Supreme Court of the State of Idaho maintained a district court ruling to permit an eight thousand animal-unit facility owned by Big Sky Farms, approximately one and a quarter mile from Minidoka. The court not only ruled in favor of Big Sky Farms but also used the legal and property-bearing category of "affected persons" to deny Friends of Minidoka legal standing during the proceedings. Building on scholarship about standing in environmental controversy, this chapter centers the racial, sexual, economic, and colonial underpinnings of such a potent legal term that mediates the dispute. I untether its philosophical underpinnings as a system of sexual governance constituted by race and colonialism over time, in turn triangulating systems of sexuality between Japanese Americans, the "family farm," romantic notions of animal husbandry, and the later Concentrated Animal Feeding Operation.

Recalling how a national addiction to fossil fuels facilitates a particular vision of Anglo-American modernity, chapter 5 examines how land lines shape contemporary sexual politics in the region. "Petroculture and Intimate Atmospheres" draws from narrative interviews and my own reflections to map how queer subjects manage the violence of heteronormativity and the petroculture state by crafting intimate atmospheres. Overall, in this chapter I argue for shifting gears to reimagine sexual imaginaries as tethered to a structure of queer living inside the infrastructures that oil made. This argument is part of a broader history that took hold in the twentieth century, what Stephanie LeMenager calls "living oil."[84] Here, I build on LeMenager's work by focusing on what living infrastructures can offer queer studies, especially queer ecologies and geographies. As a counterpoint to the endless extractivism of settler colonial sexuality, I close by turning to the collective Queer Nature. Based in Boulder, Colorado, when we met Queer Nature is a collaboration that teaches survival skills, while also circulating their own creative frameworks of regeneration. They offer a way of thinking about energy as reciprocity, tracking the intimacies, land lines, generations, and matter of grief that affords potential for a decolonial queer ecology.

Violent Inheritance: Sexuality, Land, and Energy in Making the North American West forwards the argument that sexual modernity's relationship to energy and land necessitates a grounding interpretation within regimes of organizing life of the North American West, a deeply contested, multifaceted geopolitical project. Each chapter illuminates how situated publics manage and contest the layered dimensions of the region's making and manifestation through the politics of vitality. The conclusion, "Infrastructures of Feeling and Queer Collaborative Stewardship," considers how residual cultures offer political possibility in contrast to how Williams prioritized the emergent as more politically capacious.

As a term, *regeneration* holds the tension between the reproduction of infrastructural violence through culture; on the other hand, it references political imaginations of a futurity dependent on systemic transformation. The conclusion begins to think through how regeneration as a queer and decolonial orientation might be guided through collaborative stewardship. Defined as a process of care that also works with and against epistemological boundaries, collaborative stewardship offers a hopeful framework for reimagining queer environmental politics. The environmental ethic of *steward* prioritizes ethics of care. Stewardship in this case is to learn and model a settler obligation and responsibility to relinquish logics of possession as the grounds for intergenerational kinship. In the context of calls for justice, regeneration offers an embodied political imagination. Calibrated to conditions of violent inheritance, justice tethers past and present, shifting between the known and the felt. The lesson in these places of contestation is not "how do we return" as if we could ever mobilize a world unchanged by Capitalocene settler violence. Rather, we might ask how do we relate and regenerate? The question "What might we do with violent inheritance?" renders these openings possible. By turning to the land lines of sexual modernity, I highlight the capacity of publics to sense, perceive, feel, and make intelligible the systems of order, classification, containment, and control that organize ways of living in the North American West. How those publics unearth, make visible, or repurpose infrastructure through acts of revitalization underscores a regional future not yet known but felt, as if on the edge of crossing a precipice.

CHAPTER I

Cartographies of Sexual Modernity

Often when I have camped here, it has made me want to
become the ground, become the water, become the trees,
mix with the whole thing. Not know myself from it.
Never unmix again.

—Owen Wister, *The Virginian*, 1902

Deboarding the Columbian Express upon arrival in Chicago after several days of travel from Philadelphia, Owen Wister gallivanted from the train station to his temporary stay, then sauntered back to the station yet again en route to the 1893 world's fair. This summer would take him between and betwixt Wyoming, Chicago, Philadelphia, and elsewhere. Ambling through heavy crowds gathered in the sticky summer heat, Wister made his way somewhat aimlessly, stalling time until he would later meet for dinner with Theodore Roosevelt and other men on Wooded Island. Wister suddenly felt bewildered and *seized* by the grandiosity of his surroundings, a captivation that intensified with each passing hour. Wister reflected, stunned, "I did not look at anything in particular, but merely swam in the atmosphere of beauty and brilliance and stateliness that poured from everything." As he made his way toward the lagoon, he braced himself once again as he stared at the Beaux Arts buildings in a stupefied fashion, the white sheen of Columbia's body amplified by the basin's water. Suddenly, the tiredness registered; his energy drained and intelligence diminished. He reflected, "I became so deluged with this splendor that, as I say, all thinking power ceased, leaving a pleasurable elation of body and spirits that carried me on when we landed, through more new vistas of astonishment. It did not make the slightest matter where one went. I wandered at haphazard seeing everything but looking at nothing."[1] The sensorial overwhelm and depletion of it all would shift only later that evening.

Wister later met with his company in the afternoon at Hunter's Camp, an islet located south of Wooded Island. Structured by marshland, the whole of Wooded Island was an extension of the horticulture exhibit located just west, connected to the island by a bridge over one of the fair's lagoons. Instilling the contrast between stately urbanism and a promised respite in a Japanese Ho-o-den, planting exhibits, and long tree-buttressed walkways, here visitors could find a brief retreat from the overwhelm of the illumination. On the islet the men gathered in a small structure named Hunter's Cabin, a small log cabin structure built to commemorate the rugged "pioneer." Funded by Roosevelt's Boone and Crockett Foundation, the cabin replicated pioneer fashion. Adorned with skinned and tanned animal pelts, hunting gear, and leather stockings, the interior was a monument to nostalgic artifice. Cast against the grandiosity of its surrounding buildings, Hunter's Cabin concretized the pioneer as a figure of masculine vitality and a modern past: an extractive subject capable of generating energy through the mastery land seized for a "manifest destiny." Here Wister joined Roosevelt and other club members for a lengthy, revitalizing dinner, the meal "well and simple," "camp fashion," with whiskey and beer.[2] At dinner's end the men lingered amid the peristyle to imbibe in the illumination—lights and fireworks glimmering on the water. As the crowds receded and quiet dissipated throughout the grounds, the men moved back to the cabin for cigars and later rejoined to their own dwellings, all in the rhythm of their homosocial interlude. Wister narrates the vigorous simplicity of Wooded Island, cast against the stimulating and gradually debilitating splendor of the fair's center near Lake Michigan. As he would recount after a later trip back to Chicago, this feeling of overwhelm would pass as he became more and more accustomed to its surroundings.

More than a simple sum of its parts, the 1893 Chicago World's Fair, as we encounter it in Wister's observations, was the concretization of a world view that understands a white nation and people as both tied to land and capable of *revitalizing* movement. In this chapter I show how that revitalization operated as an imagined consequence of transportation networks and city planning rather than as a discrete property of any given location. Wister's recollections underscore an assumptive logic of vitality as produced in motion, made possible through a belief in climate as a technology of energy generation. That revitalization relied on the fundamental interconnection of *urban* and *nature,* not as opposing terms but as interconnected pairs generative of *friction* as a technique of bodily energy management.[3] By the time of the fair, Wister was arguably familiar with friction as a response to overwhelm and exhaustion. Prior to this trip he had already traveled west a number of times in search of respite, and with each excursion his reputation hastened as the acclaimed western writer from Philadelphia. On the advice of his physician and cousin, Dr. Silas Weir Mitchell, in 1885, Wister's illnesses prompted his first journey to a friend's ranch in Wyoming. A nineteenth-century "nerve doctor," Mitchell diagnosed Wister with "neurasthenia," meaning a deficit of nerve energy, something of an umbrella term for fin de siècle nervous maladies.[4] Wister in particular was a progeny of what Mitchell called "the west cure," a treatment capitalizing on what the latter believed to be the arid and strenuous West's therapeutic qualities.[5]

Wister delivers a story of vitality not as an innate disposition but as one *deeply* embedded in networked capacity, or the ebb and flow of vital energies made in both technological and social networks.[6] The bodily capacity of whiteness and heteroproductivity linked *city* and *nature* together through rail and forged cultural narratives of transcontinental thinking wherein nature was rendered a form of capital. The center of neurasthenia's interpretive clusters reflected a broader culture of *vitality*. Neurasthenia captured complaints associated with the condition of modern life and rendered them objects of medical scrutiny, particularly their environmental etiology.[7] Neurasthenia's clusters of symptoms, regimes of classification, and therapeutics also reflected a broader culture of medical models of energy, scientific racism, misogyny, and apprehension of "modern" troubles, including sexual function or white women rebelling against marriage.[8] To trace those networks of actualizing energy, I interpret Wister's observations twofold: first, the scene of depletion mimics the sensory overload of an electrified city, and, second, his journey to the pioneer cabin parodies the formative West cure on a much smaller scale yet instills the function of reconstituting energy through friction afforded by nature. Wooded Island, and especially Hunter's Cabin with its pioneer artifice, spatialized that place of restoration for fairgoers, creating a nature deeply intertwined with the social process of vitality production.

Indeed, the cultivation of sex as energy—a capacity to be produced, managed, and regulated to protect whiteness through a language of heredity—was but one consequence of the "commodity machine" of Chicago's emerging metropolis.[9] I open with this story of Wister gallivanting in Chicago because his recorded observations and reflection elucidate the fundamental connection between sexuality, environment, and vital energy production, a domain of sexual modernity underappreciated in North American histories of sexuality. Scholars of the medical humanities, sexuality, and disability have well established the power of neurasthenic cultural imagination in facilitating western myth, especially in Wister's and Roosevelt's respective biographies, as a romanticized story of the West as a space of vital energy. For example, historian Peter Boag traces how sexologist's typologies of sexual inversion and nervous exhaustion helped shape the rhetorical power of frontier myth.[10] Speaking to neurasthenia's longevity, Julian B. Carter notes how its emotional vocabulary, rooted in twentieth-century popular culture, outlived its timespan in medicine.[11] Finally, Alexandra Stern's vital scholarship emphasizes how twentieth-century eugenicists often revitalized the story of the neurasthenic migrating from degenerate landscapes to the vital atmospheres of the West, especially California.[12] Together this work establishes an important rhetorical dimension of making inheritance: connecting appeals to hereditary as energy, as well as their later moments of reinvention across space and time. In colloquial terms *reinvention* refers to scenes of argumentative creation that draw on already existing myth or stories. In the context of this book, inheritance travels through the social life of the archive.

The purpose of this chapter is to denaturalize western myth as a consequence of extractivism, defined in the introduction to this book as the ideologies undergirding a model of economic production that rely on the depletion of matter rendered "resource." In doing so my aim is not to celebrate elite white men in the making of the region (though the predominance of men in the West cure in addition to medical writings of neurasthenia necessitate dwelling with this iteration of masculinity), nor is it to suggest neurasthenia is exceptional to a range of sexual disorders operative at the time.[13] This is a book about confronting the naturalized and overwhelming weight of Anglo-American modernity that lingers as a violent inheritance on the landscapes of the North American West. Denaturalizing this familiar myth of masculine somatic energy that proliferates in western myth and memory returns to scenes, knowledge systems, and networks of its making. Connections between neurasthenia and western myths are well established, but what this work does not do is trace how the actualization of vitality is made possible through particular conditions of energy extraction. In other words, I map the conditions where "sexual modernity" is rendered possible.

This chapter argues that climate and environment, from infrastructure to environmental landforms, were central to the production of the "modern sexual subject," defined by a porous white body who imbibes and inherits environments ordered to maximize bodily capacity. I examine the crucial, though overlooked, networks of capacity building: tethers between eastern cities, nonurban lands of the North American West, and Chicago and the world's fair as visions of future city life. Throughout these spaces medical systems of knowledge deploy the ecological and sexual body in ways that emphasize friction and thermodynamic energy, or the capacity of individuated bodies to convert climatic energy to do the work of reprosexual (not necessarily heterosexual) whiteness. In what follows I examine several nodes in this network: first, the medical writings and knowledge systems undergirding the classification, etiology, and therapeutics of neurasthenia broadly and for men in particular; second, Wister's writing from his experience with the West cure; and, finally, how the imagery of a mythic frontier and Wild West intersected with the landscape of the Chicago World Fair of 1893. Together these underscore that critical dimension that sexuality studies calls sexual modernity: medical models of somatic energy production and perceived vital capacities of land and climate for actualizing that energy to materialize a civilized sexual subject. Consequently, this approach reframes sexual modernity as a capacity produced within an intensive network between urban and nonurban lands.

This argument draws from two central threads. First, neurologists and medical climatologists configured western lands as therapeutic places to extract and convert vital energies from their purified surroundings. Specifically, the West cure included a set of techniques rooted in "rugged" habits. Rugged is a type of friction, an environmental relationship that generates force. In this equation bodies become rugged as they extract and convert vital energies, restoring in turn vital energy central to racial logics of heredity. In the decades of 1880 to 1900, neurologists and biologists such as Mitchell, George Beard, and John Harvey Kellogg cultivated optimizing technologies in the face of a belief that climate threatened the longevity of whiteness and heredity. Rooted in anxieties that the new rhythms, sounds, and smells of modern culture would deplete energy stores of racial vitality, physicians in eastern states directed men such as Wister to "go west!" to restore their bodily stamina. Mitchell, Beard, and their contemporaries believed that an overstimulation from brainwork and poor climatic conditions created a crisis in sexual reproduction. This nineteenth-century belief in neurasthenia promised controlling climate's influence on heredity through movement, design, and technologies to secure the integrity of whiteness, sexual reproduction, and heteroproductivity. The point worth emphasizing here is that in these medical writings, climate functions as a technology of energy actualization, and what they call *nature* facilitates a social process of producing that energy—the commodity machine of "nature's metropolis," to borrow a phrase from William Cronon.[14] Consequentially, however, nature would also bear the sheen of white supremacy, one of many violent inheritances of Anglo-American modernity.

Second, the world's fair celebration of Columbus's 1492 voyage intersected with Chicago's landscape more broadly, to foster sites that dramatized these ideas about energy and vitality. In its planning stages fair managers and architects carefully arranged buildings, transportation, waterways, and exhibition to mythologize national space within the landscape of Chicago, making organization, navigation, and geography substantial to how fairgoers would learn to imagine "America" with others watching on the world stage. Competing against the reputation of the Paris Exhibition and the cultural draw of New York City, Chicago's fair would battle unruly lands and olfactory nuisance, all at great expense and enthusiasm amid constant warnings of failure. Like other cities, Chicago's reputation as perverse would draw and repel potential visitors. Despite moral and criminal policing, perversity saturated the air, emanating from the corners of vice districts in addition to the ongoing terror of disappearing white women lured by H.H. Holmes, a pharmacist and serial killer. Amid the thrill and the danger, the world's fair also became an experiment in engineering a "smart city": a trial with thousands of acres to demonstrate the ease of mobility through design.[15] Its organization connected to a broader infrastructure that centralized Chicago within a national imagination and facilitated the movement of thousands of largely white settlers to the shores of Lake Michigan to celebrate their Columbian inheritance. In total the manner by which the fair was designed to be navigated spatialized the succession of moments in entrenching a settler nation: from Columbus to the Wild West to the deluge of Beaux Arts splendor. Not simply a metaphor, the lay of the land through boroughs, planning, and physical movement implicates the production of sexual space.[16]

To fully appreciate these networks of capacity building through movement, I turn first to the sexual underbelly of neurasthenic culture. In the introduction to this book, I detailed how, under the auspices of "health seeking," temporary or long-term migrations to western states such as Colorado, Wyoming, and the Dakotas managed anxieties about the decline of Anglo-European vitality in the United States, spurned by the belief that Atlantic climate conditions affected the mechanics of life. These anxieties were particularly acute within cultures of neurasthenia, a diagnosis that linked climate, modern civilization, and brainwork to sexual enervation. Too, the culture of neurasthenia linked medical laboratories, lecture halls, journals, and sanatoriums to large-scale transformations in mobility. Treatment regimens such as journal writings, sketches, photographs, and novels treated symptoms, aligning proper energy to civilized sexuality through compositional extraction. These memory and observational practices established a hierarchy of impressibility, defining civilized sexuality as one capable of extracting vital energy from western climates. Second, I turn to the central architect of the fair: Daniel Burnham and his design process. I do so to foreground how the "White City," a reference to its overpowering electric illumination, contrasted with the neighborhoods of what John Harvey Kellogg named "Dark Chicago."[17] Inside of the exhibition's Anthropology Building, Kellogg's Battle Creek Sanitarium exhibited models of grounds, treatment regimens, and data-quantification systems. Outside of the fair's grounds, Kellogg's Chicago Mission would fixate and surveil atmospheres of vice. In turn this chapter illuminates the ecological and sexual body as a converter of environmental energy, underscoring the routing of sexual capacity through land, climate, and mobility.

NEURASTHENIA AND THE BIOPOLITICS OF NORTH AMERICAN CLIMATE

In 1881 New York neurologist George Miller Beard published *American Nervousness: Its Causes and Consequences*. In the book's preface Beard distinguishes neurasthenia from "simple emotional excess [and] organic disease," arguing instead that nervousness constitutes a distinctly U.S. disorder shaped by environmental influence. Although he was not alone in attention to the potent postantebellum anxiety, Beard popularized the category that encompassed a broad range of neurological symptoms, including irritability, loss of interest or appetite, anxiousness, lethargy, and lack of sexual desire. Beard attributed modern civilization as the primary culprit, specifically the emergence of modern infrastructure: "steampower, the periodical press, the telegraph, the sciences, and the mental activity of women." Civilization proved a constant factor in the etiology of nervousness, but secondary and tertiary symptoms included "climate, institutions—civil, political, religious, social and business—personal habits, indulgence of appetite and passions."[18] Beard's and Mitchell's invocation of "civilization" and "climate" underscore how neurasthenia guided and regulated a hierarchy of impressibility, the anxiety that particular climates affect the reproductive vitality of white settler bodies.[19] Their classification and clinical examination of neurasthenics provide two insights: first, how climate shaped normative cultures of sex and, second, how sexual knowledge also triangulated psychiatric disabilities and race to techniques of biopower by the end of the nineteenth century.

Investments in therapeutics and cures conditioned the usage of the term *climate,* particularly for scientists and moral reformers. Decades prior medical geographers as far west as California carefully detailed environmental data and its promise or peril to carefully managing the health of the body.[20] Prior to genetics or the much later emergence of epigenetics, Lamarckians believed climate acted on the body in ways that would threaten the generational reproduction of whiteness. Indeed, drawing from racialized and species distinctions, Beard and Mitchell repeatedly invoked arguments that heredity conditioned responses to climate. Reproduction and heredity surfaced as primary; thus the discovery of revitalizing techniques in climates beyond the northern Atlantic region promised vigorous bodily regeneration.

These understandings of vitality rested on thermodynamic and machine ways of thinking about energy production and consumption. Regulating vitality amid seemingly overstimulating or depleting environments through forms of sensorial discipline thus linked individual bodies to the governance of population. Deeply gendered therapeutics for neurasthenia ranged from temporary sojourns to the arid climates of the West for contests with nature, long periods of rest in sanitariums, or the deliberate adjudication of electrotherapies. Climate, built environments, and technologies contoured the biopolitics of neurasthenia and created the conditions for later attempts to order and contain western lands for capacity building.

As markers of "civilization," Beard attributes infrastructural modernity to the disorienting reorganization of bodily rhythms, ingestion of fetid smell emanating from sewers below, and the jarring sensations of noise. In the chapter "Causes of American Nervousness," Beard details the sensorial disjunctions of modern living that he assigns to "steam power, the periodical press, the telegraph," among others. Their introduction operates akin to "additional lamps interposed in the circuit" whose power was "supplied at the expense of the nervous system, the dynamic power of which has not correspondingly increased."[21] Like an electric circuit on the brink of shorting out, modern infrastructure over-stimulated the nervous system, the seat of what it meant to be a civilized and impressable subject. But cultures of work, too, came under scrutiny. Mitchell focused his ire on the abuse of white settler bodies through the depletion of mental faculties. In *Wear and Tear* Mitchell imagines that "use" of the body follows an ebb and flow of a normalized lifecycle and abides by laws of labor and rest. Tear, on the other hand, provokes scorn: Mitchell describes climates of "hard or evil usage of body or engine, of putting things to wrong purposes, using a chisel for a screw-driver, a penknife for a gimlet."[22] More specifically, the overabundance of brainwork overwhelmed the malleable subject to the point of ener-getic scarcity, an ailment Mitchell and Beard believed to be a symptom-atic crisis of national identity. Theirs was an anatomo-politics of the body that depended on the capacities of vital energy.

Race, Sex, and Heredity

The paradigm of environmental influence necessitated isolating inter-nal and external force and flow. Translated into nineteenth-century par-lance, *influence* marked the various flows that emanated within and between bodies, objects, built environments, and climatic pressure. Beard dedicated an entire chapter of *American Nervousness* to map-ping the interweaving forces of race, climate, and civilization. Climate alone could not account for the presentation of neurasthenic symptoms: Beard defined the category as fundamentally a consequence of infra-structure, political environment, and overt brainwork. Beliefs in the agentic capacities of milieu would further sediment racial categories—that is, Beard believed climate was secondary because of the absence of nervous diathesis presented by Indigenous and Black persons. In other words, neurasthenia was a racialized classification that claimed heredity and rationality made white settler bodies exceptionally impressable by their environments. For Mitchell vitality became the biomarker of white heredity as reproduced across generations. Thus, Mitchell and Beard in turn attempted to reduce the perceived complexity of influence by stabi-lizing relationships between heredity, race, and climate.

For Mitchell tear of the body exacerbated fears of genealogical de-cline. The overabundance of brainwork brought on by civilization drained the capacity of the body for racialized vigor and vitality. Mitch-ell believed that vitality was strongest in situated and "sturdy contests with Nature." In *Wear and Tear* he describes vitality as a question of living closer to nature to promote "vigor." In a long passage Mitchell describes friction with nature as restoring a hereditary connection to prior generations:

> The man who lives an outdoor life—who sleeps with the stars visible above him—who wins his bodily subsistence at first hand from the earth and waters—is a being who defies rain and sun, has a strange sense of elastic strength, may drink if he likes, and may smoke all day and long, and feel none the worse for it. Some such return to the earth for the means of life is what gives vigor and developing power to the colonists of an older race cast on a land like ours. A few generations of men living in such fashion store up a capital of vitality which accounts largely for the prodigal activity displayed by their descendants, and made possible only by the sturdy contest with Nature which their ancestors have waged. That such a life is still led by multitudes of our countrymen is what alone serves to keep up our pristine force and energy.[23]

Herein Mitchell paints a picture of an enclosed nature bounded by whiteness, in which the stars, rain, water, and sun enhance a long-lost vigor of an "older race."

Following this logic, if those who experienced nervousness were fundamentally of good "stock" descending from European civilizations, then a shifting U.S. climate must be responsible for depleting racial vitality. Linking population to climate, Mitchell suggests connecting the presentation of nervous symptoms to "ascertain how much our habits, our modes of work, and haply, climatic peculiarities, may have to do with this state of things."[24] "City" and "nature" provided powerful contrasts when demarcating "inheritance" from "climate." Fixing the variable of inheritance as a matter of heredity could help Mitchell craft etiology and delineate environmental influence on behaviors such as vice, degeneracy, and nervousness.

Mitchell deployed sexual difference to stabilize impressibility with racial difference.[25] Centering reproductive inheritance in *Wear and Tear,* Mitchell writes, "In studying this subject, it will not answer to look only at the causes of sickness and weakness which affect the male sex. If the mothers of a people are sickly and weak, the sad inheritance falls upon their offspring, and this is why I must deal first...with the health of our girls, because it is here as the doctor well knows, that the trouble begins."[26] The possessive adjective "our" marks possessive attachments to white girls as responsible for continuing the (re)production of a vitality of whiteness. Similarly, in Beard's catalog, he argues that rationality and emotion distinguish the clinical presentation of nervous diseases. Of one of his more telling distinctions, Beard argues nervous diseases observed in nonwhite settlers derive explicitly from the emotions and unfold in distinct phases.[27] Rationality, in turn, is within the province of whiteness, and civilization remains the primary force in cultivating neurasthenia.

While Beard and Mitchell aligned neurasthenia as primarily rooted in civilization, with climate a close second, they departed in prescribed therapeutics. Mitchell believed time at the edges of civilization in the arid mountainous West would prove restorative—a view of "wild nature" as matter to be transformed into somatic energy. By contrast, Beard studied the body as a racial matter bound by physical laws of energy stimulation and depletion. Beard turned to electricity to safeguard population against the fear of incapacitating whiteness through perversion.

Sexual Neurasthenia, the Electric Body, and Perversion

American Nervousness treats "nervous diathesis" as categorically distinct from neurasthenia, visualizing movement from hereditary predispositions to ultimate manifestations of exhaustion. What Beard called the "evolution of nervousness" implied ongoing overstimulation from modernization in addition to a lack of mental and sexual hygiene (see fig. 1). Movement from the base of the tree to its upward branches illuminates applications of force from the external climate and interior predisposition—the culmination of which was sexual pathology and later insanity. In short, what he named "sexual pathology" included both exosomatic and interior forces. Beard identified four typologies of neurasthenia: cerebral, spinal, digestive, and sexual. Although Beard invoked logics of sexuality in his discussion of race and species, arguing that exhaustion threatened the "vigorous stock" of "long-lived ancestors," he also believed that sexuality was the most important of classifications of neurasthenia.[28] When Beard and his collaborator Alphonso David Rockwell used "sexual neurasthenia," they linked together a lack of sexual desire, compulsive masturbation, and perversion. By these logics sexuality must be secured to ensure reproductive capacity. Disciplining sexual perversion through biotechnologies would include hydrotherapies and electrotherapies. "Sexual normalcy" was, in short, managed by the modern obsession with energy.

Sexual Neurasthenia: Its Hygiene, Causes, Symptoms, and Treatment was first published in 1884 under Rockwell, Beard's collaborator. As in

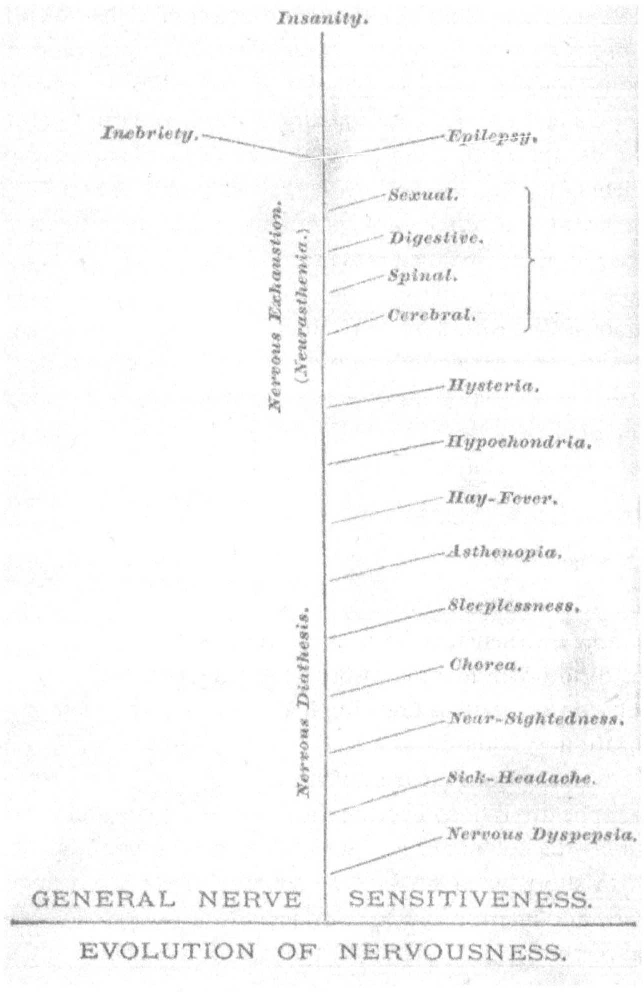

FIGURE 1. *Evolution of Nervousness*, 1881. Diagram published in Beard, *American Nervousness*.

the preceding text, Beard argues that the cause of neurasthenia could be attributed to the particularities of the North American climate and the "excesses" of modern civilization, including "evil habits." The text's introduction reads as an apprehensive attempt on Beard's part to manage the reception of *American Nervousness* in the United States, which did not find universal favor within medical institutions. But Beard believed that ideas of the mind necessitated their own evolution and thus argued that, in contrast to his previous work on the subject, his typology of sexual neurasthenia would find a ready audience. Most work on the matter was of German origins. One of these authors he listed was Richard von Krafft-Ebing, whose initial examination of neurasthenia was published in *Ueber Irresein durch Onanie bei Männern* in 1878 (roughly translated to "About Insanity by Masturbation in Men"). Beard claimed that few, outside of a select circle, had interest in his typology until Herbert Spencer visited the United States in 1882. Spencer, Beard believed, aroused a "shadowy interest in this subject in America."[29]

Sexual Neurasthenia clarifies Beard's schema. As diagnostic criteria, the text foregrounds hygienic problems: "true spermatorrhoea, its nature and effects; involuntary emissions, when pathological; impotence, its varieties and treatment; the relative harmfulness of nature and unnatural methods of producing emission; sexual excess as a cause of nervous diseases; reflex nervous symptoms from morbid conditions of the glands and urethra; the effect of nervous and other diseases on the genital function." In contrast to his earlier work demarcating exosomatic and interior forces, Beard now clarifies his evolutionary paradigm grounding sexual disorders. He believes this and previous works "rebuild our knowledge of the nature and phenomena of nervous and mental diseases on the broad basis of physics."[30] Beard seeks laws of matter and energy that course throughout all of the natural world that could serve as guiding principles for all matter.

In contrast to the mechanical view from Mitchell's writings that believe in the restorative capacities of nature, Beard's anatomo-politics of the body is *electric*. Perhaps as a byproduct of his experiments with medical electrotherapies, Beard describes the psychology of sexual perversion through the mechanics of positive and negative charge:

> When the prime conductor of an electrical machine is fully charged with positive electricity, it tends to discharge itself in proportion to the tension of the electricity; and the electricity upon it seeks for its opposite, the negative of electricity, to equalize itself. A wave of the sea, thrown up by the wind, tends to fall more and more in proportion to its height, in obedience to the law of gravity; and when it falls it leaves a trough in the sea in its place. These physical facts suggest a law which runs through all nature, which the inanimate as well as animate world obeys: reaction follows action, and as a necessary result of action; violent and excessive exercise of any function finds relief only in the opposite condition—in perversion.[31]

If perversion ran amuck of natural law, Beard believed discipline and therapeutic management could stem an unfolding crisis to racial supremacy. Beard and Rockwell proselytized electrotherapies, the study of which allowed them to refine neurasthenic typologies. The pair classified electrotherapies as a "stimulating sedative tonic," a complex variation that ran against the more traditional uptake of medical electricity at the time. Beard and Rockwell clarified electricity generated tension as a tonic within the nervous system, enabling a "fit" response to external stimuli. They also rejected the definition of "stimulants" as technologies of arousal, opting instead for a view of "stimulants as those agents that correct, intensify, or economize the forces of the system." Their work *The Medical and Surgical Uses of Electricity* is a tome characterizing the history of therapeutic electricity, its physics, and instructions for its use across a wider variety of nineteenth-century maladies. Beard and Rockwell devoted one chapter to diseases of the genital organs, in which they advocated its cautionary use in cases where the patient had hope for recovery. For those patients with sexual neurasthenia, electric therapy meant the insertion of a catheter electrode to "galvanize the spermatic nerves and testicles."[32] Without these interventions—which at times led to death—Beard and Rockwell warned against the inevitable diagnosis of "insanity" and movement into an asylum.[33]

Beard and Rockwell were not the first nor the last to use electricity to regulate sexuality, but their writings certainly illuminate a biopolitical culture in which climate and infrastructure were central to classifying and diagnosing practices of sexual perversion. Beard and Rockwell illustrate natural law by calibrating sexual *desire* to corporeal energy: in the case of sexual neurasthenia, "exhaustion of the sexual organs, through excess or masturbation, brings on first indifference to the opposite sex, then positive fear or dread of normal intercourse; confirmed, long-standing masturbators of either sex care little or not at all for the opposite sex; are more likely to fear than enjoy their presence, and are especially terrified by the thought of sexual connection." These forms of excess are relational and oriented toward objects: partners in excess exchange and circulate feelings of "irritability, aversion, positive hatred and disgust." But within his theory of sexual perversion, indifference moves along various intensities, completing a circle in which "sex is perverted; they hate the opposite sex, and love their own; men become women, and women men, in their tastes, conduct, character, feelings and behavior. Such, as appears to me, is the psychology of sexual perversion, whenever and wherever found."[34] In addition to electrotherapies, Beard advocated marriage for those who were otherwise unwed.

Beard's theory of the nervous system as a generator of somatic energy provides a logic for the management of reproductive sexuality, to protect white supremacist logics of heredity. Or, another way of putting it is that "sexual aberration" produced by climate in addition to heredity's fungibility necessitates a "proper sexual education." Even Sigmund Freud recounted his clinical mission to separate sexual neurasthenia from more generalized anxiety neurosis. Freud typified sexual neurasthenia as "excessive masturbation and too numerous nocturnal emissions," neurotic behaviors he believed could be alleviated through "normal sexual activity" that he cast as "its own reward."[35] But how did these ideas of corporeal energy and nerve force become linked to land? Therapeutics for neurasthenics depended on logics of movement, making mobility a critical technique of sexual normativity. If we look more carefully at the theory and prescribed therapy for neurasthenics, movement is a constitutive aspect of maintaining sexual normalcy against the perceived external environmental influences on the body.

Go West, Young Man: Energetic Capacity and Therapeutics of Western Migration

In July 1885 Wister boarded a locomotive out of Philadelphia to embark on his first journey to Wyoming Territory. Gazing out the window with a journal in hand, Wister penned his daily impressions of the passing land and the feel of the air as the railcar pulsed forward in time. Moving from the density of Philadelphia to Pittsburgh, Wister closes the first day by marking the conditions of what he must leave behind, perhaps alluding to a Miltonian hellscape: "Now we've left the region of spitting chimneys and heaps of smouldering coal—and the moon is shining quietly down from a clear sky on fields and woods. Those furnaces are hateful—they seemed like rows of grinning hellish mouths." His mood shifts with the change in atmosphere. As if Wister was on the edge of being devoured by the eastern city's climatic conditions, he senses a different feeling as the train moves deeper into the western horizon. The sky is clear, quiet. By July 6 Wister had arrived at a Wyoming ranch, feeling and later marking down the "immensity" of his surroundings. Bathing in the creek each morning and spending his nights in a tent, Wister begins to feel the tempo of a different climate. Only a few days after his arrival, Wister reflects, "This existence is heavenly in its monotony and sweetness. Wish I were going to do it every summer. I'm beginning to be able to feel I'm something of an animal and not a stinking brain alone."[36] Feeling his body adapt to the new stimulus, Wister believed his brain and body became more physically adept.

On the advice of the same Dr. Silas Weir Mitchell, Wister traveled to Wyoming Territory as a progeny of the West cure. For bodies suffering with depleted energy, Mitchell encouraged long stays living amid "Nature," stripped of modern artifice. Practiced as a form of nature conquest, camp cure was taken by luminaries of the nineteenth century, including Wister, Roosevelt, Frederic Remington, and Walt Whitman, among others. Published six years after *Wear and Tear,* Mitchell proposes in *Nurse and Patient, and Camp Cure,* the idea of returning to "barbarism," wherein men could ease their anxieties amid contests with nature. Although sojourns to the countryside and temporary stays in boarding houses or hotels afforded respite from daily energy drains, he did not believe this mass commonsense would provide the intensity necessary to alleviate symptoms. Rather than "use the remedy in a weak form," Mitchell underscored a dramatic shift in climate, slowing down from the steady drain of commercial time, and to cultivate a sense of purpose in learning of those surroundings to commit the experience to memory.[37]

Western climates—particularly Montana, Wyoming, Colorado, and New Mexico—were valued because of their reverse temperature extremes and air quality in comparison to those to the east. Medical climatologists helped to produce this data, circulating their findings in medical journals directed to the treatment of neurasthenia and tuberculosis.[38] With intrepid elevations and rarified air, climate and activities on the edge of civilization promised restoration. Mitchell emphasized the need to cultivate relationships with those men who lived at the edges of civilized life: "While speaking of men's ways in camp I should not neglect to say how much of its enjoyment comes of the contact with the guides, woodmen, and trappers, and the simple minded, manly folk who live on the outposts of civilization—the 'lords of the axe and the rifle.'"[39]

Mitchell believed these technologies of recording and preserving experience fostered memory, aides to reanimate reflection. Those who traveled west did not do so aimlessly; their purpose included activities that brought pleasure, such as photography, writing, sketching, or botany. Unrestrained by the multitudinous tasks of the city, men could choose how to organize their time in these pursuits. These were not outside of the scope of treatment. But when Mitchell discussed writing and sketching, he framed them as techniques to incorporate the landscape's energy into the masculine settler body. Mitchell described sketching thusly: "It is a capital exercise and it is curious to see how, when you sit down to put in words just what you see before you, it fixes the landscape forever in your memory." Mitchell believed the camp cure would be most effective for those "gifted with keen powers of observation," a nod to rationality and modes of sensorial discipline believed to distinguish white settlers.[40]

Although Wister's travels circulated in the form of the popular novel, *The Virginian*, other popular figures displayed their somatic transformations in the pages of major newspapers. Roosevelt's time in the Dakota Badlands is perhaps most well known for his cultivation of the "rough rider" persona. Prior to his self-described "hardening," the poor health–ridden Roosevelt was ridiculed by newspapers for his effeminacy: a "squeaky voice and dandified clothing, referring to him as 'Jane-Dandy,' 'Punkin-Lily,' and 'our own Oscar Wilde.'"[41] The linkage of "our own" marks national possession in both effeminacy and sexual enervation. For the public Roosevelt's transition from national dandy to daddy provided an aesthetics of land, capacity, and the cultivation of masculine vitality.

Even his attempts to craft a masculine persona met skepticism, and it was not until 1886 when eastern audiences determined that the West had visibly changed his body. As Sarah Watts notes, no longer seeming overly eager and overdressed (as he did in early studio portraits), Roosevelt's persona aligned with his embodiment of a new found ideal of somatic masculinity—he had incorporated the West into his body rather than adorned its elements as an artifice. He had, among other possessions, consumed indigeneity.[42] For example, the *Pittsburgh Dispatch* declared, "What a change! He is now brown as a berry and has increased 30 pounds in weight...a voice now hearty and strong enough to drive oxen."[43] Roosevelt's *The Winning of the West* and his later speeches would proselytize the strenuous life as a means of cultivating "American," vital, white settler masculinity, not only the embodiment of a vision of citizenship but as the grounds for a U.S. imperialism.

For men the biopolitics of neurasthenia privileged migration to western lands to train sensorial management and innervate masculinities, defining in turn the relationship between culture and nature as extraction for settler wellness. Medical cultures linked the ecological body of sex to its capacity to be transformed by energy: electric, hydro, or more ephemeral atmospheres. For queer studies and the environmental humanities alike, it's worth asking more deeply why the idea of "modern sexuality" emerges precisely within a massive technological, social, and economic reassembly of global energy regimes: the shift from the long nineteenth century of coal to an age of petrol that would dominate the American century.[44] Indeed, the conflation of *sexuality* as a category of social experience remains eclipsed from both the environmental humanities and the emerging energy humanities as long as it continues to be underscored as a matter of individual possession, constituted outside of settler colonial environments. Here I am in conversation with those who argue for a queer studies attentive to genealogies of the "modulation of matter," shifting away from, following Dana Luciano and Mel Chen, "fantasies of possessive individualism...[and toward] critical discussions of the commercialization of 'life itself.'"[45] Shifting to Chicago's World Fair of 1893—the White City of Columbian inheritance—further concretizes a sexual culture of energy grounded in settler colonialism in which nature would be a resource of extraction for whiteness and wellness.

SEX ENERGY IN CHICAGO

The expansion of the settler body into the space of a racialized occupied frontier created a foundation for the grandiose spectacle of the 1893 world's fair in Chicago. Wister's narrated meeting with Roosevelt on Wooded Island elucidates what the reformed neurasthenic could do amid such an overstimulating spectacle. Although the immediacy of his encounter prompted exhaustion, Wister also narrated his recovery at Hunter's Cabin. He again reflects in his journal months later that he had fewer debilitating experiences in later encounters. At the fair additional figures of frontier memory would compete for narrative mastery of the region's emergence as an apex of U.S. identity. Amid an annual meeting of the American Historical Association, Frederick Jackson Turner would deliver his "Frontier Thesis," a lament to the closure of the frontier on the basis of the 1890 U.S. Census.[46] Buffalo Bill Cody and the Congress of Rough Riders of the World performed the storied Wild West that fairgoers may have previously encountered in dime novels or sketches. Settler colonialism did not end with the closure of the frontier; it shifted in style. The world's fair delivered a vision of modern life as it was lived and imagined, a vision made possible through mechanization, extraction, and modern biotechnologies. More to the point, these networks of capacity building also served a critical pedagogical function in the service of making the totality of a settler, energy rich nation walkable and knowable.

Largely forgotten, webs of accumulation and production bring connections between sex, energy, land, and infrastructure to the foreground of the modern—and thus *sexually* modern—imagination at the end of the nineteenth century.[47] In this section I turn to networks of capacity as they appear in the landscape connecting Chicago, the world's fair, and the now mythic West. In retrospect Wister's reformed sensorial management speaks to the importance of design to facilitate movement to and within the White City's grounds. As a smart city, its social, environmental, and medical milieu shaped affective responses and attendant sensorial practices. Individual bodies moved, and muscle, trains, and mobile walkways facilitated the entanglement of national identity through mobility and land. The chains of production linking extractive practices and mentalities at multiple scales, land, and environment centered sex and energy as commodities. Yet warnings against vice and moral aberration provided one crucial contrast to the "pure," vital energy of the White City's grounds and exhibition spaces. None was so clear as Kellogg's medical missionary in the South Side and his exhibit of biotechnologies for moderns seeking engineered vital energy.

John Harvey Kellogg's "Dark Chicago"

A medical missionary who proselytized the gospel of biologic living, Kellogg trained others to incorporate religious teaching into medical practice. Originating at Kellogg's Battle Creek Sanitarium, the formal teaching of medical missionaries evolved from the School of Hygiene in 1878 to the more formal Adventist American Medical Missionary College in 1895. During this time the South Side of Chicago served as a zone of experimentation and laboratory for how to cure moral aberration and degeneracy.[48] Kellogg's mission of physical health and spiritual fitness concentrated within what he called "the urban slum dweller."[49] Speaking about the need for physical and spiritual fitness for Chicago's poor, Kellogg joined Jane Addams and C.C. Bonney, chief promoter of the Parliament of Religions at the 1893 fair, in addition to other moral reformers. Here Kellogg justified his vision by appealing to vice: "The homeless, destitute man is always a sick man. He is sick morally, mentally, and physically."[50] Brian C. Wilson details the medical missionary work of the Chicago settlement house that operated as a "poor man's sanitarium," with signatory Kellogg therapies ranging from "vegetarian foods, laundry and bath facilities, a clinic for hydropathic and electrical treatments, and nondenominational worship services." Entwined with his efforts in social purity, Kellogg's mission of biologic living promised securitizing "vital energy" against the "malignant ulcer eating at the vitals of our society," a cancer he named as rampant "unchastity."[51]

In early May 1893 Kellogg opened the Chicago Branch Sanitarium, located at 26 College Place, where anyone from local residents to visitors at the world's fair could indulge in various treatments and diets. The vision for a medical missionary school took shape soon after, as Kellogg asked the police chief to take him to the "dirtiest and wickedest place" in the city—identified as Skid Row at the south end of the Loop.[52] In his 1897 lecture "Darkest Chicago," Kellogg recollects the South Side, emblematic to him of "all cities" in the United States. Combining visual images layered with a documentary style and the genre of an anthropological tour, Kellogg details for his audience the atmospherics of vice and religious impurity. "You cannot find a large city in the United States that will not have in it places which are darker than any to be found on the dark continent. The darkest spot,—the place where true religion shines the dimmest—is not to be found in heathen lands; the very darkest places—the very leper spots of humanity—are to be found in our large cities."[53] His anti-Black imperial cartography juxtaposes Chicago's "impurities" by appealing to his audiences' attachment to an extracted white nature in the countryside. Thus, Kellogg's "nature" optimizes and strengthens bodily constitution for "those of us who live in the country, and have abundance of fresh air to breathe, and who associate every day with the things of nature, that are pure and sweet and good, the conditions of our large cities, the physical darkness, degradation, and crime, and the smoke and the soot and the dirt—the physical impurity, and worst of all the moral corruption and impurity." In other words, Kellogg constitutes a white supremacist nature as therapeutic practice—an environmental relation of sexual purity and social dominance. Kellogg narrates his own nervous trepidation while grounded in Chicago, configuring breath as a point of contagion amid atmospheres, dark places, and city death rates.

To wit Kellogg's "Darkest Chicago" lecture gleans the cultural environment for engineering the White City as a direct opposite to spaces of enervation, degeneracy, and poverty, linking city design to the "perfection" of human form. The Chicago plan, argues Neil Harris, attempted to perfect ongoing experiments with the control of massive crowds and land acreage. Between the turnstile design, the provision of water premised on the prevention of disease, the containment of bathrooms, and the general sensory atmosphere, the fair embodied an obsession of order and control.[54] The idea of the city was newly dependent on infrastructure for water supply, sewage, railways, policing, and traffic control; each deployed to optimize the health and hygiene of fairgoers. Kellogg and temperance reformers believed medical missionary work could morally and physically rehabilitate individual bodies over and against debilitating environments through the use of biotechnologies. These would be showcased by the fair's cultures of categorization and display.

Together Kellogg and the White City suggest a different story of sexual modernity, one that emphasizes land, movement, and climate as central to its making. Kellogg embraced the conception of a modern ecological body that could be refined and calibrated to produce innervation by redesigning and managing exosomatic landscapes. In the Anthropology Building, Battle Creek Sanitarium installed a large exhibition space to model the grounds of the Michigan Sanitarium. The small-scale models (like dollhouses) provided a "bird's eye view" of the grounds, over five separate buildings. A write up in *National Popular Review* described the sanitarium's surroundings as enriched by nature, for "nature has done much to enhance the value of this favored spot for the institution."[55] Scattered across the exhibit were models of the physical culture rooms (a combination of massage and Swedish manipulations and movement); the laboratory (for diet research and bacteriological examination); and doll-scale models of Kellogg's system of "healthful dress."[56] Finally, another section of the exhibition displayed five of Kellogg's mechanical apparatuses developed to facilitate the movement of waste out of the body in addition to improving circulation. The kneading machine excited the bowels; a vibrating chair stimulated capillaries of the whole body; vibrating bars targeted the stimulation of arms and chest; a trunk-shaking machine "*bestir[ed]* the torpid liver"; and, finally, the breathing apparatus stretched open the clavicle from the back shoulders to enlarge the chest cavity.[57] The juxtaposition between spaces of vice and vitality matter in light of much of the foundational scholarship in queer studies connecting the sexual valences of vice to demographic and population analysis of urban environments that dates to the early eighteenth century.[58]

In consequence what we call *modern sexuality* is a cultural energy regime that makes extraction of life a pedagogy for ways of living and actualizes that pedagogy through movement, infrastructure, and environmental landforms. The contrast between Kellogg and fair architect Burnham—whom I turn toward next—is not that different from moral reform arguments in cities ranging from San Francisco to Boston or elsewhere. Yet herein lies why an explicitly *ecological* theory of sex matters in nature's metropolis. Kellogg's vast network of sanitariums intersected with the world's fair and settlements throughout the Midwest and Rocky Mountains. Chicago matters for its central location in creating biotechnical and social arrangements of commodity production—one of which I argue was sex. As Cronon has argued, Chicago is actually a dense network of infrastructure connecting rural hinterlands to the city. This network became an extraction machine: bodies, minerals, agriculture, and electronic technologies all made objects of scrutiny. Whereas Kellogg produced bodily and spiritual order through science, Burnham produced order through architecture and design. Here bodies of the nation and world would pilgrimage and converge, becoming subjects who could actualize that extractive pedagogy of the settler nation state.

Making Extractive Subjects through Pilgrimage to the White City

In this section I interpret the White City as optimization through movement taken to its extreme. Scholarship about the World Fair itself is an academic industry, and one central takeaway is that 1893 served a crux of modern imagination through architecture, city planning, infrastructure, and design. Even so, following Harris, the fair encompassed a medley of interests and motives, challenging the ability to center Chicago as driven by singular narratives.[59] These interests include congressional debates about location, architectural firms capitalizing on its location and design, ongoing transitions within Chicago and the Midwest, not to mention conflicting vernacular cultures that shaped why individuals or communities across the United States or globe would travel long periods to arrive at the fair. Among all these the sexual dimensions in particular have been vastly underlooked. Some underscore vice districts or the modern underbelly of exploitation and murder, most notoriously captured in the story of H.H. Holmes, a pharmacist and serial killer who kidnapped young women working in or touring the area.[60] My argument is not that sexual modernity originates in Chicago but rather that the White City enacts grounds for rethinking sexual modernity at the scale of city planning, conceptually yoking land to the biopolitics of infrastructure. In this way sexual modernity shared dimensions of energy production linked to heredity premised in optimization.

The commemoration of the four hundredth anniversary of the conquest known as the Columbian voyage ignited a national competition over federal recognition and congressional appropriation for a U.S. based fair.[61] In the 1880s Chicago branded itself as an emblem of U.S. modernity, a porous city "open to new influence" yet deeply connected to the rural character of U.S. identity. In April 1890 Congress selected Chicago, and the state of Illinois followed with the creation of a corporation authorized to finance and furnish the grounds in addition to regulating all activity at the fair. In due time D.H. Burnham and Frederick Olmstead were selected as two of the fair's planners—director of works in addition to landscape architect. Between Burnham and Olmstead, planning the fair would become an experiment in planning the cities of the future, wherein architecture and land align in visions of order. Burnham believed "the White City materialized the American citizen's yearning for a beautiful, orderly, and unified urban scene."[62] A confluence of federal and state legislation and national character, Chicago represented a land-heavy imagination of future cities—one deeply networked to the expansive infrastructure of the Midwest.

Reiterating a settler command of nature embodied by a Columbian inheritance, the planners marshaled design and architecture to control and reorganize the movement of bodies, water, electricity, and transportation—in short, relational webs of life and meaning. Design and construction pitted national character and reputation against the very land, climate, and waters that made the site possible. In a letter Olmstead described the site of Jackson Park as "swampy"; Lake Michigan's body pushed against the shoreline, "encroaching on the land," necessitating a plan to contain its fluidity and secure the integrity of the shore. The northern inlet covered with native wood would become Wooded Island—the very location Wister met with Roosevelt and others after being depleted by the illumination. Wooded Island, Burnham imagined, would provide an "episode of scenery in refreshing relief to the grandeur of the buildings." Early landscape design coordinated transportation to the detail of how patrons would arrive in the city from their respective points of departure, where they would enter the grounds, and what order of buildings they would ascend. Additionally, design capitalized on regional infrastructures of electricity, steam, gas, water, and sewage. Above all, perfecting architectural and interior design was critical to the global perception of the United States. Burnham in particular implored that the success of the exhibition "is not so dependent upon the expenditure of money as upon the expenditure of thought, knowledge, and enthusiasm by men known to be in every way endowed with these qualifications and the results achieved by them will be the measure by which America, and especially Chicago, must expect to be judged by the world."[63]

Planners layered movement into and throughout the fair's grounds that staged a succession of a settler colonial past and present. In the grand basin these included Frederick MacMonnies's Columbian Fountain, statuary that tethered meanings of state, power, and time to movement and discovery of knowledge.[64] At the east end the Statue of the Republic shimmered against the water in gold-leaf finish. Statuary of muscular bears, bison, and national frontier archetypes dispersed along the edges of the peristyle. Together water, light, stone, and gold concretized a vital energy of national civilization. As a consequence, the layout constituted both a perceptible structure of occupation through the knowledge of "discovery" and the mythic resources necessary for affective attachment to the settler nation state, grounded in foundational violence, the frontier, and ongoing imperial geographies emplaced in the Midway Plaisance.

Herein lies the grounds to make the structure of the settler colonial nation walkable and knowable, movement producing the modern extractive subject of civilized sexuality. In Lauren Berlant's *The Queen of America Goes to Washington City,* they recount stories of national pilgrimage connected to fantasies of national form that "produce normative political subjectivity and create spaces of exaggeration, irony, or ambivalence for alternative, less nationally focused, or just more critical kinds of political identification."[65] For the first time Chicago was a place where "citizens" could travel and sense the nation and its past in its totality. That nation embodied ironically in the name White City, for its iridescent glow in the sun and the pulse of electrical currents was not lost on its critics. Vociferously opposing the marginalization of Black leadership from exhibition operations, Frederick Douglass, Ida B. Wells, and others circulated twenty-two thousand copies of a pamphlet excoriating the fair's segregation. In its pages Douglass named the vast transatlantic infrastructure that made the exhibition and modern imaginations possible, writing, "The first credit this country had in its commerce with foreign nations was created by productions resulting from [enslaved] labor. The wealth created by their industry has afforded to the white people of this country the leisure essential to their great progress in education, art, science, industry, and invention."[66] By naming the chain of labor and production disregarded in the showcasing of this white city, Douglass points out that progress and mobility of the nation is tethered to the forward moving, modern subject who extracts bodily energy and capacity from those marked for death and disposability.

As a space for the self-knowing settler subject, the breadth of interior displays and documentation entangled scientific racism, settler mythologies, and theories of U.S. history. Exhibition goers arrived in Chicago riding the pulse of steam power just south of the Transportation Building. In the Auxiliary Building U.S. historian Turner delivered his paper to a special meeting of the American Historical Association. For Turner "frontier" was a category based on population and scale as much as it was a nostalgic attachment to western environments as places of transformation for white settlers. Turner, perhaps more than others of his time, shaped a narrative of U.S. history and national identity as premised in the displacement of indigeneity—a land grab that would make settlers and their political systems "indigenous" to the transformation of the greater West. The agent of this history was the "frontiersman," based on Turner's reading in 1889 of Roosevelt's *Winning of the West*. Drawing from Turner's personal copy of Roosevelt's book in the Huntington Library, Ronald Carpenter notes Turner "heavily underlin[ed] passages about *'individual initiative'* and the hunters who became the 'peculiar *heroes of the frontier.'*" Using Roosevelt's myth making as a typology, Turner traced the "The Hunter Type," a gendered category of the white masculine subject as a historical agent. This category was fundamentally spatial, grounded in Roosevelt's seemingly homoerotic attachment to the mobile settler's embodiment of masculinity. The Hunter Type, as portrayed by Roosevelt, were men who "'found too little elbow-room in town life' and 'loved to hear the crack of their long rifles, and the blows of the ax in the forest.'" In his correspondence with Turner, Roosevelt emphasized his commitment to the frontiersman as historical agent in conquest. Roosevelt was, in his own words, "more interested in the men themselves than in the institutions through and under which they worked."[67]

Similar to Roosevelt's postneurasthenic transformation, Turner's archetype of historical agency depended on a somatechnic of space that organized both social and individual body. In his treatment Cronon distinguishes Turner's nostalgia for a mythic West and the geographic realities of the metropolitan Midwest. Whereas Turner believed the movement from rural to urban would mark the end of the frontier, Cronon emphasizes how western settlement shaped the economic and political relations *between* rural and metropolitan. In Cronon's words, "City and country formed a single commercial system, a single process of rural settlement and metropolitan economic growth. To speak of one without the other made little sense."[68] Yet, with Roosevelt, Turner's nostalgia for an explicitly rural West and the rural roots of U.S. culture would structure myths of national identity for centuries to come. Turner and Roosevelt's agents of so-called U.S. civilization were fantasies of bodies made vital, able-bodied, masculine, and modern through violence or by taming the so-called wild environment. Though largely intended for a professional audience, Turner's eulogy would not be the only space commemorating foundational violence.

Adjacent to the Transportation Building and south of the Plaisance, Buffalo Bill Cody and the Congress of Rough Riders of the World's theatrical Wild West show occupied the corner of Stony Island Avenue and Sixty-Third Street. Although the show was not part of the official programming of the fair, spectators experienced it as such, and the show's organizers certainly tried to bill it so, goading fairgoers to "remember the location." As they walked from the midway to the exhibition proper, spectators encountered enactments of what would become ritualized scenarios of western conquest, rehearsing formulaic episodes believed to be a component of public education and history. Though it was certainly theatrical, Cody billed the show as "realism" akin to a "Wild West Reality," in contrast to the imaginary fantasies offered by the popular delights of the midway just a few blocks north. This blend of performance and "realism" afforded the coexistence of fiction and reality, where a historical space was translated into myth in the primal scene of the exposition.[69] As the United States hosted the world, this iteration of the West took on significance to U.S. audiences themselves vis-à-vis an imagined transnational spectatorship.

Regeneration of the Wild West through mythic space positions the region as an entrée to modernity. The adjacent location of the two theaters: one, dedicated to the ritualistic performance of a national past, and the other, an embodiment of a futuristic modern imagination, shaped how white settler bodies could tour the space of the exhibition. The spatial layout afforded movement from the Wild West show *to* the White City. Their relation embodies a kinesthetic melding of Roosevelt's popular interpretations of western history: the present is the culmination of civilized progress and the metropolitan is the desirable consequence of a frontier past. Spectators move from the spectacle of violence to the modern era, from frontier to a metropolis, becoming in turn sexually normative agents of history themselves through myths of national heritage. This feeling body turned time-keeper embodies what

Dana Luciano calls *chronobiopolitics,* the "sexual arrangement of the time of life."[70]

Whereas the Beaux Arts design and meticulous landscape signaled neoclassical monumentality, building interiors tell a different story of Anglo-American modernity's relationship to life. In *Book of Builders* Burnham recounted the economic and timeline barriers in harmonizing interiority with their stately facades.[71] Instead, interiors showcased the cavernous guts of steel shaping the backbone of the exhibition's exterior. Patrons would meander open floors to view merchandise or exhibits cordoned off into compact order. Lack of harmony itself was not a perceptual problem, as department stores and other world's fairs familiarized the experience.[72] But within the web of commodity production that was Chicago, minerals, technologies, agriculture, botanicals, and even human beings were transmogrified as merchandise. In total the commercial aspects of the fair performed and celebrated the creation of value through the extraction and mechanization of life.

The Anthropology Building and the Midway are most notorious in the display of extracted human beings meant to showcase civilizational hierarchies.[73] Drawing travelers from across the world, the zeitgeist informed anthropologists and sexologists alike.[74] Traveling to the United States from Berlin, sexologist Magnus Hirschfeld toured the White City among a broader Midwest excursion. Although Hirschfeld is generally remembered as contributing to movements to decriminalize same-sex attraction and eroticism, his position was shaped by a belief in dispositions of two categories: "civilized" and "primitive" peoples.[75] Exteriors emphasized tradition, order, and control, giving material form to the heredity logics of whiteness as monumentality. But the interiors gave form to ideas of newness, progress, and optimization together embodying the tensions constitutive of beliefs of U.S. identity.

In contrast to previous world's fairs, mines and mining were granted elevated stature. Take, for instance, the Mines and Minerals Building located among those in the Court of Honor. The *Official Directory* recounts the congressional act authorization of materials for display, declaring "products of soil, mine, and sea" of the utmost import. The state did not prospect this as "dead" matter but as central to the mandate of national vitality. The exhibition hall of the Mines and Minerals Building was nothing less than a monument to extraction: the conversion of compressed time and matter to resource "to the uses of man."[76] Patrons could mingle alongside "qualitative" examples of mined materials—including coal, petroleum, and natural gas. Some states even transfigured

FIGURE 2. *Silver Statue of Justice*, circa 1893. Montana Exhibit, World's Columbian Exposition, Chicago. LOC number 89712765, Library of Congress, Washington, DC.

the abstraction of "liberty" into silver statuary (see fig. 2), creating a national body melded by whiteness's drive to accumulate and exhaust matter for the sake of self and national becoming. Linking together layout and design, the world's fair concretized the ideological dimensions of the sexually extractive subject that modulates capacities of life, binding surfaces and undergrounds to a settler sovereign. On this read sexual modernity was always a matter of land and movement, ordering nature to cultivate extractive subjects as the makers and inheritors of a transcontinental national infrastructure and an aspirational future.

ARCHIVING INTIMACIES, REPRODUCING SEXUAL MODERNITY

These ideas and their connected networks of capacity building encompass the violent inheritance of Anglo-American modernity, inscribed into land lines. When Wister's papers arrived between 1951 and 1981 in small batches at the University of Wyoming libraries, "western heritage" dominated the logics of their archival preservation. One of the

FIGURE 3. N. Orwin Rush and unidentified person, with one of Owen Wister's journals, n.d. Folder 23, box 3, Owen Wister Papers.

reasons this chapter opens with Wister's written reflections of his time in Wyoming and the Chicago World's Fair is precisely because I want to account for the social life of the archive. As much as inheritance mediates a social relationship, it simultaneously references a shift in recorded culture, as I detail in the introduction to this book. Specifically, we might inquire how his attraction to an energetic life through his writings rhetorically transitions into a new generation's enticement toward a vital, somatic masculinity. These kinds of relationships to modernity enact inheritance as seemingly settled belonging, mobilizing an affection for the past to guide interacting with the present. Take for instance, this captured homosocial moment over one of Wister's journals by N. Orwin Rush and an unnamed colleague (see fig. 3).

Holding Wister's small travel journal in an undated photo, Rush lingers with his unnamed colleague against the backdrop of library shelves stacked with leather-bound portfolios. Rush was appointed director of libraries in 1949. His eyes meet the open pages with boyish curiosity, thumbing its fragile pages in his open hand. Both figures resemble men of the middle class, clad in suit jackets with pops of textured neckties.

The moment feels pedagogical, as if the lips of the man to the left move toward an utterance while his younger colleague takes note of a cusping revelation. In this scene the viewer witnesses generational transfer, historical wonder, and a moment when myth comes alive. Although this photograph doesn't suggest much in the way of historical evidence, its *punctum* offers an abundance of generational mood. Whereas the fair itself was nothing short of a monument to westward movement and expansion on a municipal scale, Rush and his boyish companion offer another, more intimate moment. Together they gaze at Wister's time at the outward edges of civilization with men of long axes, marveling at his sensorial aptitude for not erupting too quickly amid the spectacle of the world's fair.

Preserved within the locus of university archives as "western heritage," the journal mediates masculine homosocial intimacy and cultural inheritance: from Wister to Rush to the body of the man on the right, who might represent an abstraction of younger generations of white settler masculinity. In other words, generational mood circulates akin to a love triangle, a mythic daddy bromance of western conquest. Stripped of its historical realism, the photograph can be interpreted as a temporal doubling: an entry point to climates of cultural production and the consequences of inheritance as a relationship to unknown generations of settlers. The photograph is instead multidimensional. For interpreters of nineteenth-century western climates, the object of the journal offers a first-person retrospective of neurasthenic travel, the writing of *The Viriginian,* and in this chapter Wister's travels to the Chicago World's Fair. Wister's travels train his gaze toward the more-than-human world; the convoy also serves his need for introspection and cultural production. More to the point, the journal's transformation into archival object also renders perceptible the making of land lines.

The purpose of this chapter is to underscore the social ecologies that underwrite the production of sex as energy, inviting a deeper inquiry of sexual modernity as an extractive energy regime. I've centered elite white men in this account not because they offer the pinnacle of understanding this argument. Rather, their dominance in western myth as *vital* subjects requires denaturalizing and unsettling. Through scenes of inheritance such as what we encounter in Wister and Rush, those residual techniques of bodily capacity serve as deployments of white masculine heritage, transfigured as affect—a romantic attachment to myth subtended by ongoing extractive projects. In turn land lines make sex not only a matter of desire or the emergence of structures of normalization.

Rather, the centrality of land lines to sexual modernity makes space, orientation, and movement dimensions of biopower. Myths of movement so celebrated in the work of people like Wister keep alive these ideas of white settler sexual normativity as dependent on energizing motion. As traces such as the journey take on a social life in the archive, demonstrated by Rush and his colleague, so too do they reproduce a place to cultivate nostalgic attachments to the vigor of regenerative violence.

CHAPTER 2

Settler Intimacies and the Social Life of the Archive

No place exerts its full influence upon a newcomer until the
old inhabitant is dead or absorbed.

—D. H. Lawrence, "Spirit of Place," 1923

Like Wister before her, Grace Raymond Hebard was a central architect
of western myth. Trained in the science and art of mapmaking, Hebard
first emigrated from Iowa to Wyoming to work at the Cheyenne surveyor general's office in 1882. Here Hebard translated surveyor notes
into cartographic form, constituting territorial authority over newly
possessed land.[1] Hebard carried her love for mapmaking as she later
ascended as a member of the land-grant professoriate at Laramie's newly formed University of Wyoming, first as campus librarian and later,
in 1906, as professor of political economy. With her faculty appoint-
ment, Hebard rerouted her energies into the collection of stories and
ephemera to aid her composition of Wyoming settlement, particularly
stories of individual "pioneers."[2] In due course, in her public life as a
historian, suffrage activist, and progressive, Hebard traveled by automobile throughout the state, delivering speeches or gathering matter
she believed pressed a sentimental past into a tangible durabilities.[3] She
consumed oral stories, newspaper clippings, buffalo skulls, nonhuman
vertebrae, and fossils. A Progressive Era white settler feminist, Hebard's
sentimental collecting was rife with *wanting:* a desire to inherit and possess a place of settler vitality in a time wherein the pioneer had passed,
particularly women. She would communicate these desires in speeches;
in her letters resolving a resting place for the materials of her intimate
friend Agnes Wergeland; and perhaps, most acutely, in her sentimental
maps of Wyoming.[4] Her desire to possess an arid and intrepid western

landscape seemed to burrow deep beneath her skin, into her bones and breath so that a western romance invigorated her every step. As a producer of impressible, national space, Hebard's archival remains shape the sentimental grounds of a modernizing West.

As I argued in the previous chapter, the proper subject of sexual modernity embodies a forward-moving pioneer capable of transferring land's energy into bodily vitality. In Hebard's historical writings, commemorative address, and active role in regional suffrage for women's access to the ballot, she postures an account of the progressive sentimental pioneer who is emotionally tethered to the national body through the settlement of national landscape. By "sentimental" I mean a feeling cartography of sympathy that melds distance and intimacy, an "intensity" that moves between human and nonhuman forces.[5] The "sentimental pioneer" encompasses a subjectivity constituted by indigenizing whiteness and policing the racial homogeneity of the national body, with entwined processes of violent replacement and absorption.[6] Hebard's attachment to the pioneer threads two moments in her professional career: first, her textual romance with the mythic figure Sacajawea and, later, her public role in the Americanization movement. Hebard's nostalgia and affectionate treatment of her subjects provokes anything from celebration to accusations of overt romanticism, particularly in her production of national space compressed through local places of nationalist "progress."[7] These charges range from her tendency to embellish or even manufacture historical evidence, a controversy that continues to call into question her claims of Sacajawea. My approach is not to amplify these debates; I want to be clear that I agree Hebard's historical writings center dubious claims and manufactured evidence, which also places her well alongside other white men of the time who celebrated a nationalist and imperialist project. Rather, my investment in Hebard is to think more critically about what her affective attachment to the pioneer and racial homogeneity *does* in producing a settler feminist sense of place within national space and how those affects circulate when encountering her archival remains.

Those remains are scattered across the University of Wyoming campus, but her collections are housed largely at the institution's repository within a legacy collection at the American Heritage Center (AHC). Hebard's more well-known memory as a suffrage activist graces a downtown mural named *Wild West Social Justice,* a dedicated place to memorialize "hidden figures" of Wyoming's civil rights past. But the inner workings of her deeply felt relationship with Wergeland—longtime confidant, housemate, and, as I insist here, intimate friend—remain something of a mystery. By intimate friend I mean the epistolary contours of their relationship suggest their mutual entanglement and adoration.[8] This mystery was unraveled during the 2010 Queering the Countryside conference in Indiana, wherein for me Hebard's memory veered in a queer direction. To me Hebard was the architect of every Wyoming fourth grader's intimacy with field trips to ruts left by wagons on the Oregon Trail, which we encountered long before pixelated frontier gamer culture. But, in an exchange of geographic biographies, another conference participant inquired, "Have you heard about the lesbian professors in Laramie with the shared headstones?" The comment lingered in the air, creating something of a punch line for all queer archive detective stories. Set out on a hunch, the researcher digs deep in a search for evidence of a queer past, going so far as lingering in graveyards, listening to wind chimes shake with the breeze. Queer archive stories are rife with the complexity of detection and seduction, revealing, among all else, the complicated politics of historical anachronism and recuperation. So too I found myself *wanting* Agnes and Grace, not so much to hail them into the grand parlor of "Wild West lesbians"— a laughable premise for some alter-Hollywood. What I wanted was to know *how*—in this place of all places—such a connection was possible.

But, in the process of coming to know Hebard, Wergeland, and their social world, my relationship with them would pivot into an inquiry of *wanting:* What was I desiring from them and why did their displaced memory make me feel *want?* To me this is a question about how one engages with the problem of violent inheritance, moving through the desires to revitalize the past: to imbibe, energize, and feel under one's fingertips their dust and memory. Generationally, I would inhabit a relation to Hebard through accounts in New Western feminist regionalism that worked tirelessly to recuperate "woman" into narratives of national contribution.[9] In this chapter, however, I place pressure on discovery as a practice of archival imagination to understand recuperation relative to extractive energy regimes. When presented with a story of lost love rendered through the social form of queer archival gossip, cavorting with Hebard and Wergeland's intimate friendship to represent a "queer place" in the Rockies need not be a conclusion to scenes of archival labor. Specifically, I situate Hebard's writings about western settlement and her later teachings in the Americanization classroom as a nodal point for thinking through regional grounds of sexual modernity. By this I mean Hebard embodies a sexual politic wherein the sentimental tethered her love for land *and* woman, a narrow vision of settler feminism inscribing extractive world making into her labor.

This chapter questions how mediation contours relationships between memory and imagination, thinking intimately with what archival stories hold. Rather than recuperate a lost figure of state craft, I ask instead how archival imaginations might regenerate relationships: to the past, the land, and queer and feminist politics. Etymologically, recuperation invokes *resuscitation,* energizing life and breath. I argue by contrast that the critical memory practices of imagination and regeneration interrogate possessive desire representative of settler subjectivity. As an introduction to a thought practice and critical method deployed across the book, this chapter grounds the *how* of regeneration through careful attention to archival space, design, and information infrastructures: tensions and friction generated in the relational materiality of bodies, in this case queer colonial intimacies.[10] Archives are, among other things, affective routes of perception, feeling, imagination, and desire. Part of the perception of Hebard and Wergeland's kinship takes shape through the auditory and kinetic culture of the AHC, their queerness enlivened, constituting the grounds to grapple with the violent inheritance of settler feminism in making the North American West.

Archival mediation includes one example of land lines I take up throughout the book. As the conclusion to the previous chapter makes clear, the social life of the archive encompasses scenes of mythic production, transferred and circulated within later generations through sentiment and sediment. Hebard was a political actor who shaped her environment and surroundings materially and symbolically, but those ideas were spatialized long after her death because of their transference into a political myth of regional and identity. The transference of memory garners favor with lessons of bodies taking up space in the world—of authorizing one's deep attachment to the grounds of their sense of place. Located in a quintessential scene of possession in a "heritage archive," this chapter traces the grounds of Hebard's sexual modernity as they move between the layers of her possessive environment and their transference and reproduction into the land lines of the AHC. My goal here is not to merely historically contextualize Hebard's intimate friendship with Wergeland—reading their friendship within contexts of categorical classifications of sexuality by doing what Peter Coviello calls an "anticipatory reading" of intimacies in the wake of American sexology.[11] Rather, I situate those intimacies within emerging structures at the turn of the twentieth century: the land grant university and frontier commemorative culture. These radically transformed the land and incorporated landscape into an expanding region and nation. This chapter in turn challenges the AHC's information infrastructure by reimagining connections between the sentimental cultures of civilizing the West embodied by Hebard's public role and semipublic-semiprivate spaces of female friendship.

THE SOCIAL LIFE OF THE ARCHIVE: FROM RECUPERATION TO REGENERATION

To trace land lines at the AHC means starting with architect Antoine Predock's invocation of deep time as a well of creativity rooted in environmental commonplaces. He describes his vision by conjuring regional sensibilities through the Laramie orogeny, the primary uplift event that formed the Rocky Mountains: "Throughout Wyoming, there is a sense of landscape in transition. The appearance of this 'archival' mountain can be thought of as parallel to the slow but certain geologic upheaval."[12] As myth becomes material through concrete and glass, Predock transposes orogeny as the possession of Western Man, a symbol of nature and culture impressed within regional consciousness. This geologic imagination extends to the vast miles of archival space dedicated to the preservation of settlement. Heritage imaginations tend to romanticize individual ingenuity and discovery, two frames of archival inquiry also at the heart of recuperation. The curated environment of the AHC maintains this individualist heritage myth throughout its information infrastructure, constituting an ambient environment of historical feeling also at odds with the vast epistolary bureaucracy of rail, petrol, and mining.

Completed in 1993, the art museum and archival spaces that encompass the Centennial Complex fuse an archival imagination with mythic architecture embedded in the regional landscape. From the outside visitors encounter concrete and sandy bricks nestled between shimmering black roofing tile and tall, oblong window frames to take the shape of a mountain emerging from the horizon (see fig. 4). The AHC's architecture and axial alignment enfolds the structure within the geography of Laramie Peak and dominant memories of the settlement of the U.S. West during the transitional period between the frontier and Progressive Era.[13] In consequence design's juncture with narratives of geologic change creates an atmosphere for historical feeling, all working together to make "heritage" palpable. My attention to atmospheres

FIGURE 4. Centennial Complex, American Heritage Center, October 15, 2012. Laramie, Wyoming. Photo by author.

places *mediation,* more than merely a descriptor of the AHC environment, at the center of my inquiry into land lines. In particular visitors may move through the energy regime of white settler extractive culture through the archival spaces' mediation of heritage. Archival encounters create an opportunity to hold the tension between recuperation and regeneration in queer archival labors.

I take as my starting point that archival spaces are fundamentally *generative.* By this I mean the ordering elements of the archive give way to both sensations and story work integral to the recitation of memory, an orientation proving particularly vexing for those invested in questions about sexual histories. Interdisciplinary scholars carefully reassert the import of archival spaces for cultural labor over and against the legacy of modern imaginations that favor origins and transparency.[14] My attention to the complexities of the archive's social life builds on these insights, specifically processes of acquisition, classification, and the information infrastructure so central to how individuals actually experience these environments as a kind of queer detective. As K.J. Rawson and others have argued, the cultural power of archives resides in these particular techniques of organization and labor and impress knowledge of gender, sexuality, and race into a web of intelligibility.[15] In other words, classification and its discontents make sexuality in the archive a terrain of knowledge in itself. These techniques matter because archival knowledge practice builds on the legacy of earlier infrastructures. My approach takes these orders as the grounds for challenging the praxis of "recuperation" that has long served LGBTQ archival theory and practice and works with "regeneration" to illuminate how narratives around Hebard and her relationship with Wergeland produce a particular relationship to sexual modernity.

By recuperation I broadly refer to the politics of national "contribution." While colloquial critiques of recuperation may emphasize the question "What do we do with bad actors?" I'm less interested in determining how to modulate an affective relationship to settler feminism and white supremacy in suffrage movements. Rather, I see this question as one mode contemporary publics engage in when asking, "What should we do with a violent inheritance?" Pushing against the desire to recuperate actually enables wrestling with an extractive politics of knowledge—that *wanting* I referenced earlier. Revitalizing mythologies of what Carolyn Steedman refers to as the "general fervor to know and to have the past," detecting seduction in the archives indexes a peculiar coupling between knowledge and desire.[16] *Wanting* locates both absence and presence as an index of desire: the gossip "Do you know those lesbians?" and the absence of hard evidence to substantiate such a claim. In this way wanting is a wish for enclosure in the space between body and historical object.[17] Wanting the archive turns toward an understanding of intimacies as fundamentally spatial, enmeshed within ordering mechanisms that positions the archival queer's relation to the archive as *to know* and *to have*. Queer archives collapse the space between to know and to have, intensifying knowledge as a field of desire, and desire as a field of knowledge. But, in the context of heritage, to know and to have turns over to extraction and possession. Etymologically, *heritage* is "that which has been or may be inherited: any property, and especially land, which devolves by right of inheritance."[18] Although the contents of the archive illuminate the particular techniques and periods by which land in the West became central to twentieth-century

U.S. settler colonialism, the archive itself is part and parcel of this inheritance imagination.

"Vexed actor" is a problem because of *our* attachments. Recuperation in a settler idiom, ultimately, says more about *us* and *our* desires. A resuscitation of heroic individuals, to note their contribution to the biopolitical nation-state, no longer feels sustainable, and for some it never has. I ask in earnest: Whose West? Whose heritage? Whose energizing? These questions map both possessiveness and loss that lie at the heart of the ethics of recuperation. Queer and feminist scholars have long emphasized the limits of recuperation of figures on the basis of their contribution to national or colonial projects. The challenge, then, is to demarcate the losses that can be sustained by decolonizing queer feminist social ecologies, to move somewhere toward a potential future wherein settler romance no longer seems a sustainable nor just place to inhabit. If, as Antoinette Burton suggests, the archive is a place of loss, then the question becomes how that loss might generate and sustain an unsettled relation to the past.[19] Loss often prompts desires to restore, to close a gap. But what of an elsewhere, a beyond? Feeling remains evoke imagination and (re)generative potential.

To contemplate the possibilities of regeneration requires a different historical imagination, toward the creation of an antiextractive relationality. Imagination offers a powerful rhetorical resource in thinking and feeling as a historical body. Despite their ordering mechanisms, heritage imaginations are never guaranteed; relationships to the past are fundamentally bound up in the vital and vexing question of interpretation, positionality, and power. The archive generally is a place of power and authority, a place of loss, and a place rife with the possibilities of normalizing and disobedient desires.[20] To borrow from Steedman, "The archive is ...a place of dreams." Steedman locates atmospheres of archives within the imagination of historical writing that undercuts modern forms of writing history as scientific practice. The confluence of historical imagination and the physicality of archives—touching, wanting crushed by disappointment, inhaling dust—generates "memory's potential space, one of the few realms of the modern imagination where a hard-won and carefully constructed place, can return to boundless, limitless space, and we might be released from the house arrest that Derrida suggested was its condition."[21] In other words, imagination and physicality collide in the foreground of those vital and vexing moments in which queer bodies interface with archival logics, systems, and strategies of containment.

The juncture between sensation and imagination is a meeting place for structures of desire made intelligible by the consequences of particular archival orders. Here the process of maneuvering information infrastructures depends on routes ordered by perception, sensation, and imagination. Sensation is one of many ways an archive's context becomes legible in concert with the properties of organization and cataloging that inhere in a careful selection process; spaces enable and constrain visual, tactile, auditory, and olfactory encounters between objects and bodies, and the accumulation of sense patterns translates into mood, though in what follows I attend most closely to touch. In meandering through the routes that organize my attention in the AHC, I have tried to balance the pressure of both indexical markers of historical representation and sensory techniques of memory that challenge how materials may be encountered, storied, and remediated. The split between the indexical and performative in this case denaturalizes settler perception and disrupts the categorical frames of western memory that constrict how contemporary audiences of the AHC may remember its settlement. This is what I mean by the grounds of embodied, imaginative, and regenerative practice. Toggling with those systems and practices enables archival queers to "recall and renew the historical imperative to apply critical pressure to the type of knowledge we inherit in relation to sexuality and gender and the manner through which we inherit it."[22]

These fluctuations generate possibilities for different relationships between bodies and the archive. A confluence of historical imagination, built environment, and researcher positionality shapes conditions to *feeling historical*. Working against a practice of recuperation and identification, regeneration activates what often disappears into the background of cultural and environmental inquiry. In this case the AHC *moves* researchers to a settler's orientation to the past. But that does not mean the confluence of built environment and information infrastructure overdetermine what encounters become possible. Queer play features scenes of critical disobedience: to normative and racialized genders and sexualities, to the unspeakable registers of desire, and to the archive's mission to contain and categorize.[23] Making ambience the generative point of contact between inheritance and imagination means access takes on a different texture. Thus, if we reimagine access as an entanglement of bodies at the crossroads of environment and infrastructure, we might conclude that bodies engage archives in ways that generate queer possibilities: tactile intimacies and generative twists, turns, and torques both relational and strange.[24]

Whereas the space of the AHC as a whole mythologizes orogeny, archival labors generate erogenous layers of contact, making it possible to glimpse Hebard and Wergeland's intimate friendship. Hebard's collection follows the logic of heroic memory and individual biography, inhering her own epistemology of place as a sentimental pioneer. Shortly before her death and on a return visit to her alma mater at the University of Iowa in 1932, Hebard illuminated her attachment to ideologies of hard work and historical change: "Perhaps my greatest heritage is that I am a pioneer daughter of pioneer parents."[25] Here Hebard produces a claim to belonging through the logic of sexual modernity, tethering familial inheritance to land and hierarchies of bodily capacity, a relation that moves between private and public lives.

The broader argument I'm making here is that moving through the ecological and social inheritance of sexual modernity to contest the relational webs of extractive world making depends on regenerative rather than recuperative imaginations. Negotiating what is actually Hebard's violence of sentimentality necessitates toggling between the desires undergirding recuperation and an anticolonial archival imagination. The former works to resuscitate sentimentality *for* Hebard through the "vexed" attachment to settler feminism, shaping in turn *our* relation to her and, even further, the communicative structures of settler colonialism. By contrast, regenerative frameworks insist that the staging and remembering of historical figures matter in understanding our—meaning, settler—relation to them. To interrogate the *want* for Hebard means confronting the colonizer within, whose relation to sexual modernity is one of inheritance.

GRACE RAYMOND HEBARD'S GROUNDS FOR SEXUAL MODERNITY

In 1928 Hebard created "The History and Romance of Wyoming," mapping county lines, illustrating historical scenes, and commemorating western literature, all framed by icons of statehood.[26] The map elucidates Hebard's skill as a draftsperson and mythmaker, transforming land into a landscape of settler knowledge: the Union Pacific Railroad, old pioneer routes, places of outlaw myth, and scenes of romanticized violence. Romance and history entangle through a cartography of desire, whose use value lies in an affective purchase to transform the land into an extractive commodity. Cartographic science and survey photography have long been central technologies of ordering space in settler cultures: they create a common sense of connections linking settler bodies and social imagination within a shared sense of place.[27] They also function as protean material of infrastructural time.[28] Not only does Hebard's production of settler vitality depend on a land dispossessed of Indigenous relations, but the romance of possession also produces proper and improper subjects of sexual modernity.[29] In my discussion of her prominent public roles, I focus on Hebard's relation to sexual modernity in two moments: her relentless research and writing about Sacajawea and her later work in the Americanization movement in the region. With Sacajawea Hebard constitutes the subjectivity of settler feminism as one who "consumes" indigeneity, the transfiguration of kinship ties to land. In teaching citizenship courses for the Bureau of Naturalization, she also sediments a relationship to the extractive nation-state as a biopolitical agent who protects "heredity" in the region.

Hebard planted the seeds of a controversy that would linger throughout the rest of her career. After publishing a 1907 essay in the *Journal of American History* titled "Pilot of First White Men to Cross the American Continent," Hebard implored her readers to reevaluate what they came to learn of the transcontinental expedition of Meriwether Lewis and William Clark. Their journey had recently resurfaced in public memory, given a national exhibition in Saint Louis and Portland. Recounting the expedition, Hebard made a spectacular claim: "The most hazardous and most significant journey ever made on the Western continent—a journey that resulted in the greatest real estate transaction ever recorded in history and gave the world riches beyond comprehension—was piloted by a woman." This claim of "woman," ostentatious for her time, rhetorically places her in the center of regional and national extraction—the making of real estate to produce capital: it "gave us the breadth of the hemisphere from ocean to ocean; the command of its rivers and harbors; the wealth of its mountains and plains and valleys—a dominion vast and rich enough for the ambition of kings."[30]

This person was Sacajawea, a Lemhi-Shoshone woman taken by force.[31] Hebard was not alone in her intrigue—she "discovered" Sacajawea's story after reading Eva Emery Dye's *The Conquest*. Dye and Hebard later shared correspondence about the mutual interests in manifest destiny, particularly the matter of Sacajawea's name and her likeness, place of death, and later burial. In fact, Sacajawea also inspired broader interest, striking the heart of many activists in the western region of the United States. In the case of women's suffrage, Michael Heffernan and Carol Medlicot argue that Sacajawea become a "national" icon for woman's contribution to the making of America, inscribing her likeness into the commemorative landscape of the nation.[32]

In the early twentieth century, Americans at the Saint Louis World's Fair and Lewis and Clark Exhibition in Portland once again found interest in the story of Lewis and Clark and the formation of the nation as a landed mass constituted through a process of settler "discovery." Alongside these spectacles of white nationalism and settler colonialism, Dye's book reanimated attention to Sacajawea. Hebard complimented Dye on her "extoll[ing] not unduly the devotion of the little woman to the cause of Lewis and Clark on their marvelous trip."[33] Hebard corresponded with Dye and disputed two core facts: the date of Sacajawea's death and the place of her burial, which she claimed to be located in Wyoming on the Shoshone Indian Reservation, later named the Wind River Reservation. Previously, evidence had suggested Sacajawea died near the Missouri River around 1812 and was likely buried in the Dakotas. Hebard made reference to this fact of death and burial in her early essay and continued into her book-length history of the expedition. The dispute of vital statistics is one place wherein Hebard pivoted to a "sentimental politics of life" that governed Sacajawea through a possessive and biopolitical reanimation of her likeness.[34] In disputing her burial, Hebard animated Sacajawea's body as a place to inscribe white womanhood into the national landscape. Through her career-long claims to the "accuracy" of Sacajawea's biodata and burial, Hebard produced terra nullius—erasing indigeneity through its consumption to produce an indigenous settler subjectivity.[35]

Hebard was, in short, a necromancer, and Sacajawea was made pliable to the whims of constituting a settler nation state. A number of scholars have formally contested Hebard's account, arguing her historical writing is rife with romanticism and mythic invention.[36] But in reading her archive, I argue her sentimentality is precisely the point—for me, the question is what her affection for land does in producing national space. Hebard's sympathy for Sacajawea presented conditions of seeing "woman" in land, in turn recuperating a person already taken by capture and violently reanimating her corpse to inscribe her memory as a "national pioneer."[37] Her historical writings are no more sentimental than the homosocial eroticism of masculine imaginations of the West and nation that I foreground in the previous chapter. Instead, Hebard's sentiment for land and white "woman's place" in that land drives her practice of recuperation. Hebard's archival imagination embodies the production national vitality: an extractive politics that energizes evolutionary whiteness as a primary condition of landedness.

Hebard and Dye describe Sacajawea in sentimental language, affixing the latter's bodily characteristics in racist tropes of white femininity. Dye fixates on facial features, writing that she was a "modest princess of the Shoshones, heroine of the great expedition," her "hair neatly braided, her nose fine and straight, and her skin pure copper like the statue in some old Florentine gallery. Madonna of her race, she had led the way to a new time."[38] Dye sentimentalizes morphological data (hair, skin, nose structure) to produce a femininity that traverses time and space.[39] In practice these markers of "race" typical of scientific racism came to the fore when New York sculptor Bruno Louis Zimm sought an Indigenous woman who might resemble Sacajawea's likeness.[40] According to Hebard, Zimm studied ethnology for a year and, on the advice of missionary John Roberts, created a sculpture of Sacajawea using the likeness of Virginia Grant, who at the time lived at Carlisle Indian Industrial School in Pennsylvania. Carlisle was a flagship residential school, a place of state violence, and a vector in a broader network of residential schools in North America.

Imperial commemoration of Grant as Sacajawea bares racist logics and settler ways of thinking about heredity and possession that are central to sexual modernity's extractive capacity. Dye and Hebard believe Sacajawea's story is a feminist inheritance of national contribution and work within sentimental grammars to recuperate her as such. I interpret Hebard's Zimm story as one that *concretizes* racist thinking of blood and heredity. These land politics of Sacajawea amplify critiques of settler feminism as premised in "woman as pioneer" and "Indian Princess." An imperial feminist politic, the "Indian Princess" consigns the bodies and sexualities of Indigenous woman to be appropriated as the lovers and saviors of colonizers.[41] The characteristic of a saint—or in this case pilot—who facilitates conquest is one side of what Rayna Green originally called the "Pocahontas perplex."[42] Moreover, Chris Finley (Colville Confederated) emphasizes heteropatriarchal and colonial mythos, noting how conquest becomes justified through heterosexualization.[43] The Sacajawea myth is a story about woman and her possession of land first constructed by terra nullius. Consequentially, the "inheritance" of settler feminism creates a kind of relationality wherein "'native' resources include Indigenous cultures and peoples themselves."[44] Incorporation of Sacajawea into the national body through the racialized category of woman exemplifies a sentimental politics of life that sustains a hierarchy of bodily capacity, grounded in western lands and producing the social space of nation through the category of woman. Moreover, as Hebard fervently researched the Lewis and Clark expedition for her 1907 article and book-length study published in 1933, she also worked in the region to consolidate the borders of heredity and inheritance through nativism, herein calibrated to migrant bodies.

Approximately a decade later Hebard passionately engaged in regional naturalization work, policing boundaries of racialized homogeny. Her classes at the University of Wyoming largely attracted students who worked as laborers for Union Pacific Coal Company, Central Coal and Coke Company, and Megeath Coal Company, among others. Hebard served as a proxy for the Department of the Interior in addition to the U.S. Department of Labor, which housed the Bureau of Naturalization. Although some scholars examine Hebard's role in western Americanization movements at length, my emphasis turns to her work as a regional accent of state biopower.[45] Among others Hebard circulated arguments to other settler feminists concerned with the suffrage implications of marriage for "American women" linked to "foreign men." She questioned how the migration of "undesirable" people would affect a national heredity and corresponded with national bureaucrats about lesson plans in civics, hygiene, and the cultivation of selfhood.[46] This proxy localized the biopolitical nation at the scale of the Rocky Mountain region, in which Hebard and others engaged the labor of producing national subjects.

One of her more highly cited pieces of eugenics literature, Hebard's 1921 editorial "Why We Exclude the Ninety-Seven," justified the heredity logics of "homogenization" that grounded the basis of a new immigration law restricting the admittance of "undesirable" migrants. Linking racial homogeneity to a national future, Hebard wrote, "No nation, with the possible exception of Russia, has the population problem of the United States. Observe her heterogenous people. Homogeneity can only be maintained by admitting in greatest numbers those who are acceptable for assimilation within our national people. If we believe in heredity—and who does not?—our task, though economic, is vastly racial. The stock we have permitted to land represents millions of unborn future citizens." Hebard grounds her anxiety of the capacity for assimilation in a number of techniques. These include the capacity to learn and use English, the perceived porousness of heredity from intermarriage, and the preference to relocate in cities rather than open lands in the West. Drawing from sociologist Edward A. Ross—who also coined the term "race suicide" as a justification for eugenics—Hebard argued settlements in cities embodied enervation: "prisoners of ignorance and inertia." She clarifies earlier sentiments about the impressibility of land in maximizing hereditary based on the capacity for energetic evolution. She explains that the new law created new responsibilities for "native-born women," writing, "To assist in the work of Americanization for the foreign women is for each native-born woman a duty, if she be ambitious to bring the status of women up and beyond the sphere of unintelligent voters."[47]

In the classroom Hebard met the Bureau of Naturalization's preferred requirements for productive educators, which defined the ideal teacher as someone who "1. Should be sympathetic, energetic, resourceful, and dignified. 2. Should have a real interest in the foreign born and the conviction that other races represent different, not inferior, civilizations."[48] An undated document by the Department of the Interior, titled "Syllabus of Tentative Course in Elementary Civics for Immigrants," makes clear the desired outcome of naturalization. The subject "citizen" is one proficient in matters of food (protecting food sources to ensure good health), clothing, water, and fresh air and understands interiorized self-regulation.[49] Moreover, Hebard's own lecture materials focus on cultivating a civic-minded and feeling body through nationalist rituals. For example, in a series of ten lectures, her students had to detail in English the formation of federal and state government, formative political or national figures, and national rituals of citizenship.

Beyond her public writings about the "threat" posed to national heredity from migrants, Hebard also collected materials from her professional networks that likely informed her thinking about naturalization. Hebard's files include notes from a lecture by June Etta Downey, a professor of psychology and philosophy at the University of Wyoming. Downey delivered a lecture to a psychology class in 1916, titled "Immigration Tests at Ellis Island: Scale of Psychology in Immigration." Here she reiterated the practice of medical examinations at Ellis Island used to detect forms of "feeble-mindedness," among other so-called undesirable traits.[50] The question Downey posed to her class was a one of the construction of medical knowledge: "How do we *know* that the medical experts are capable of *knowing*, after what is necessarily a superficial *examination*, that [the] immigrant is of a low caste; is an idiot or an imbecile." The bulk of her lecture followed with a eugenic screed—a lament of inheritance, heredity, and a will to police the purity of populations. Downey would die in 1932 after becoming ill while she attended the Third International Eugenics Conference at the American Museum of Natural History in New York City.[51] Downey's preoccupation with the ocular regimes of knowledge produced some uncertainty of measures in selective immigration. Disability historian Douglas Baynton notes how the "defective" migrant contoured eugenic immigration law, a national context of "all-pervasive ethic of competition, of national survival and the human race. The heritability of virtually every personal characteristic...and the deplorable fecundity of degenerates evoked the specter of racial declension."[52]

Thus far my attention to the social ecologies of Hebard's professional life aims to illuminate how the locus of the settler body constitutes an extractive subject whose selfhood materializes through belief in energizing forces from land and climate, securitizing bodily constitution of whiteness. Hebard crafts the category of woman through the extraction of vitality from land. These gendered energy regimes reframe Scott Lauria Morgensen's articulation of the biopolitics of settler colonialism, clarifying "modern sexuality became a method to *produce* settler colonialism, and settler subjects, by facilitating ongoing conquests and naturalizing its effects."[53] Following Hebard's land lines into her archival remains at the AHC pose a number of questions about the contours of the feeling, historical body. Archival logics prioritize Hebard as a public figure and "pioneer" of masculine-dominated institutions such as the university. On one hand these logics elide the relevance of her private life as publicly meaningful. On the other the frustrating absence of intelligible markers of sexual relationality, or descriptive techniques organizing Hebard and Wergeland's intimate friendship, generate conditions to toggle with a desire to grasp hold of Agnes and Grace, to resuscitate their lives enmeshed in the violence of civilizing sentiment.

To detect queer traces of Hebard and Wergeland in the space of the AHC necessitates reading against the archival grain, making absence present along the lines of epistolary encounters in lesbian historiography. My encounter with Hebard's and Wergeland's materials called me to move beyond the surface of singular documents. Rather, my gaze lingered around the walls of the reading room, my fingers on the thickness of photographic paper, inhaling the dusty residue of Hebard's possessive wonder. These moments are rarely accounted for in making sense of the archive's relationship to historical imagination. Making the space and atmospherics of the archive matter in Hebard and Wergeland's intimate friendship also negotiates the violent inheritance they leave behind—a "woman's place" that forgets its violent condition of possibility. The question I want to shift toward now is how the archive reproduces the grounds of sexual modernity and how those land lines become intelligible.

QUEER INTIMACIES, SETTLER ARCHIVE

Virginia Scharff characterizes Hebard as "not one to search for a cowboy to take her away.... With a PhD, a lot of energy, a sense of mission, and room to move, a woman, in her view, didn't need a man to have an empire."[54] Hebard and Wergeland met as professors at the University of Wyoming when, for the first time, women entered the ranks of faculty at U.S. coeducational institutions. Women such as them disturbed conventions of gendered labor in academic professions: their movements into "serious" academic disciplines such as political economy and history respectively challenged academic norms for labor in addition to social expectations for normative kinship.[55] Like others, both Hebard and Wergeland remained unmarried, opting for the kinships afforded by female intimacies in the social rank of the academic profession.

Similar to the map that frames the entrance to the reading room of the AHC, Hebard's remnants are traces of her roles as a public historian during a transition between mythic wildness of frontier living and the sentimentality of early twentieth-century progressivism.[56] Hebard collected stories of settlement, fossils, and nonhuman bones; hairbrushes and combs supposedly used by mythic figures (including Sacajawea); and patriotic memento flags and "vote for women" pins. As a recent emigrant from Iowa, Hebard and others believed the western landscape afforded opportunity and political promise, especially for the status of women relative to the progression of capitalism. Hebard's interests in white women's right to civic participation amplified her sentimentality of the transitioning frontier.[57] For Hebard, "pioneer" was a form of political romance and self-identification. Because she embodied the ethic of a pioneer woman—in rank, vocation, and mobility—her collection is one of the AHC's most widely circulated holdings.

These public histories often ignore the depth and intensity of intimate relationships entangled between a public persona and her private life, what Kathryn Kent calls "semi-public/semi-private spaces."[58] Hebard's kinship with Wergeland was arguably the most important of her female friendships, evidenced by public remarks, their shared residence at the Doctor's Inn, and familial headstone in Laramie's Greenhill Cemetery. Surrounded by a concrete border, Hebard and Wergeland were buried side by side under a colossal pine tree, their relation made durable through a black marble marker that reads, "Hebard Wergeland."

I first encountered Hebard's and Wergeland's papers in 2012 as separate holdings, but their provenance indicates previous intimacy. Wergeland's papers were given to the AHC by Hebard after Wergeland's death in 1915 and continued as part of the Hebard Collection until separated in 1998.[59] Although now distinct, Hebard's papers contain fragments of Wergeland and their relationship. The fragments point to the arbitrariness of categorization for archival access and often appear as misplaced letters, objects, or forms of address. Their entanglement exceeds the archive's ability to contain and to separate, generating moments of surprise. These are the gasps in which archival infrastructure become apprehendable.

But these fragments also reveal standards of historical value at work in preservation. Correspondence gestures toward what has been lost, casualties of specific preservation missions tethered to geographic boundaries or national affinities. These fragments are most evident in correspondence between Hebard and Maren Michelet, who was charged with the preservation of Wergeland's photographs and writings after Wergeland's death.[60] Michelet, the educational secretary for the Society for the Advancement of Scandinavian Study, took up the challenge of locating a public space in Minnesota to preserve Wergeland's materials for future generations. Yet Michelet died unexpectedly from illness in 1932 before being able to secure Wergeland's belongings.

At the news of Michelet's death, Hebard contacted Michelet's benefactors to ensure the protection of Wergeland's materials. In a letter to William Michelet, Maren's brother, Hebard expressed a need to preserve Wergeland's memory: "When Miss Michelet was with me the year after Dr. Wergeland's death in 1915, she agreed that it would be something of a historical tragedy to have Dr. Wergeland's collection of pictures left without a permanent home. As time went on the indications seemed to have been that the Norwegian women of Minnesota would erect a handsome museum for the collections of Norwegian women's work and for other material. Miss Michelet was to make a provision in a codicil of her will for this, but death took her, as it many times does unexpectantly."[61] Hebard encouraged William to give care of these materials to Belle K. Middlekauff, a close friend to Maren. Though willing to follow the wishes of Hebard and her late friend, Middlekauff noted the difficult of settling matters of the estate. Middlekauff was encouraged by members of the Michelet family to settle the estate in ways that seemed contrary to Hebard's initial wishes. She wrote, "We all knew the Historical Society would take only such material, relating to *Minnesota* men and women."[62]

For students of the archive, these exchanges illustrate the challenges of preserving material that has not been invested with public value, often the case with women's archives. In her letters Hebard amplified why Wergeland matters: one of the first Norwegian women to earn a PhD, a noted poet and professor. Hebard often used a heroic tone to describe those whom she feared might become forgotten from the historical record. Yet, indicative of what materials accrue value, Wergeland's memory remained placeless. Neither Middlekauff nor Hebard could store the materials at their homes and agreed to dispose of some materials at public libraries near Minneapolis.[63]

Some materials identify objects that may elaborate the context of Hebard and Wergeland's kinship. This includes the diary that Michelet used to craft *Glimpses,* Wergeland's intimate biography; portraits of Hebard and Wergeland; and a gold ring. Although *Glimpses* mentions the diary, the portraits and the ring are objects of loss. In a letter to Hebard tucked into a red journal embossed with the name "Norse Kvinder, 1914–1924," the writer laments, "I am sorry, that the portraits of you and Dr. Wergeland are not in the book. My illness is the reason for it. I was ill just when they should have been arranged."[64] In reference to another disappeared token, Hebard composed a letter to Middlekauff to inquire about Wergeland's ring and requested its return: "In checking over some of Dr. Wergeland's material I find that I am short on a gold ring, like a wedding ring, with a small but very superior diamond set in the gold."[65] Middlekauff replied that the ring had been reset and given to one of Mr. Michelet's daughters. Middlekauff regretted the timing of the exchange with the later request by Hebard.[66]

These exchanges highlight how primary documents can draw attention to the mechanics of the archive, enumerating the conditions of preservation, through which materials accrue public value or become privatized objects. The fragments reference discussions of relational media that bind together Hebard and Wergeland's kinship: photographs and a ring; what was preserved references objects outside of the boundaries of standards of value at the time of Wergeland's death. At this moment in the reading room, standards around preservation value collide with the absence of historical materials and enumerate the arbitrariness of archival orders. Yet, if the prerogative is to provide "proof" of Hebard and Wergeland's intimate friendship in the face of such an evidentiary constraint, then how do queer detectives proceed?[67] What becomes possible in response to the contingent "what if" that might speak to the nature of their desire for each other? These questions insist toggling with the matter of sexuality's mediation.

In what follows I reassemble the routes taken in the archive, assembling a map that organizes attention from folder to folder, box to box, and everywhere in between. As I trace these routes, my own body putting pressure on archival orders, I engage photographs, letters, and tokens, among others as remnants of material cultures. Too often these are flattened as vehicles of symbolic meaning rather than media central to the generation of intimacies between bodies. To me this is the distinction between recuperation through sexuality as *identificatory* or representational and regenerative intimacies as materialized within time-binding media. Thus, to map performances of reassembly as an embodiment of disobedience gives way to archival scenes of generative story work that write back to archival heteronormativity. As these unutterable fantasies move as one works their hands against the sensory grains of the archive, the gaps in the archive respond from moment to moment, giving over to a sensory repetition that soon becomes realized as feeling, enabling transformative conditions for imagination and language.

TACTILE INTIMACIES

Scharff describes the women as "passionately involved" on the basis of Wergeland's poetry.[68] In her recollection of their intimate friendship, Scharff reproduces a version of "Thy Hand," originally published in Norse and later translated by Michelet.[69] Notably, the version reproduced by Scharff does not include referents to Hebard. However, a draft of the poem in Wergeland's papers include fragments that tether Hebard into her world:

SEPT. 17, 04. 10 P.M.

May I sing thee, dear, the song of thy hand?
No lovier possession shall heaven me send!
I see thee now, as I saw thee, lend
To the music rapt attention, forward bend—
While the music rattled and muttered in storm
My heart sang a song of a different form;
My eye swept thee up in a motion so fleet
And kissed they sweet self from head to feet,

Sh, never was love more tenderly near
And whispered its secret to soul and ear—
But thou spoke too and the speaker so meek
Was the gentle hand reposing 'gainst my cheek.
The supple, the always active hand
for others,—if blackened—white in the end,
that had done so much and loved so much,
had lifted loads, smoothed paths with a touch,
as a blossom it lay against thy hair,
a white dove's wing, so peaceful and fair,
Resplendent with life, with thought and will
It slept 'gainst thy face, dreambound and still.
It seemed of velvet and is as of steel,—
Yea! Gifted with power to guide and turn the state's weel,
An emblem of life, with its towering aim,
Its pulsebeat of love, its longing without name
Much travailworn, eloquent of care,
But great beyond words! Oh my heart! Let it rest there!

(A.M.W.)[70]

"Thy Hand" fantasizes about entangled corporealities touching bodily surfaces. The text realizes bodily desire by its imagined sweeping motions and the duration of such affection ("no lovier possession shall heaven me send!"). A first clue of their connection, the draft contains the referent "dear" amid detailed intimate contact, which is otherwise lost in Scharff's reproduction.

Bound by print media, the address magnifies by turning the page over, touching its dimensionality, type face, and paper form. On the symbolic level the poem's content and style express desire between Wergeland and imagined "dear." As an object of exchange, however, these sentiments accumulate value within circuits of relationality. Void of these circuits, archival orders impress together a symbolic and material nexus of intimacy. Turning the page over reveals that Wergeland's typescript was produced on Hebard's stationary: in the upper left-hand corner of the page the header marks, "GRACE RAYMOND HEBARD LIBRARIAN." The collision of symbolic meaning and materials of an epistolary tradition produces a queer moment, piercing the gut.

Wergeland's poem touches and sweeps me into their world. For a moment I relish the covert pleasure of devouring the typeface of tactile intimacy, only to realize the environment of the reading room: an assemblage of chairs and desks in a public archive, at times populated by other bodies poring over materials. The lines of the archive become clear. The transference of desire between object and body becomes interrupted in the moment of realizing the act of reading what feels like a protolesbian love poem in the middle of a reading room with others walking by, casually talking about the wind. The interruption marks queer sociality and the social life of the archive, the interjection of queer feeling into an otherwise public space. The presence of others magnifies feelings of the covert: "And whispered its secret to soul and ear."

The interruption elucidates positionality in archival spaces, affording a moment to feel the textures of Wergeland's desire within converging discourses of racialization embedded in U.S. settler society.[71] The flux of settlement shifted hierarchies of familial dominance and redefined coeducation and female independence but maintained a class belief in the virtue of white femininity, as "pious, virtuous, genteel, refined, soft-spoken, well-dressed."[72] These virtues extolled the sensibilities of "civilization" in addition to the "cult of true womanhood" situated within evolutionary ideologies of race and racialization. These sentiments appear in lines such as "gentle hand reposing 'gainst my cheek" and "a white dove's wing, so peaceful and fair."[73]

This moment of initial revelation hardens a desire to occupy the position of archival detective, seeking additional traces that collapse the distance between knowledge and desire. Moving away from the origin of my search in Scharff's account, I inspect the photographs on file. Yet, in contrast to the richness of the poem, photographic memory remains largely absent, despite reference of their presence in the letter tucked between the pages of "Norse Kvinder." Public records detail their close relationship, yet only four photographs have been preserved of Hebard and Wergeland together. These occupy public spaces of the university in commemorative scenes: women holding space in the library or donned with regalia and staged near the entrance of university buildings. Those photographs contrast what remnants one wishes to trace, knowing the depth of their intimate friendship. Hebard and Wergeland built a life together in the Doctor's Inn, a large home south of campus, and yet the only photographs preserved in this space feature Hebard herself. When the collection does reference Hebard's kinship, Hebard is nation maker, daughter, or sister, collapsing the relationship between familial bonds and national citizenship. Unsatisfied, I requested the original photo file, much larger than what was digitally accessible. Hebard's photo file represents the confluence of her public and private life: public speeches and commemoration of pioneer monuments, gardening at the Doctor's Inn, presentations of flags, and work at the university. Yet among these public moments are also analogue snapshots that bear material traces of intimate photographic culture.

With "intimate photographic culture" I wish to displace in some capacity that superiority of the index in making sense of photographs. The index delineates historical value for what a photograph contains; usually this is a faithful referent to a "real" person located in time and space.[74] But when photographs inhabit circuits of exchange, their value also is relational, not merely indexical. As relational media, photography becomes a generator of affection and desire.[75] For instance, snapshots pasted to a family scrapbook evoke a different intimate feeling in comparison to the photo of a secret sweetheart kept close to the heart in a locket. In turn the materiality of photography *mediates* intimate friendship and reveals social conventions of expressing otherwise private feelings. In the context of archives, researchers become entangled by circuitous desires and tactile intimacies.

These snapshots evoke dimensionality, emphasizing their capacity to be handled, with contact between hands, skin, paper, and dust. In the worlds of Hebard and Wergeland, many of these photographs were exchanged as intimate objects, trinkets, or tokens, invested with emotional value that create and sustain a bond. The backs of photographs, often ignored as empty spaces devoid of evidence, may feature archival histories or fragments of the routes they travel across time and space, handwritten reflections of the photo, or the bumpy sensation of glue and torn paper from mounting and display in more intimate locations. These are felt objects in which sensation and feeling collide.

As a form of material culture, a relational approach does not elide indexicality from the generation of intimacies; rather, the indexical and material intensify each other at the limits of their respective affordances. Imagine, for example, a hand grasping the edges of a photograph to hold attention with the scene depicted. Hebard wears a white dress, shoes, and gloves, with an umbrella perched in the curve of her neck and shoulder; she returns a taut look to the photographer. She clutches her leather briefcase under her arm and next to the side of her body, waiting on the camera to work the light.

If we shift from the indexicality of the snapshot, then we may feel traces of their previous use: torn brown display and glue streaks that shimmer in the iridescent light from the ceiling. The written word

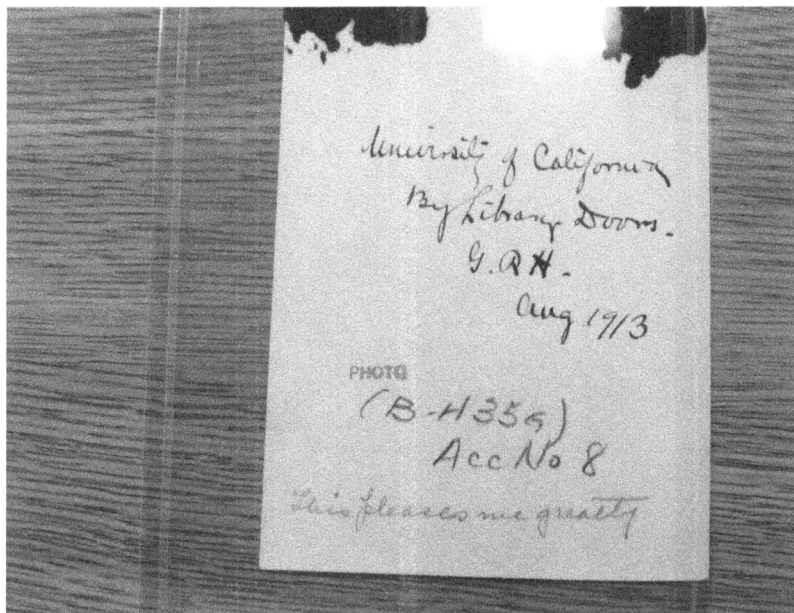

FIGURE 5. "This pleases me greatly," August 1913. Hebard Photograph File, American Heritage Center, Laramie, Wyoming. Photo by author.

details the photograph's production and later archive. Commentary on the back moves us: "very pleasing happy schoolgirl" and "this pleases me greatly" (see fig. 5). Our imagination wanders toward the "what if" of Wergeland as the intimate spectator in this photographic exchange.

Hebard's briefcase appears often across the collection, its repetition a reminder of her place as an intellectual and public position, at other times a peculiarity. In another Hebard stands with Old Main in the distance, her posture places an emphasis on the briefcase itself, as if she's handing it over to the spectator outside of the frame. The photograph is a composition of lines and looking, the pathway of the sidewalk moves toward the horizon as our eyes move upward to the windows above Hebard, both looking back at the spectator. Her grip on the briefcase repeats the nature of the demand—it is not at her side, the strap not draped around her shoulder (see fig. 6).

The AHC stores Hebard's briefcase in a large flat box with other oversized and carefully curated objects. I lift a ragged pink silk scarf as the briefcase appears, unlocked, leather worn and covered with ink

FIGURE 6. Grace Raymond Hebard with briefcase, n.d. Old Main, University of Wyoming. American Heritage Center Digital Collections.

stains. I came to this box after working my way through haunted objects like a grayish-green felt hat, a hairbrush supposedly used by Sacajawea, fossils and rocks that left residue on my fingers, and dried and cracked vertebrae—all spooky and shiver inducing, all tokens of settler spatialities, the impression of human settlement on western environments, and Hebard's romance of the West. I lifted the cover of the briefcase to

FIGURE 7. Grace Raymond Hebard's briefcase, n.d. Box 76, American Heritage Center Collections, Laramie, Wyoming. Photo by author.

reveal two gold embossed names aligned directly above the buckles: to the left "A.M. Wergeland" and to the right "Grace Raymond Hebard, Laramie, Wyoming" (see fig. 7). I greeted the embossing with a gasp.

Hebard's name appears worn by time and contact with the fold-over top. Wergeland's initials appear new. The difference in the clarity and strength of the embossing suggests two different times. Although the story of this briefcase is perhaps the most difficult to understand, my queer intuition ponders if Grace etched Agnes's name on her briefcase to carry Agnes with her after her death. Perhaps cliché, but Hebard was nothing short of sentimental, and this was especially clear when the woman who was a part of her world moved through the process of dying and encountered the world of the dead.

IMAGINING IN DECOLONIAL MODES

Recuperation and regeneration offer distinct modes to engage narratives of Hebard and Wergeland; their contrast also produces different relationships to sexual modernity and its consequences. As civil and *civilizing* subjects of the biopolitical nation, Hebard and Wergeland both cultivated a place in the nation as settler feminists. This chapter reads their relationship to sexual modernity through a structure linking *pioneer* and *womanhood* to a landed whiteness that leverages *woman* as a political identity. My treatment of Hebard illuminates how gendered whiteness grounds a civilizing mission of sentimentality, governing a landed nation through the circulation of affect, especially the emotional tether to land. Land, from the eugenics standpoint of Hebard, energizes whiteness, protects heredity, and must be passed on to future generations through the possessive imagination of heritage. This is what it means to *consume* indigeneity—to absorb landed lineage and replace structures authorizing intimate relations with place.

But a regenerative relationship requires feeling remains in ways that engender capacious historical imaginations reflexive of the losses we might create otherwise. María Lugones reminds us that the coloniality of gender is a "complex interaction of economic, racializing, gendering systems in which every person in the colonial encounter can be found as a live, historical, fully described being." The anticolonial and antiextractive ethos of regeneration foregrounds a material and relational practice of desire as disobedient to the logics of the archive and the archiveable. Critical disobedience offers a conjuncture for decolonial, feminist, and queer perspectives. Lugones's notion of "fractured locus" initiates epistemic resistance to colonial genders.[76] Later Walter Mignolo articulates "epistemic disobedience" of the colonial-modern system, a sensibility that must be situated as emergent in situated, geopolitical practices.[77] Decolonial perspectives encourage queer critics to put pressure on the modes of inheriting the imaginative metanarratives we use to guide archival practice and craft queer memories. Further, queer critiques of settler colonialism ensure that gender and sexuality are central analytics to the memories of settled nation-states.

The first chapter reframed Chicago's relationship to the North American West as a nodal point in systems producing energetic capacity. This read underscores "capacity" as a critical dimension of sexual modernity, one that tethers nation and whiteness to sex as actualized with infrastructure and climate. As the very grounds of settler subjectivity, those relationships become occluded as they become remediated from lived to documentary culture, a lifecycle of mediation intrinsic to land lines.[78] Recalling her relationship to Sacajawea and Virginia Grant, Hebard's consumption and displacement of indigeneity to indigenize her own sentimentality for the land-grant institution was implicitly and explicitly a consequence of the residential school era in North America. Building on a dimension of capacity and grounds within sexual modernity, the next chapter now turns to capacity as the resource of settler futurity and the settler state's dominion over the figure of the child.

CHAPTER 3

Childhood and Settler Aesthetics of Violence

The industrial school is the principal feature of the policy known as "aggressive civilization."...There is now barely time to inaugurate a system of education by means of which the native populations of the North-West shall be gradually prepared to meet the necessities of the not distant future; to welcome and facilitate, it may be hoped, the settlement of the country; and to render its government easy and not expensive.

—Nicholas Flood Davin, "Report on Industrial Schools," March 14, 1879

Exiting the alabaster hue of marble floors and the opulent ambience of the Fort Garry Hotel, I step into the palimpsest of memory that constitutes Broadway, the east to west stretch of highway that is a core of the genesis of a place named Winnipeg. Leaving behind my châteausque resting place for a day of walking throughout the city, I amble toward the Red River that flows to the east of the Canadian Pacific railyards. The Fort Garry Hotel shares its namesake with a now historical landmark approximately a block from the grounds of the hotel. The preserved site of Upper Fort Garry braces the intersection of Broadway and Main Street, though it might escape immediate attention. As I look to the east and across the railway tracks, a silver orb jettisons upward into the sky. In 2008 the Canadian Museum for Human Rights (CMHR) broke ground at the confluence of the Assiniboine and Red Rivers. Opening to the public in 2014, the CMHR became a monument to Canadian power and appeal to a mythic multicultural nation. As the first museum to be built outside of the capital city, it is a place that embodies all the contradictions of its surrounding landscape and subterranean layers. And because of those contradictions, publics representing different state and land relations within Winnipeg have since its emergence contested the CMHR as a reproducer of colonial relations.

One such controversy centered how the museum memorialized Canada's colonial history of residential and industrial schools, particularly after the Truth and Reconciliation Commission's (TRC) stated need for redress to school survivors for the violence of the church and state. In Canada the residential school system comprised a vast network of state-funded and church-administrated institutions scattered throughout the territories, in operation from the mid-nineteenth century to as late as 1996. The schools themselves were explicitly designed to rupture the kinship ties and languages of Indigenous children stolen from their families. At the time of my visit in the spring of 2016, the museum included a handful of exhibits renarrating residential school timelines, administrative capacities, and afterlives of the schools into the child welfare system. All these narratives were organized largely in the first-floor room named *Canadian Journeys*. As I traveled to Canada as a white non-Native and U.S. citizen who benefits from the settler state through my training and employment at land-grant institutions, I wanted to consider how recollections of violence may invite multiple and conflicting models of responsibility. At the time of my visit, the United States had not yet in its history structured a national commission dedicated to examining its colonial history. I wondered what kinds of comparative lessons that Canada's state-sponsored reconciliation process might hold. Relative to the inheritances I map throughout this book, state-sponsored reconciliation renders a paradox of calls to come together all the while intensifying extractive projects and pipelines under the auspices of an entitlement to land made legal or rightful to settlers only through a vast administrative apparatus of violence.

Although museum studies scholars have overwhelmingly established how national museums constitute political subjects through sanitized depictions of the past, this chapter illuminates the importance of engaging in situ encounters with settler aesthetics of violence as an entry point to witnessing violent inheritance. Of course, for some this relationality is explicit in most interactions within Canada as a settler state; for others these relations may be more ambient and implicit. Calls to reconcile with formative violence fundamentally question the structures of settler inheritance; simultaneously, those invitations may generate both evasion and responsibility. Some critics excoriated the museum's absence of explicit reference to residential schools as spaces of genocide and sexual abuse, underscoring a lack of accountability, especially following the mandates elaborated by the TRC. Testimony before the TRC recounted the depths of sexual abuse by priests and nuns, assault and punishment used to force children into compliance, and the intentional exposure to disease and illness. As I detail later in the chapter, the museum countered with a justification of audience accessibility, arguing sexual violence and the frame of "genocide" is too fraught for their imagined audience of readers at a ninth-grade reading level. In their claim to protect access in the CMHR's immersive environment, the museum appealed to constructs of "the child," a presumably white, youthful visitor whose innocence must be regulated and protected from difficult memories. Buffy Sainte-Marie, an iconic Indigenous musician who performed at the CMHR's opening ceremony, said in October 2016 that the museum remains "too soft" in its depictions of residential schools, encouraging the museum to exhibit an "adults only" gallery. In some ways the elision of historically accurate information isn't all that surprising: the CMHR is an extension of the Canadian nation and thus tells "official" stories of only those genocides recognized by the state.

My goal in this chapter is to linger with how these elisions and other disputes render the museum itself a contested space, one that at the time of this controversy invokes protectionist appeals to "the child" to maintain interpretive, curatorial, and, by extension, sexual authority. I'm not interested in understanding these debates as an issue that centers apolitical decisions about representation nor in engaging the well-tread yet nonetheless important ground in museum studies that treats institutions as spaces of forgetting.[1] Rather, I situate the invocation of "protecting the child" within a constellation of colonial power relations. These make apparent the operations of sexual authority as a paternal relationship, in which the museum tightly curates and constrains an expansive emotive field. Mapping these power relationships inside and beyond the CMHR's walls, I highlight the multiple structures which potential audiences navigate—at times critically, at times less so—as they grapple with their own mixed relationships to settler colonialism as a violent inheritance, be it in Canada or, in my case, the settler colonial United States. U.S. and Canadian residential schools administratively overlap, even as they share different state trajectories.[2] To the extent that museumgoers shape and are shaped by their relation to different settler colonialisms, they may also navigate violent inheritance as an active process of meaning making and feeling.

Specifically, I attend to how the CMHR becomes the physical and affective grounds to contest and reinforce colonial categories of child and childhood. Both these categories are rhetorically vexed, operating back and forth between singular individuals (child) and the more abstract notion of childhood that manages competing hierarchies of protection, innocence, immaturity, and paternalism. In a colonial context these terms carry an even deeper contextual meaning; for example, Philip Deloria's work in Indigenous studies has long argued that child and Native are categories rhetorically paired.[3] For sexuality studies the figure of the child looms large in Michel Foucault's narrative of sexual modernity and in various critical engagements with his notion of power and subjectivity, such as Kathryn Bond Stockton and Robin Bernstein.[4] I discuss childhood as a (de)sexualized figure of the settler state in greater detail later in the chapter, but, in short, the "pedagogization of children's sex" functioned as one of the four "unities" that account for sexuality as a "dense transfer network" of administration and population management.[5] The question that remains is how these different accounts interface, enabling a vocabulary to map the rhetorical work of the child in two modes—one administrative and the other memorialized—that fundamentally reenergize ongoing colonial authority. The paternalistic justification of the museum to censor their exhibits illuminates childhood's affective charge—that some histories are too dangerous, too disturbing, too *mature* for broader understanding.[6]

Taking up childhood as a figure of sexual modernity and paternal colonial authority, this chapter builds on recent and not so recent literatures on childhood as a technique of racialization and colonial biopolitics. Childhood constitutes a crucial vector for what J. Kēhaulani Kauanui (Kanaka Maoli) terms "colonial biopolitical governmentality." Kauanui anchors the term in her examination of settler colonial legal structures and land-based occupation encompassing paradoxes between Hawaiian nationalist movements and the disidentification of Kanaka with U.S. interior national policies of recognition. For her colonial biopolitics encompasses "the governing of Indigenous life, death, reproduction, gender, sexuality, relation to land and property, and other sites of state power over both physical and political bodies...while providing a means to demonstrate that settler colonialism is a historical and ongoing form of governmentality in which Indigenous life is simultaneously eliminated and assimilated, affirmed and negated." The operative logic of Canadian settler colonialism is the "elimination of Native *as* Native" to dispossess land through the layering of regimes of property and colonial recognition.[7] When viewed through the lens of Canadian settler colonialism, Kauanui's definition emphasizes different domains of administration and logics governing Indigenous life: state power targets the elimination of Indigeneity and its replacement with settlers as North America's mythical original inhabitants.

Moreover, her concept offers a countergenealogy of biopolitics stemming from Foucault, who fails to grapple with North American settler colonialism but whose theories nonetheless have been used to describe their workings. For example, Ann Stoler's landmark work built on the geographic and structural limits of volume 1 of *The History of Sexuality* and placed coloniality at the center of modern power, emphasizing the *imperial* linkages between, among other things, the sexualization of children and domestic hygiene in the wake of expanding empires, shoring up "political operations...as an index of society's strength, revealing of both its *political energy and biological vigor.*"[8] Geographer Cole Harris locates residential schools as one of the formative sites of biopolitics in Canada, noting that "Native children were subjected to rigorous time-space disciplines, watched, and weaned as much as possible from their Nativeness."[9] I need to underscore Harris's geographic approach here, encompassing land and the site of the body. Biopolitical logics position indigeneity as encompassing *land* and, as we will see later, reproductive capacity—including the regeneration of cultural structures.

More recent interpretations underscore this entanglement of environment, land, and sexuality in biopolitics: as a "bare inhabitance," as Mark Rifkin puts it; "amalgamation," as Scott Lauria Morgensen has it; or "colonial biopolitics" according to Kauanui's theory.[10] At the center of my own inquiry is sexual authority as a node within a constellation of environmental and infrastructural violence. I believe we can learn broader lessons in mapping this constellation through ongoing challenges to the CMHR as a structure and content generator. Infrastructure (including land), as I've argued throughout this book so far, functions to actualize political energy of the biopolitical state. In the context of residential schools, the biopolitics in North America follows a logic of amalgamation, or logics of elimination, by producing civilized life.[11]

Accordingly, this chapter argues the monopolization of protection functions through the museum's land lines, materializing a broader constellation of colonial relationships inclusive of sexual authority and infrastructural violence. I track these relationships through scenes that emphasize the museum as a contested space—an object of sustained criticism from its planning stages to opening day to design and water infrastructure. Those struggles metonymically serve as contestations of the state itself.[12] The reproduction of sexual authority as paternalism in the scene of the museum is one way to understand the museum's land lines and relation to the regime of sexual modernity.

In what follows I draw from controversies over the CMHR's creation and curation, as they relate to materials of Canada's official policy on Native sovereignty and identity. First, I contextualize childhood within colonial biopolitics by rereading key administrative documents responsible for the systemization of shifting management systems. In these documents child and childhood are used as analogies at the level of *population* as much as they reference individual children. These include the Bagot Commission's *Report on the Affairs of the Indians in Canada* (1845), Egerton Ryerson's *Report on Industrial Schools* (1847), and Nicholas Flood Davin's *Report on Industrial Schools for Indians and Half-Breeds* (1879), or the *Davin Report*. These reports also reflect shifting terms for these institutions: "manual labor camps," "industrial schools," and, finally, "residential schools." These shifts in language are important in that they explicitly reference the shifting institutional function of these spaces in relation to operating in loco parentis to Native children. Moreover, the reports' movement from work to industriousness and finally to residential confinement respectively trace an extractive regime, rooted in logics of individuation and the (always incomplete yet incredibly violent) obstruction of reproductive capacity.

Next I move to narrate key museum controversies, in addition to two exhibits dedicated to the memorializing of the residential school period. The first exhibit, *Childhood Denied,* is part of a permanent and official gallery, created and curated by the CMHR. I juxtapose this reading with an encounter of the *Witness Blanket,* installed into the museum's *Expressions Gallery* between December 2015 and June 2016. Located on one of the upper floors, the *Witness Blanket* was housed in a gallery that hosts temporary exhibits, often highlighting timely materials or individual artists. The *Witness Blanket* is a project created by master carver Carey Newman (Kwagiulth and Coast Salish) and takes shape as a sweeping installation composed of objects recovered from residential schools and survivors. The contrast between the exhibits illuminates radically different logics of collection, witness, and care from artists, community members, and the Canadian state. Interpreting the CMHR's settler aesthetics and strategies of emotional regulation help us understand the possibilities and limits of its attempt to model responsibility. These highlight how the institution itself is not solely a container of violent inheritance but a materialization of biopolitical strategies of violent colonial governance.

This chapter's readings shift across administrative language, academic scholarship, and individuals in space. Similar to earlier chapters, I use *Indigenous* and *indigeneity* as analytics to describe Native relationships to land and political sovereignty.[13] These are not themselves settler-based racializing terms in this context. In writing about administrative documents from the Department of Indian Affairs and state officials, their terms of "Native" or "Indians of Canada" *do* operate as *state-imposed* racial terms through biopolitical governance.[14] My aim is to map the modes of governance that the colonial state requires, carefully tracking a racial imaginary *and* the legal and cartographic modes that erode Indigenous nation sovereignty. Canada's legislating of "the status Indian" is one of many ways the state constrains nation-to-nation sovereignty.[15]

DAMAGE-CENTERED RESEARCH AND THE ETHICS OF WITNESSING

One cannot fully grapple with the formation of North American sexual modernities without acknowledging residential schools as technologies central to settler colonialism. I expand on this central thesis of queer Indigenous studies with greater detail in the next section but for now want to underscore that sexual modernity and settler colonialism are *not* parallel to each other; rather, they are mutually imbricated processes of land expropriation.[16] Encountering the *Witness Blanket,* I was motivated by a long-standing interest in anticolonial critiques of sexual violence, in addition to ongoing struggles for Indigenous sovereignty.[17] One of the critical dimension of settler colonial critiques from Audra Simpson (Mohawk Kahnawake) includes how state frames of "recognition" and "reconciliation" enact a liberal horizon of justice. Simpson emphasizes the "time of reconciliation" as a technique of ongoing possession: "when the difficult past would be reconciled to the present even as that past itself remains structured through a geopolitical dispossession, starvation, death, and ongoing legal forms of dispossession."[18] Even as Canada has offered a former apology for its history of residential schools, the ongoing circulation of reconciliation discourses also structure the frames of meaning making around "violent inheritance." Reconciliation—the coming together of multiple factions in the absence of settler *disinheritance* maintains settler geopolitical authority. Disinheritance would highlight a far different imagination of action because it requires relinquishing what was never ours to possess from the beginning. Thus, one of the questions that lingers for me is how "witnessing," as modeled by Newman's *Witness Blanket,* juxtaposes state-sponsored frames of reconciliation.

I've conceptualized *inheritance* in this book as an active process of meaning making around histories of extractivism even as they may not seem related as such. In the context of Newman's project, witnessing entails a physical encounter with remnants of residential schools. He describes those objects themselves as story keepers, witness to both violence and survivance. To witness in Newman's project entails multiple though variable kinds of action or emotional response. For Newman, who identifies as an intergenerational survivor, affected by a relative's experience, witness remembers, honors, and promotes healing through resurgence of language and tradition.[19] Settlers such as myself may be more or less willing to incorporate responsibility, which Newman also acknowledges in his dedication statement: "For the people who want to learn and for those who feel guilt. For those who walk beside us and those who are, only now, ready to walk beside us."[20] Overarchingly, witnessing accounts for in situ moments in which an onlooker takes responsibility for what they encounter. One responsibility includes relationship to violent inheritance as a structure of meaning and feeling structured as a settler logic of intergenerational kinship and land-based capital.

But how one shifts from encounter to the ongoing, active witness remains less perspicuous, particularly in cases where these moments are structured by institutional spaces. As a communication scholar, I know how vexed state museum spaces can be, and there is no way to guarantee that audiences come away with singular experiences that align their beliefs, emotions, or desire for action. Still, it's important to ask: What is the museum designed to elicit from its imagined audiences, and how do these designs engage (and elude) the body's emotionality? To this end I examine different invitations to witness that emerge in curatorial contexts and the sorts of political subjects museums produce (or fail to produce).

For me as a white non-Native and U.S. citizen, witnessing might at the very least entail tracing systems of interconnected violence between the United States and Canada. In my attention to witnessing as a contrast to state-sponsored reconciliation, I wonder how the former may support enacting different relationships. Those relationships might take shape under the auspices of collaborative stewardship. Detailed more robustly in this chapter's conclusion in addition to the book's concluding chapter, collaborative stewardship serves as a framework for the later acquisition agreement made in 2019 between the CMHR and master carver Newman. Collaborative stewardship is a framework more closely grounded in reciprocity and antithetical to the extractivism of settler systems of inheritance.[21]

By engaging with the museum's justification for censorship of particular sexual content, in addition to how they invite museumgoers to process their emotional reaction more generally, I hope that readers can reflect on how state institutions circumvent responsibility to those they've harmed and call on state citizens to potentially act in similar ways. However, regardless of how deeply I reflect on the ethics of writing and researching historical systems of violence, a focus on residential schools comes with a tangle of challenges. First is what Eve Tuck calls "damage centered research," which supplants resilience and resurgence with a focus on experiences of violence.[22] This focus can exacerbate already existing extractive relationships, particularly about sexual violence. I have lingered with the question of whether reproducing scenes of violence in this text is a pathway toward witnessing. Or should I linger with the various alibis of the state in evading the scale and scope of violence in making and maintaining a colonial regime? My focus has largely been the latter. I have made an explicit choice not to reproduce detailed horrors of specific scenes here, instead making references to arguments circulating in the press, public writing, and documentation of testimonials during the TRC proceedings.

Even prior to the 2021 discovery of unmarked graves at several former residential schools, the extent of physical and sexual abuse in addition to chronic exposure to illness constituted a tortuous regime well documented in various registers: by early investigations and inquiries, in community knowledge, and by scholars and TRC reports. As this book goes to press, forensic investigations in Canada are continuing to unearth remains at places such as Kamloops Industrial School and Marieval Residential School. As more investigations are under way, given the long documentation of genocide, we know upward of tens to hundreds of thousands will be found. The fact of the graves was never a secret; no, their burials spurred cover-ups and denial. Meanwhile, on June 22, 2021, the U.S. secretary of the interior, Deb Haaland (Laguna Pueblo), called for the first U.S. national investigation of federal boarding school policies. In particular her memo directed the Department of the Interior to identify archival records, burial sites, and former school locations.[23]

I hope a frame of witnessing might be generative to imagine and enact different relationships in remaking these legacies of violent inheritance that also presumes an entitlement to land in both the United States and Canada. In particular witnessing constitutes an active process of "collaborative stewardship." I ask what *responsibility* these critiques of "reconciliation" and the legacy of residential schools generate for settlers and non-Natives. The risk of this question is to recenter the settler subject. My aim, however, is to underscore the debt attending reconciliation for those who benefit most from durable structures of dispossession or, to echo the words of historian Roger Epp, "How do we solve the settler problem?"[24] Can witnessing create the communicative conditions necessary to make a world of *disinheritance,* a social relation of relinquishment of the grounds suturing settler entitlements to land in North America?

CHILDHOOD AND THE BIOPOLITICS OF RESIDENTIAL SCHOOLS

In the mid-nineteenth century, the Canadian government shifted official policy toward "Indians in Canada," the phrase used to gather First Nations, Inuit, and Métis under an administrative rubric of "civilizing" (rather than earlier, more directly military control). Although industrial schools and religious missions had selectively operated before this time, the turn to a systematized federally financed residential school system would follow the recommendations of the Bagot Commission's report.[25] The commission would argue for an assimilative strategy to facilitate a number of colonial imperatives: the acquisition of lands to be integrated into the state's holdings; domestication of Indigenous peoples into an agricultural life; and, through education, the cultivation of "civilized habits," Christo-religious thoughts, and feelings.[26] Ensuing administrative documents built on attempts to assimilate, proffering a range of different management systems for residential schools as state-financed and church-managed institutions. This section details how these reports invoked child and childhood as analogies that authorized paternalistic settler colonial governance in addition to literal embodiments of children.

Three reports in particular structured management systems: the Bagot Commission's *Report on the Affairs,* Ryerson's *Report on Industrial Schools,* and the *Davin Report* intended to rupture the influence of familial lands. I primarily focus on the latter two, signed in 1847 and 1879, because, as administrative language shifts around child as a construct, these reports also move from implicit to explicit references to eugenic fantasies of a settler state's dominion over the reproductive capacity and kinship of Indigenous peoples. This reading matters precisely because it maps residential schools in the broader story of this book: that settler sexual modernity functions as an extractive relationship. "Elimination" both expanded colonial land regimes and worked to produce civilized subjects. I paraphrase Cole Harris: these institutions did not so much discipline or normalize as much as their function was to *remake* stolen children into usable workers.[27] This connection builds on critiques in Indigenous studies of Foucault and Giorgio Agamben that call for and theorize more complex vocabularies of biopolitics and necropolitics, given the land-based strategies and context of elimination. First, I share a map of key terms that highlight the function of land and the rhetorical power of child and childhood in the affirmation and negation of Indigenous life and lands. Second, I examine key passages in Ryerson's and Davin's reports, mapping the linkage between these terms and state-sanctioned eugenic policy. Across these I show that the Canadian nation-state framed inheritance as the expansion of a territorial land base through forced labor in addition to the targeted elimination of Natives as *native,* to echo Kauanui.

As the chief superintendent of education in Upper Canada, Egerton Ryerson penned a report for the Indian Affairs Branch, regarding management principles in "manual labor camps" for Indigenous children and youth. Ryerson divided his report into three general sections: the terminology and designation of these sites, what role the government should have in oversight and management, and, finally, a breakdown of general regulations to create a replicable and efficient system. Ryerson took issue with the designation of "manual labor schools," insisting they instead be called "industrial schools." Over the time of the operation, the names for these sites shifted (manual labor, industrial, residential), and shifts in those terms highlight changes in policy or what the state believed to be their function in the colonization process. Notably, Ryerson also argued for a specific time breakdown between "labor" and "instruction." In the summer he called for twelve hours of labor and two to four hours of instruction. In the spring, when labor was more intensive, Ryerson believed all instruction should cease. By calling the sites "industrial," Ryerson wanted to emphasize their connection to "domestic" and "spiritual" education as well as the technological promise of Anglo-Canadian modernity. He was clear that, in contrast to the manual labor sites, the industrial school would emphasize work: "making industrial farmers" and "learning is provided for and pursued only so far as it will contribute to that end."[28] In practice "learning" looked like the colonization of thought and spirt through largely land-based work.

Work continued to be at the center of what Ryerson referred to as "Indian economics," which insisted the colonial project of civilization fails in the absence of "the influence of, not only religious instruction and sentiment but of religious feelings." He believed that "the Native," typified by emotional excess and immature intellectual development, necessitated religious feeling "to improve and elevate his character and condition."[29] "Indian economics" centered agricultural time, domestic education, and religious instruction through structures of work; the industrial school, then, created *industrious* future agrarians: potential masters of transactional relationships, bookkeepers, and self-sufficient managers. This system, Ryerson believed, would require—by which he also meant ground—government oversight through occasional inspections in addition to the outsourcing of financial bookkeeping to the children themselves to protect the institution from claims of malfeasance.

Recall from the introduction to this book that "work" is a central modality of energy, in that one of the primary operations of modern energy is the transformation of matter to usefulness. I expand on agriculture's energetic dimensions in the next chapter; here I want to emphasize that in this arrangement settler colonialism takes children as the "matter" to transform into present and future use for the settler state. By present I mean children had already been stolen from their families and lands, and by future I mean that Ryerson (and later administrators) desired their *domestication* into a "productive," agricultural life, cultivating lands taken from their own bands or others. Moreover, by this time children in manual labor schools were already subject to disease exposure and neglect. In *Dying from Improvement,* Sherene Razack notes that First Nations were believed to have an *unclean nature* by colonial standards. Residential schools, as extensions of colonial hygiene and enculturation, promised to "save the child." Instead, governing authorities would expose children to fatal disease or chronic underfeeding, creating conditions that facilitated their death.[30] In Ryerson's imagination *industrial* functions as the pivot between intellectual incapacity and self-sufficiency, promising the economization of life. Ryerson's linkage has enormous stakes for how I am thinking about inheritance in this project. Arguably, he uses child and childhood as proxy for cultivating energy for the settler state. In this iteration industrial schools tethered a physical geography of forced containment with the logics of paternal governance, all the while implicitly invoking *energy* as an authoritarian relationship. This nexus of producing life while also negating that very life partly accounts for the complexity of biopolitical and necropolitical logics of governance as we see here. Inheritance in this iteration is the violent redirecting of lines of caretaking into the theft of land and life.

After the passage of the Indian Act in 1876, Prime Minister John A. McDonald's government accelerated a policy of aggressive assimilation, aided by a legal regime. Bonita Lawrence calls attention to how the act instills strategies of classification, which culminated in the kinship regulating the term "status Indian."[31] In 1879 the new confederation questioned again a different management system, driven by the expansionist fantasies of McDonald. On assignment from the prime minister, Nicholas Flood Davin completed a tour of residential schools in the United States. In Washington, DC, Davin met with Carl Schurz, secretary of the interior; E.A. Hayt, commissioner of Indian Affairs; and chiefs representing the "Five Civilized Tribes."[32] Davin's tour coincided with the opening of the Carlisle Indian Industrial School, operated by Lt. Richard Pratt. Following his meetings in Washington, Davin traveled to Minnesota and toured a mission-run contract boarding school.[33] Davin's report created a philosophical justification for compulsory education. Similar to Ryerson, his calculus argued first for the need to target children as objects of colonial policy, followed by a suggestion to institute a "contract" system in which the church, on contract from the state, would manage daily life in the schools. To highlight key shifts in the *Davin Report,* I address Davin's rhetorical methods. First, Davin oscillated between the *construct* of childhood as a colonial abstraction to forward population-based arguments that Indigenous peoples were immature, emotionally excessive, and intellectually inferior; and, second, Davin extended arguments in favor of state policy targeting individual children as access points for Native *amalgamation* into the body politic. In short, Davin explicitly used eugenic principles to make the case for a contract-based management system.

Throughout his report Davin articulated his understanding of the childhood analogy's possibilities and limits for defining the scale of colonial policy. Undoubtedly, he believed a system that forced residency in remote areas would rupture the influence of familial lands. This appeal to the locus of "influence" functions through registers of scientific racism. In no uncertain terms, he claims, the child "who goes to a day school learns little, and what little he learns is soon forgotten, while his tastes are fashioned at home, and his *inherited aversion to toil* is in no way combated." By framing "aversion to toil" as a matter of inheritance, Davin invokes "Native" as a *racial* category of population and state biopolitical governance. Simultaneously, he uses "child" as a "racial" analogy and object of scrutiny to tether individual children to the metric of population. Davin further shifts between population and an analogy to assert paternal authority:

> The Indian is sometimes spoken of as a child, but he is very far from being a child. The race is in its childhood. *As far as the childhood analogy is applicable, what it suggests is a policy that shall look patiently for fruit, not after five or ten years but after a generation or two.* The analogy is misleading when we come to deal with the adult, and is of course a mere truism and not a figure of speech when we take charge of the Indian in a period of infancy. There is, it is true, in the adult, the helplessness of mind of the child, as well as the practical helplessness; there is too, the child's want of perspective; but there is little of the child's receptivity.[34]

From the start Davin analogizes childhood—associations of immaturity, potential for change, and malleability—at the level of population. When framed as an abstraction for population, childhood differentiates between "perspective" and "receptivity" to mark intelligence against the capacity for coercion. He uses the temporal logic of maturity to construct the relation between a child as *individual* and child*hood* as a colonial construct of racialized ability.

Davin's logic follows a progressive metric of maturity consigned to the site of the body, an intimate geography of colonial biopolitics that spans generations. His third sentence in this passage explicitly appeals to a eugenic logic of governance: that policy success can be measured "after a generation or two." This is a progress narrative, yes, but, more to the point, a eugenics temporality presumes an intervention in reproductive capacity whose consequences can be observed in the future. Producing shifts in bodily comportment and disposition, capacity could be determined through the incorporation of elements such as an English education and success in *producing* heterosexuality through a colonial gender system that organizes life in accordance to a binary of masculine and feminine.[35] Gender in this case is also sexualized. In separate boys' and girls' education, each child learned the habits of future "husbands" and "wives" within autonomous households.

Architects and design enabled and constrained physical contact with visiting family members and the assembly of children with their family members. The remote locations produced geographies of displacement:

specifically, attachments to place, identity, and language.[36] The carceral nature of individual schools includes four characteristics: remoteness, building materials, layout, and standardization. The isolation and remoteness of schools from reserves enabled both control and resistance. In the former, a senior official in the Department of Indian Affairs, Hayter Reid, argued that "the more remote the institutions and the greater distance are the points from which pupils are collected, the better the success."[37] On the other hand, remoteness from the schools in some cases enabled some families to resist enrollment. That potential for evasion shifted, however, once the expansion of trains and automobiles collapsed distance between band locations, Indian agents, and school grounds.[38]

By pursuing a contract system, Davin also forecasted the financial feasibility of this model on the basis of proposed site soil quality, timber availability, and access to water. These environmental considerations were not ancillary to governance strategies but part of a broader structure of control. Calculating the cost of building and operations with the resources to be generated by individual schools, he argued that Canada's wealth of timber resources would make the schools economically feasible. In 1920 Duncan Campbell Scott, then deputy superintendent of the Department of Indian Affairs, testified for Bill 14, An Act to Revise the Indian Act. The amendment intensified the capacity of the state to mandate schooling through compulsory attendance while simultaneously expanding the authority of Indian agents to punish Indigenous parents who resisted. In an appeal to the primary authority of the parental figure, Scott argued enforcing parental separation was justified given *all* Indigenous persons were legally wards of the Crown.[39] Residential schools, he argued, fulfilled the state's treaty obligation to provide education in exchange for land. In other words, like an abusive father, he framed the violence of civilization as an extension of a benevolent Crown. All the while, these juridical attempts to civilize were met with resistance.

As much as these reports underscore the colonial biopolitical logics of the schools themselves, they also highlight the structural production of a Canadian settler relationship to "rightful inheritance." In other words, entitlement to land functions as violent settler nativism. "Elimination" operates in multifaceted ways through state-sanctioned inheritance of what is now known as Canada: through structures of law and policing the "substance" of Native identity, in addition to intensive surveillance. Elimination also speaks to dimensions of chronic exposure to disease, sexual violence, and strategies of confinement. In the context of creating the institutions that would be called "residential schools," child and childhood functioned as the abstractions holding together a power structure of targeted elimination.[40] Administrative documents again and again hinge on colonial conceptions of childhood that naturalize the state's power over Indigenous nations as they analogize Natives as children. Policies that render "Native" as "child"—a ward of the state and also an "underdeveloped" human—racialized civilization as historical maturity.

In linking residential schools to the energy regime of sexual modernity, I interpret the logic of amalgamation as the transformation of matter (yes, *children*) to use value for a settler empire. The state imagines children as potential for the future of the nation, underscoring how settler colonial states regard "subpopulations" as matter to extract and fuel settler futures. As many historians have emphasized, residential schools emphasize "virtuous" practices, emotional containment, and learned self-management at the level of population, while simultaneously invoking a relationship of paternal dependency. Paternalism enacts a colonial relationship through assumptions of virtuous authority and dominance. The historical narrative captured by the Bagot Commission report exemplifies this assumed paternal relationship, noting that a shift to religion and education would facilitate the colonial goal of "raising themselves from the state of dependence to the level of the surrounding population."[41] Thus, from the vantage point of the state, the body politics' "energy" could become revitalized through children's exposure to profoundly cruel and violent spaces, in the promise of "amalgamation."[42] The last school would not close until 1996 in Saskatchewan.

The presumed coherence of inheritance would generate a host of rhetorical challenges in the wake of public testimonies to violence during the TRC proceedings that framed action largely in terms of "reconciliation." Survivors of the residential school era would participate in the largest class-action settlement in Canadian history. The conclusion of the TRC left many with eviscerating questions about the public genre of apologia: Who benefits from these proceedings? Reconciliation for whom? And what do claims to reconciliation mean amid ongoing structures of settler governance of Indigenous lands: man camps, pipelines, and extractive projects? Where is "reconciliation" amid ongoing energy projects such as the Canadian Tar Sands, which facilitate the concentrated disappearance of Indigenous women? As the struggle over national pipelines crystallized in February 2020, land protectors throughout Wet'suwet'en Nation proclaimed, "Reconciliation is dead." TRC deliberations underscore the paradox of inheritance: ongoing performances of state apologia that accompany the state's entrenchment of property-based relationships to land and sexuality.

A tome of memoirs and oral histories emerged before and after formal TRC hearings in the early 2000s.[43] Part of the settlement stipulated a national truth and reconciliation process, which, as of 2007, gathered members of the public to share their testimony, created records, and concluded with the publication of a six-volume report in 2015. The report was clear: "In its dealing with Aboriginal people, Canada did all these things."[44] By "these things," the report crystalized definitions of "physical genocide," "biological genocide," and "cultural genocide." Together these terms recognize multiple dimensions of violence, ranging from death, interventions in reproductive capacity, and the targeted elimination of cultural structures. At the conclusion of the proceedings, then prime minister Stephen Harper issued an apology on behalf of the commonwealth. However, even as he issued a state apology, he later argued Canada does not have a history of colonization.[45]

Of its many outcomes the TRC established a national mandate to teach the history and legacy of residential schools, an iteration of which is emplaced in the CMHR. The next section lays out the state's reassertion of paternal authority in managing access to difficult knowledge about violence and sexual abuse. As I noted in the chapter's opening, it matters less that the museum *did* create an absence than *how* they did. Their curation of elision reveals an array of power dynamics embedded within infrastructures—from land to water to information. Turning toward the creation, building, and function of the CMHR, the abstraction of childhood once again governs how the state regulates sexual knowledge, in this case the curation of sexual trauma and abuse. The paternal colonial relationship is expressed through the monopolization of decision making about what to include and display, along with decisions about following the state's official narrative. Moreover, the presumed white, abstracted "universal" visitor becomes grounds for justifying its content, where elisions take shape through protection of this visitor from difficult or explicit sexual information. Here we see the regulation of childhood through management of information *access*. Positioned as the national "future," the logic follows that the mythical children must be protected from knowing acts of violence committed in their name—foreclosing an encounter with and thus accountability for their own inheritance as subjects of the settler state. As inheritors of knowledge as well as land, the insistence on the property logics of inheritance rendered settler-as-child, who under these logics must be protected by the state.

MAPPING CANADIAN SETTLER AESTHETICS AND INFRASTRUCTURAL VIOLENCE

From its genesis as a federal entity and its 2014 opening on Treaty 1 lands, the curation of human rights memory at the CMHR reproduces the colonial relationship by maintaining interpretive discretion in curatorial decisions despite calls for collaboration and by disappearing enactments of sovereignty through national aesthetics and a self-mythology of a multicultural (or "mosaic") imagination. In 2008 Parliament passed an amendment to the Museums Act that codified national recognition and investment in the CMHR. Its systemized purpose would "explore the subject of human rights, with special but not exclusive reference to Canada, in order to enhance the public's understanding of human rights, to promote respect for others and to encourage reflection and dialogue."[46] With oversight from the Department of Canadian Heritage as a Crown Corporation, the CMHR was the first national museum to be created since 1967 and the first to be located outside of the National Capital Region of the Ottawa-Gatineau metropolitan area. In this section, I describe the emplacement of the museum in the landscape of Winnipeg, underscoring how that emplacement matters to ongoing dynamics of environmental violence. Simultaneously, emplacement entangles the political operations of the museum and subsequent resistance to the state. First, we should understand how settler aesthetics of violence permeated the planning, construction, and infrastructure of the CMHR—the overlapping and sedimented histories of land use that shape the conjuncture of the present.

By "settler aesthetics of violence," I'm drawing attention to a broader context of Canadian self-mythology, in which national stories of the state's role as "peacekeeper" of the world is symbolized and iterated in monumental forms. Take, for instance, the Peacekeeping Monument in Ottawa, installed and dedicated in 1992 as a monument to Canadian forces who served as international peacekeepers. The adjudicating body detailed the purpose of the monument as such: "The intent of the Monument is to recognize and celebrate through artistic, inspirational and tangible form Canada's past and present peacekeeping role in the world. In that sense it will represent a fundamental Canadian value: no *missionary* zeal to *impose our way of life on others but an acceptance of the responsibility to assist them in determining their own futures by ensuring a non-violent climate in which to do so.*" I have italicized a great deal of this statement because, in the context of Canada's administrative capacity detailed in the previous section, the contradictions are quite clear. Residential schools operated as an explicitly *civilizing mission* to dispossess land, to impose a way of life, and to work to eradicate whole sovereign nations. Moreover, the imprint of the word "Reconciliation" on the monument itself extends these myths to public audiences, extending an aura to the land surrounding the monument as somehow neutralized of its colonial violence. The plaque reads, "Members of Canada's Armed Forces, represented by three figures, stand at the meeting place of two walls of destruction. Vigilant, impartial, they oversee the reconciliation of those in conflict. Behind them lies the debris of war. Ahead lies the promise of peace; a grove, a symbol of life."[47] Again, by placing the context of the plaque squarely within the legacy of residential schools, contradictions surface.

It is precisely these contradictions that exemplify the core philosophy of sovereignty in settler states—what Kauanui describes as the paradox of sovereignty.[48] As a communication scholar, I interpret those professions as modalities of exceptionalizing violence, recuperating narrative authority, and performing for Canadians a monumental mentality that First Nations, Inuit, and Métis are fully *incorporated* into the national body. As Indigenous studies reiterates, *incorporation* is a technique of colonialism.[49] In contrast to the celebrated settler mythologies within and beyond the museum, tracing some of the museum's relations to land and water emplaces its operations within the environment as well as violence.

As the museum moved toward an architectural reality, violations in cultural heritage protocol during its groundbreaking and later disputes over staging for the grand opening ceremony echo relations of paternal authority. In 2008 archaeologists from Quarternary Consultants criticized the CMHR's failure to follow heritage resource recommendations, specifically neglecting the terms of heritage permits.[50] The archaeological dig prior to construction unearthed over four hundred thousand cultural items over the span of only 3 percent of the total site area.[51] Reflecting on the report, some archaeologists expressed concern that negligence of cultural heritage protocol would mean that the museum would bury histories layered within the strata below the museum's foundation.[52]

Cities are rarely situated as epicenters of colonial containment and Indigenous lifeways.[53] Yet centuries of treaties in addition to restructuring through gentrification and development have transformed parts of downtown Winnipeg into a seemingly frictionless memoryscape. Commemorative signs shape perception of the historical milieu into a "meeting up" place where layers of settler containment nestle on one another. Signage tells these origin stories: the CMHR and the Forks National Historic Site are both constructed on Treaty 1 land. East toward the rivers is the Lower Fort Garry National Historic Site, built in 1830 by the Hudson's Bay Company, where Treaty 1 was deliberated between the Swampy Cree of Manitoba, Chippewa (Anishinaabe), and the Crown, signed on August 3, 1871. Between Fort Garry and the CMHR is Union Station, built as a passenger terminal thirty years after the arrival of the first transcontinental railroad in downtown Winnipeg. And just west of Union Station is Hotel Fort Garry, constructed in 1913 as a "castle of opulence," a place where current guests exchange ghost stories of railway passengers who linger amid narrow red-carpeted hallways.

In the 1970s, amid Winnipeg's centennial, the city debated how to restore and redevelop the area surrounding the Forks, including the Canadian National East Yards—land that Canadian National noted was "surplus" to their operations. Between 2000 and 2003 the Asper Foundation conducted a feasibility study for the museum, and the land for the museum was donated to the foundation from the FRC. Entering into the periphery of the CMHR, the language of Treaty 1 permeates the site's significance in the styling of settler nostalgia. "The Forks" becomes shorthand for a meeting place that shaped Canada's economic, political, and cultural terrain. This again captures a settler aesthetic of violence. A "mosaic" of places maps settler relation to land. In this case, presuming the meeting place of the Forks stabilizes for audiences a more complicated and multilayered story, in which land restructuring would move these lands and waterways from Métis stewardship to the Hudson's Bay Company to the newly formed city of Winnipeg. These kinds of stories exemplify techniques of settler inheritance; as Jean O'Brien accounts, the simultaneous erasure and memorializing of First Nations to the past accomplishes the goal of refuting Indigenous land sovereignty.[54]

But the Red and Assiniboine Rivers and broader waterways remain sites of contestation and Indigenous survivance, explicitly calling attention to the violence of meeting-place aesthetics. Zoe Todd (Métis) reframes bodies of water as flows between story, memory, and Indigenous-settler relations, disrupting the values and ways of knowing settler memory spaces such as the commercialized Forks. She writes, "Whereas cities guard their boundaries quite jealously with ring-roads and ordinances, rivers permeate broader awareness of, and responsibilities to, the watersheds with which they are enmeshed."[55] Waters permeate spaces inside the CMHR in ways that mark the intertwining of settler inheritance to ongoing conditions of infrastructural violence.[56]

In fact, the museum's third floor's *Garden of Contemplation* operates as the quintessential example of the museum's relationship to infrastructural violence. Composed of six hundred tons of black basalt spanning the floor and stone rims, the stone buttresses pools of water made to invite peace. Above, the "cloud" hovers and invites sunlight, to represent ice, air, and contemplation. As a transit space between the first two floors and the action-oriented spaces audiences encounter as they progress, the garden explicitly calls on its visitors to rest, reflect, and gain strength for their journey. These are all tropes of vital energy, and their structure becomes all the more evident in the realization that the water that soothes and calms originates in Shoal Lake. Water infrastructure here symbolizes and materializes an extractive colonial relationship. The garden in turn spatializes this extraction as a rightful inheritance, there for pleasurable consumption for visitors.

In 2007 Stewart Redsky, a member of Shoal Lake 40 First Nation, composed a letter to Antoine Predock, the CMHR's architect (and of the American Heritage Center). Redsky highlighted the cruel irony of the architect's "aquatic vision" for the garden and the ethereal cloud illuminating the brutalist exterior. Redsky outlined a history of infrastructural violence that produced water disparities between Shoal Lake and the city of Winnipeg. Securing clean water by displacing Shoal Lake territories into settler water and land infrastructure was a central component in a political dream of making Winnipeg a "Chicago of the North."[57] Redsky names ongoing relationships of violence made evident through the stark contrast of twenty-year boil advisories and flowing ripples of contemplation. Predock would remain silent, and in response Shoal Lake instituted a number of "counter museums" and tours of their lands.[58] One of those counter museums would land on the grounds of the CMHR during its opening ceremony.

Members of Shoal Lake 40 also mobilized a protest camp on CMHR grounds, joining boycotts or staged counterpresence during the Rights Fest opening ceremony. Speaking to a journalist from the *Manitoba,* Shoal Lake 40 First Nation chief Erwin Redsky described their presence as making water infrastructure visible to settlers: "'We want to let [Winnipeggers] know what is going on at the other end of the pipe."[59] Members of Idle No More and advocates of Murdered and Missing Indigenous Women gathered with megaphones alongside barricades to call attention to the elision of Indigenous genocide within Canada and the Palestinian territories.[60] While some used their presence to counter museum contents, other attendees decided to boycott the opening ceremony. A Tribe Called Red canceled their appearance, explaining their decision: "We feel it was necessary to cancel our performance because of the museum's misrepresentation and downplay of the genocide that was experienced by Indigenous people in Canada by refusing to name it genocide. Until this is rectified, we'll support the museum from a distance."[61] By contrast, the Manitoba Métis Federation decided to boycott opening ceremonies after their selection of decorated performer Ray St. Germain was denied. Museum decision makers justified the action out of their concern for a telegenic and youthful performance, a decision they believed took precedence over the Métis' right to determine how best to commemorate the opening of the museum.

Public protest of the museum as an ongoing embodiment of terra nullius necessitates recontextualizing the physical work museum spaces do on bodies of visitors, tourists, and spectators of all kinds. The performative manipulation of apologia consigns violence to a colonial past and implicates how setters immersed in its landscape become affective subjects of responsibility. Mediated by information infrastructure and immersive design, the CMHR's atmosphere creates feelings of inspiration, progress, and reflection, but those feelings short-circuit models of response and witnessing. In fact, who determines how to properly communicate sexuality and trauma reinscribes a fundamental relationship to colonial paternalism. The CMHR embodies the sexually modern through settler temporality and concretizing a "progress" narrative of darkness to light. As such, the CMHR is a tightly bound, official state narrative that elides accountability in exchange for the production and spatialization of settler innocence, in the guise of protecting future national white settler subjects.[62] This is one example by which the settler futurity of reconciliation reproduces what feels like a "rightful" or "earned" inheritance. Next I shift to the interior of the CMHR, to examine how its deployment of immersive design circumvents reciprocity by delimiting the emotional field of museumgoers.

PATERNAL MOODS AND AFFECTIVE REGULATION
THROUGH IMMERSIVE DESIGN

In this section I turn to cavernous interiors, placed squarely within asymmetrical environmental relationships. As a whole, the CMHR operationalizes immersive design, a contemporary exhibition practice that anticipates how visitors engage with spaces singularly and as a whole, with the goal of creating multisensory and profoundly emotive experiences. Casting itself as an "ideas museum," the CMHR deploys information infrastructures to curate immersive experiences of visualization, touch, sound, mood, and first-person engagement. Following John Stickler, in an era of the "reality-based entertainment" industrial complex, "immersion" and "interaction" offer competitive methods for museums to gain audiences.[63] But even this design strategy blends narrative and affective functions, aligned with a prescribed template of imagined audience. For example, in practice within the *What Are Human Rights?* gallery, this ethos is embodied by person-to-person interaction in which an individual museumgoer listens to a projected recording of individuals, who speak of their experience or about the necessity of a human rights knowledge.

As I walked under the railway tracks toward Israel Asper Way to a glass-covered entrance encased by concrete roots, the magnitude of stone, glass, and iron make it difficult to not feel diminutive. Crowds move inward to Buhler Hall, a cavernous industrial-feeling space lined with marble floors and metal beams running across the open ceiling. I purchase tickets from a docent who, after swiping my credit card, asks if I'm visiting from the States. The docent seems genuinely surprised when I say yes, that I traveled for the *Witness Blanket*. Interactions with docents may seem utterly banal and transactional, but they also function as ritualistic guest orientations and attention modulators. This docent prepared me to move forward into the museum with the option of downloading an app on my smartphone. At this visit I chose not to experience the app as a primary interface. I say "primary" because even in the absence of the app, my tour was a heavily mediated experience. Should I have plugged in prior to moving upward on warmly lit alabaster ramps into the upper galleries, I would have had access to short videos narrating architectural features of the building's accessible design. Those videos (and the app as a whole) include presentations in English, French, American Sign Language, and audio description.

After my first tour I downloaded the app to find just how much it parallels signage and self-referential descriptions of the experience the museum cultivates for its visitors. Constructed as a conversation, much of the preliminary video orientation compresses elements such as air, water, and stone into an architectural vision of progress. One of the narrators describes Predock's vision as a genesis for the CMHR's "inspirational" mood. "The building's architect, Antoine Predock, intended every part of the building to have meaning for human rights." Predock's repeated use of geology roots and routes settlement transfigured into a multicultural "meeting place." The story Predock and the museum by extension try to tell here is one of unity through design. Describing Buhler Hall, Predock notes, "The heart of the building, the Great Hall, is carved from the earth evoking the memory of ancient gatherings at the Forks of First Nations peoples, and later, settlers and immigrants."[64] This frictionless description of incorporation into a national imaginary spatialized to a gathering place offers universality as a frame of perception and understanding.[65] More specifically, these place descriptions are one of many enactments of terra nullius and a settler geography.

Choreographed as a journey from "darkness to light," the path that museumgoers move through is a tenebrous feeling gallery alongside textual declarations of Western values ranging from freedom, inclusion, dignity, and equality.[66] Progressing through an alabaster labyrinth of sweeping acoustics and visualization, each new floor expands and lightens as one walks or wheels upward from the ground floor to the Tower of Hope.[67] Predock describes this strategy as a "processional even[t]; [my buildings] are an accumulation of vantage points both perceptual and *experiential*."[68] Combined with immersive design by Ralph Applebaum Associates, the museum facilitates visual, tactile, auditory, and kinesthetic interaction, interfacing with dramatically staged human rights information.[69] In reflection of her own tour, Natalie Alvarez presses against the organization of values vis-à-vis kinesthetics: How do tropes of "lightness" and "darkness" shape audiences, given their association with "teleological narratives of western imperialism?"[70] Alvarez's question is worth reflecting here too, because they encourage considering the political function of immersion. For my purposes the curatorial control of information about sexual violence speaks to the limits of immersion as a design strategy but, more important, brings attention to the relationship between affect and norms of propriety in regulating the immersive experience.

With respect to criticisms of whitewashing residential school violence, this relationship between affect and propriety encompasses a *paternal mood.* Given colonial conceptions of childhood, paternalism embodies a hierarchical relationship of control and protection to maintain "innocence." There's no doubt the CMHR's purpose is to curate an immersive feeling space of "inspiration" that choreographs physical movement of individual bodies with a progress temporality to collectivize emotional experience. But in this instance (and in cultures of display more broadly), propriety heavily regulates immersion. Propriety, the normative scheme for moralizing dispositions and actions, is the rhetorical mechanism designed to produce relationships of paternal authority. As an interface of the state and presumed settler citizens, propriety provides the means of emotional regulation and feedback. Another way of hearing the critics of the museum is to understand how propriety overwhelmingly invokes a paternal relationship by protecting white settler subjects from an emotive field. Immersive experiences are embodied and emplaced, but they are not outside of the official narrative of institutional memory. In consequence these design strategies cultivate a tightly orchestrated emotional response that constrains witnessing and whose pedagogical function encourages the making of human rights agents that feel with the state.[71]

Underscored by asymmetries, the immersive design tries to evoke an emotional experience to move these political agents through a sequence of outrage to satisfaction and hope, even as museumgoers also actively respond to architects' and curators' designs. Beyond the choreography of the museum layout as a whole, emotional pedagogies are blatant within the app itself. For example, those who use the app may document their mood after each exhibit using a calculated "mood map." This allows visitors to plot their responses between "moved," "surprised," "inspired," and "thoughtful." A different mood map accompanies each major exhibit and accumulates responses into a range of quantified data. However, the interface constrains how one might move between an axis of surprised and thoughtful (presented as a range) over and against the axes of moved and inspired. As a whole, visitors' responses are quantified alongside these particular axes, and it is not clear what happens or who has access to that data. The limits of these options are illuminating, in their small scope and normatively positive expression. The mood map contains, regulates, and guides how visitors might express or experience emotion into quantified data with little room to name more complex emotions a visitor might feel. In my own experience, I noticed myself feeling angry, troubled, perplexed, shocked, hurt, and violated. Moreover, the map replaces relation with quantification, eliding emotions as relationships experienced across bodies, spaces, and curated material. In many contexts it is precisely these less contained flows of affect that condition political action as well as emotion.

The mood map also cues who the CMHR imagines as its ideal audience. As a domain of political knowledge, "human rights" constructs both the idea of the human and the contentious histories by which the notion of an agent of universal rights emerges across the globe.[72] Because of its location in Winnipeg and its private-public partnership, the imagined public of museumgoers encompasses largely those occupying Canada or tourists traveling across the provinces, the United States, or beyond. Entering the *What Are Human Rights?* gallery after the first descent, I walked into an open and yet dimly lit gallery space populated with a small number of other museumgoers on a brisk early afternoon. To the left I watch others read through a crescending timeline of human rights. Color coded to name in English and French one hundred key moments from ideas, events, and measures, the timeline presents human rights as an unfolding paradigm debated and codified over time. The remainder of the room visualizes the abstraction of human rights values: equity, freedom, dignity, and rights. This gallery sets the stage for visitors as they begin their journey from a point of origin, an itinerary that pairs the human rights story with a spatial syntax. In a room that begins to shape visitors as cultural subjects, the journey dramatizes the human rights struggle. In turn this means that movement from *What Are Human Rights?* to other galleries and floors engages visitors as national human rights actors. The feeling of lightness produced by a kinesthetic performance evidences one of many ways the CMHR uses design to engage visitors' emotional responses, protecting the "innocence" of visitors even as it cannot entirely control their negotiations of the exhibit. As I move forward to describe more in depth two exhibits related explicitly to the legacy of residential schools, I also consider the implications of audience and affective regulation relative to this book's argument about sexual modernity. Sexual modernity is a violent inheritance through structures of authority and an ongoing condition of ecological and settler violence.

FROM MIMESIS TO IMAGINATION IN CURATING *CHILDHOOD DENIED*

Moving down a hallway into another wide open and dimly lit space, I enter *Canadian Journeys* (see fig. 8). While the previous gallery organizes

FIGURE 8. *Canadian Journeys,* March 2016. Canadian Museum for Human Rights, Winnipeg. Photo by author.

a linear narrative of human rights touchstones across the globe, this gallery particularizes Canada's human rights history, spatialized into discrete episodes. As in other spaces, museumgoers in this room might amble over marble floors as they move and pause to individual story *niches,* the term deployed by the museum to describe segmented exhibit units that wrap around the walls of the gallery. Above each niche a collage of moving images composed of individual portraits links struggle to individual action. The luminous cascade situated above the story niches depicts both violence and resistance, transfixing into a mood of resilience against difficult histories. The design of individual-and collective action *above* difficult histories typifies the motion afforded by the gallery's name. *Canadian Journeys* provides the metacontext for the gallery in general and the residential school niche in particular.

Written in both English and French, the placard outside the gallery narrates the historical valence of the museumgoer's body: "There have been steps and missteps on the road to greater rights for everyone in Canada. This panorama of experience reflects continuing efforts to achieve human rights for all." The spatial and temporal metaphor of "road" instantiates an abstraction of "human rights" as a physical and ideological movement, in which values like freedom becomes more legible as spectators oscillate their bodies throughout the space. Notably, "road" and "rights" presume levels of national incorporation and inclusion, a frame that matters in particular for renarrating a colonial past. These curatorial strategies often juxtapose historical struggles of exclusion toward greater degrees of inclusion within a national body. Notably missing, however, are frames of sovereignty and resurgence that would not presume an incorporative relationship between indigeneity and the nation-state. *Canadian Journeys* provides a cover for the "darkness" to the emergence of a "triumphant nation." Moreover, framing a now nonlinear timeline through the spatial syntax of story niches, the gallery posits human rights struggle as an issue of incorporation into the Canadian body politic.

I walk from the edge of the gallery until I arrive at *Childhood Denied* (see fig. 9). One of the only permanent exhibits dedicated to the residential school era, *Childhood Denied* recreates the disciplinary scene of the schoolhouse, framed by a black laminate underlay. The background stages a curated photographic exhibit: some photos in black and white and few in color. Unlike other niches that use abstractions to symbolize harm, this exhibit deploys the documentary function of photography to create a historically realist interpretation of life at residential schools. If one engages the story niche linearly, as in from left to center to right, photographs themselves organize a timeline: creation, survival, and later redress. For the sake of description my depiction starts with the attention-grabbing center photograph, then shifts across the exhibit from left to right, following a spatial timeline of past and present—from residential schools to the era of reconciliation.

The center of the story niche recreates the disciplinary scene of the schoolhouse. In the foreground visitors meet the edge of a sanded, stained, and uniformly patterned wooden floor. Two wooden and steel desks occupy the center of the room, evenly spaced apart. Moving their gaze farther toward the background, the viewers realize the schoolroom replicates the photographic scene to create a mirror image to the extent that a close look reveals that the wood planks of the exhibit create a wooden elbow with those depicted photographically. The photograph creates a black-and-white "wall" for the exhibit. To the right of the image, black-and-white photographs acquired from state archives provide snapshots: a portrait of Duncan Campbell Scott, a key legal architect of the schools; a group portrait of children at Fort Qu'Appelle Indian

FIGURE 9. *Childhood Denied*, March 2016. Canadian Museum for Human Rights, Winnipeg. Photo by author.

Industrial School, wearing a European style of dress, next to their father, who wears clothes banned by school authorities; a landscape portrait of students and a priest sitting in an open field; interior shots that document likely Catholic rituals of prayers before bed; and lessons in domestic science. To the left we encounter group photographs akin to the genre of a class photo and snapshots of courtroom scenes, wherein the state language of reconciliation took shape.

How do visitors engage and make meaning out of the decision to center the schoolhouse as the background of the story niche? In contrast to the absent bodies of students in the center desks, uniformly clothed boys and girls occupy each desk in the photograph, their gaze levied toward the camera behind the frame of the photographic event. Some break from the linear gaze and look beyond the camera lens and the distant space of the spectator in their horizon. Past the tidy rows and against a blackboard located in the rear of the schoolhouse, a singular nun watches over the scene. Just above her head an icon centers the room—perhaps a religious figure, perhaps Queen Victoria. The arrangement of bodies in the space of the schoolroom is not ancillary to their civilizing function: from iconic portrait to the gaze of the nun, the transfer of power from state and religious authority produces order and hierarchy. The photographic backdrop is the visualization of the school as the biopolitical apparatus. In both its depiction and physical form, the desks function as technologies of "civilization." The app comments that Nora Bernard, a student here at Shubenacadie Residential School in Nova Scotia, initiated the class action lawsuit that led to the national settlement. The prominence of this photo and its connection to the process of the TRC gives the impression that the students caught in the museumgoers' gaze somehow anticipate the action of mobilizing demands for some sort of redress.

In the immersive foreground the two replica desks are transformed to function as screens, running video simultaneously on loop. The video includes oral testimony, spoken word from the TRC proceedings, and black-and-white video to communicate historical realism and in-color video to communicate the present. In contrast to the strategy of historical realism that animates the display logics of the photographic archive, the moving images communicate lived experience and corporeal memory. In turn the short film enables spectators to push against the linear sense of time afforded by the exhibit to consider how residential schools live as an ongoing structural legacy, connected to the generational reproduction of possessive inheritance through land.

The power of the display strategy hinges again, however, on the faithfulness of the photographic index as the basis of historical mimesis. In other words, immersion combines "reality" with "entertainment," inviting participants to submerge themselves in historical experience. Yet here lies the ruse: interpretive authority still relies on institutional frames of photographic meaning. As I argued in the previous chapters, the "index" of documentary proof does not monopolize photography's political potential. In this context historical realism depends on the faithfulness of the index to maintain temporal authority.

Childhood Denied uses a mimetic strategy to map the relation between historical actors and institutions: Duncan Campbell Scott was a key architect, the Department of Indian Affairs provided a federal body of regulatory and funding mechanisms, the church facilitated the labor of school administration, and the timber-rich Canadian landscape provided raw materials to materialize biopolitical logics. As the exhibit narrates "progress," color photographs of TRC proceedings shape temporality through a sense of closure. These carefully selected and arranged photographs perform historical realism once again. The story niche, then, uses space to map the movement from residential schools to so-called reconciliation.

But reconciliation for whom and in what form? Reflecting about the knowledge of sexual violence, Sainte-Marie told *CBC News,* "They need to know. There was an electric chair involved. There were cattle prods. Terrible things…these things need to be here, because where else can they be? They need to be acknowledged and understood." In response Angela Cassie, vice president of public affairs for the CMHR, said, "It's difficult to know what should be concealed and what shouldn't."[73] The museum promised to investigate possibilities to deepen its content, and yet this exchange reveals a number of assumptions about audience and authority. In addition the exhibit in its current form is organized around immersion, making any potential encounter with these elements a particularly challenging prospect. Remember the audience of the CMHR is at best a global public but more likely non-Native publics, given the publicity of controversies during the opening. To be clear, curators always confront the limits of space or material when they try to narrate the legacy of historical moments. Those limitations make curatorship a political practice and necessitate community collaboration in institutional stewardship.

Specifically, museum administrators countered by emphasizing the need to protect presumably white settler children (as well as potentially some adults), operationalizing techniques of propriety to shield "childhood innocence." The museum has claimed the language of settler colonial genocide is too complex for a ninth-grade reading level, the basis by which museum laborers manage the complexity of written description.[74] Sainte-Marie calls attention to the absence of historical narrative, yes, but the criticism also implicitly encompasses resistance to *propriety* as a dominant form of affective regulation through display. More implicitly, we might read Sainte-Marie's utterance of "Where else can they be?" as a potential implicit reference to ongoing coverups by the church and state and the destruction or inaccessibility of evidence.[75] Renarrating residential schools *matters* because of the pedagogical function of museums in making national subjects and sustaining national narratives as a primary horizon of historical meaning. Situated through the metanarrative of the "journey," *Childhood Denied* may invite museumgoers to make sense of residential schools as one more volatile chapter from which Canada has become a unified whole. But as Idle No More member Leah Gazan remarked during a visit, "It's the Great Canadian Myth on display."[76] And though the vast majority of the museum maintains this celebratory relationship of the nation-state, I found something different as I moved upward to the sixth floor's *Expressions Gallery.* The purpose of this upper gallery is to create flexibility in exhibition through changing themes in human rights. Herein I encountered a different memorial to residential schools, named the *Witness Blanket.*

REMAPPING AND REGENERATIVE AESTHETICS WITH THE *WITNESS BLANKET*

In this section I reflect on in what way the *Witness Blanket,* temporarily emplaced in the sixth-floor gallery, disrupts the paternal setter aesthetics of violence. In my framing I suggest the *Witness Blanket* enacts "remapping." Tiara R. Na'puti (Chamoru) defines remapping through Native and Indigenous scholars' "practices that address colonial mappings of land, bodies, and lives…that underscore the intertwining epistemic, relational, and geographic forms of violence."[77] In what follows I trace the remapping practices of the *Witness Blanket* that facilitate a regenerative aesthetic through a focus of collaboration, sovereignty, and listening in different modes for different subjects. Designed by Newman, the *Witness Blanket* is an installation of more than nine hundred reclaimed and collectively acquired photographs, textiles, bricks, glass, material objects, administrative papers, and architectural ruins. Collected from every residential school operative in Canada, Newman's collaborative vision was to acknowledge the structure of settler governance yet center orientations of survivance, transformation, and witness. Objects originate from the sites of former locations but also come from institutional archives, Native Friendship Centres, and Indigenous schools and

FIGURE 10. *Witness Blanket,* March 2016. Canadian Museum for Human Rights, Winnipeg. Photo by author.

universities.[78] As the exhibit makes clear, Newman's commemorative purpose is to "hono[r] the children who were forced into the Indian residential school system in Canada." I detail in this chapter's conclusion important developments in the relationship between the CMHR and the *Witness Blanket,* but for now I need to acknowledge my analysis of this encounter is limited to the specific time frame of March 2016.

Initially on display between December 2015 and June 2016, the *Witness Blanket* spans almost the total length of the center gallery, with space remaining for museumgoers to move in front and behind.[79] As a whole, the *Witness Blanket* is composed of two large square panels divided by a smaller rectangular panel, on either side of a central doorway (see fig. 10). A master carver, Newman describes how the confluence of "witness" and "blanket" enact his traditions: for Kwakwaka'wakw, blankets are pieces of identity and lineage worn in ceremony and, for Coast Salish, blankets are used to "honour, uplift, and protect." In both of these oral traditions, "witness" is a practice of memory keeping in addition to listening and reflection. Newman narrates his creative process as determining how to tell a "whole story," one that does not end with the brick and mortar of schools and those who designed them but also spaces such as Big Houses and sweat lodges that have shaped the continual work of healing.[80] The *Witness Blanket* is, in short, an embodiment of magnitude.

Individual objects include fragmented places, memories, or stories: prayers, clothing, braided hair, concrete ruins, photographs, report cards, a torn-up ice skate, children's shoes, door knobs, light sockets, and pieces of an apple tree collected from the site of Saint Michael's, where Newman's father was enrolled. Mounted below each panel twenty-four copies of the statutes of Canada, from 1857 to 1938, including the Indian Act, constitute the blanket's foundation. Other fragments include a section of a copper roof from the Manitoba Legislative Assembly and a piece of used green carpet from the House of Commons chamber. In a public lecture to the Sooke Fine Arts Society, Newman reflected that inclusion of pieces of churches, government buildings, and leather-bounded copies of legal code materialized an idea of "reconciliation." He described the *Witness Blanket* as a visual representation of the idea. Simultaneously, Newman's collection and classification offer a testament to the resilience of survivors. He noted the "need to highlight or include the culture that still survives. The language that is resilience. Language and culture are connected. The victory that we can claim that we survived."[81] As a whole, the *Witness Blanket* exposes and displays rather than resolves and reconciles the violence of the past.

A few specific pieces lingered with me in the context of earlier debates over the proper display of sexual knowledge. These pieces offered material reference to spaces of explicit abuse, in addition to institutional design elements used to limit contact between family members and facilitate violence to community systems. For example, in *Picking Up the Pieces* Newman contrasts the design of the schools with the design elements of Big Houses to underscore relationships between design and need. He reflects how the living beings of Big Houses shaped his process of collecting materials from former sites. These include standardized red bricks, imposing exteriors, and segregated spaces to facilitate surveillance and separation from family members. Rather than assert a binary of traditional/modern, the stark contrast between community and state structures can be described as a transformation in the time of childhood from fields of care to fields of control—a crucial shift in relationships of energy. Or, as Newman summarizes, "That connection among community members was damaged by separating families and taking children away from their homes, and the damage was reinforced by making sure that the residential school buildings themselves felt like institutions instead of homes."[82]

Fragments of institutional affects are layered throughout. On the first large panel to the right of the center door, two small turquoise identification plates read, "Girls" and "Boys." Taken from the Gordon Residential School at the time of its demolition, these designated gender bathroom plates also speak to the broader institution of gendered practices within the schools.[83] Gender segregation also facilitated day laborers, couched in the language of civilizing skills acquisition. To the left of the door, eight green and maroon merit badges line an axis of a smaller panel. The 1,493 total badges issued after 1942 were awarded for demonstrating gendered skills in housekeeping, sewing, poultry keeping, and knitting. Emma Gladue kept these badges as evidence of coercive forced labor because sewing skills were used to produce items like tea towels for commercial sale.[84] Her memory keeping documents what was taken from her, evidence of exploitation and expropriated labor. The badges themselves are objects of a violent inheritance: she saved a record of "merit" actually operative as an extraction of time and energy.

Newman imagined the door at the center as a crux of the *Witness Blanket*'s experience, connecting their imagination with the lingering traces of touch and fingerprint oil that remained. He collected the door from the infirmary at Saint Michael's prior to its demolition, where many of his family members were sent. Newman describes the infirmary door as a gatekeeper, registering "behind closed doors" of shame and abuse. For this reason Newman created a doorstop so that the door could no longer be closed. And for survivors of Saint Michael's, reminders of the infirmary resurfaced particularly bad memories, prompting Newman to make alterations to the door through the addition of objects such as a scale, a plaque, and writings by Nancy James and Katherine Palmer Gordon, who speak to the process of reclaiming Indigenous histories and cultures. On the inside of the door, Newman mounted George Littlechild's (Cree) drawing *The Priest and His Prey*. Depicting an older priest in his collar with an ominous stare and arms clenched around a sleeping student wrapped in a checkered blanket, Littlechild created the image after listening to testimony at TRC hearings.[85] It was not until after he had donated the drawing to the *Witness Blanket* that Littlefield shared that the testimony of abuse inspiring the image was from Newman's uncle, Edwin.

I've highlighted these specific elements of the *Witness Blanket* because they illuminate a dynamic temporality of resurgence that counters settler maps and notions of trauma and temporality: the idea that trauma is rooted in "stuckness" in the past or that "progress" encompasses a linear narrative that we experience in visitors' movement through most of the CMHR. By contrast, these pieces highlight in a public-facing way the necessary work of critical Indigenous gender, sexuality, and feminist studies interpretation, which confronts the colonial-imperial operations that displace indigeneity and replace it with terra nullius.[86]

More so, the *Witness Blanket*'s imagined audience departs from the dominant audience presumed by the museum itself. By imagined audience I mean that all cultural production includes clues about who a work is for, even as what reception theorists call "real audiences" can be more expansive. The *Witness Blanket* imagines and prioritizes its audience as survivors of the residential school system themselves, particularly as Newman found inspiration for the project in his own father's survivance. Further, the exhibit includes an acknowledgement of the artist's aim to tour the provinces. A pamphlet to the exterior of the exhibit provides information for those who may be retraumatized by visual triggers. As an example of the types of feeling responses to the exhibit in other locales, one survivor responded, "For me, it's…it's… it's painful. Because I'm a survivor of…of…that. So when I first came here, I felt that…The first thing it does is bring out an anger, in…in… in a survivor, because that's where your thoughts go. And when I work with my coworkers here, I…I…I always tell them about healing, I will always tell them I will never heal. I will never heal from that experience. It's because as long as you have a memory, I will not heal from that."[87] Other publics might include those who are intergenerational survivors or children of those who were forcibly taken but survived to become elders. This visitor's clarity that meaning making happens not to promote resolution but expressly in the absence of any clean ending emphasizes the difference between the mood of the other floors and the ambient affect attending the *Witness Blanket*. Further, the language of "witness" complicates the entangled lineages of generations, settler and colonized.

The exhibit space further encourages audiences to compose and display their own reflective engagement. On either side of the gallery, a placard lists instruction for museumgoers to record their participation in reconciliation. *Bearing Witness* invites an ethic of listening, reflection, dialogue, and engagement. It is not clear if these materials are produced by the CMHR or Newman, but they connect the whole gallery to an in-depth engagement with his work: "Each piece of history tells a story. Many of these stories remained untold for generations.

These items witnessed the loneliness and abuses children suffered. But they also represent the children's act of courage. Each contribution calls upon the viewer to bear witness and hear its story. You are invited to participate in reconciliation by listening to the stories of survivors and their families, and by leaving your own message."

Across the room a computer keyboard and paper notebook create space for participants to record their thoughts and feelings in response. Projected onto a concrete wall as a word cloud in French and English, participants include words in an enlarged font such as "resilience," "*honte*," "survivor," "hope," and "honour," which give the impression of dense usage. Smaller fonts include acts of apologia: "I am sorry," "regretful," "wrong," and "injustice." The interaction between the *Witness Blanket* and museumgoers reconfigures the metaphysics of witness. It also contrasts from the much more highly circumscribed scope of the mood maps on the lower levels of the museum. Typically, "witness" calls forth an idea of human actors mobilized to utter testimony of catastrophe. In a stark contrast to the museum's mood map, the projection cloud invites participants to record feelings without the same level of curator-imposed circumscription. This is a meaningful emotional disruption that recalibrates the witnessing potential of viewer engagement, if it also offers an occasion for private reflection and the unspoken and unwritten as well. It's hard to say if this disruption is a consequence of the temporary qualities of the *Expressions Gallery,* but the notable rupture of paternal guidance shifted how I found myself engaging with and experiencing the museum space. Beyond the short online testimonial at Vancouver Island University, I did not encounter recordings of additional survivors of residential schools encountering the *Witness Blanket.* For me and perhaps other settlers, the questions that *could* come from this encounter may render a political demand for settler audiences: What will you do with this legacy, given its ongoing presence for your benefit? This invitation to act, knowing that a future is not enclosed by a settler temporality, seems to be at the heart of Newman's framework of witnessing and emphasizes the contrast to the permanent exhibit of *Childhood Denied.*

In stark contrast to the historical realism of *Childhood Denied* that interpolates the spectator into a position of settler temporality and emotional containment, the *Witness Blanket* creates an occasion for something different. One of these differences includes regenerative potentials. Leanne Betasamosake Simpson (Michi Saagiig Nishnaabeg) argues that for Canada to imagine the possibility of "reconciliation" requires

a decolonization and reeducation project "grounded in cultural generation and political resurgence." Given the evidence of ongoing abuses
by Canadians and the federal government that can also be observed in
the United States, Simpson asks, "How is reconciliation possible?" She
contrasts this settler imagination of evading accountability with "na-
tion-culture-based resurgences," specifically the regeneration of political
and intellectual traditions through a deep commitment to anticolonial
interrogation.[88]

Regenerative aesthetics offers a political imagination and emotional
horizon that *do not* presume the integrity nor Indigenous incorporation into the settler state. "Reconcile" portends a desire to bring back
together again, desires that are largely settler fantasies, violently projected as mutual and shared. Instead, Simpson's Nishnaabeg theoretical perspective offers regeneration as at "the core of re-balancing
relationships."[89] Simpson's focus on relationships and reciprocity reso-
nates with what I believe the *Witness Blanket* offers for its various audiences. It demands a reciprocal relationship and unsettles the property
logic of inheritance. Paternalism enables the ongoing conditions of possibility for settlers and the state to evade responsibility to stolen lives,
genocide, and ongoing violence. As a conclusion to this chapter, I turn to
developments in the relationship between Newman, the *Witness Blanket,* and the CMHR.

TOWARD COLLABORATIVE STEWARDSHIP

In October 2019, three years after the tour recounted here, Newman
and the CMHR entered into agreement through ceremony conducted
in Kumugwe, the K'ómoks First Nation Big House on Vancouver Island.[90] Dozens of people gathered, asked to witness what would become
a historic moment. That ceremony finalized a year-and-a-half process of
negotiating a legal agreement that assigned the CMHR as steward and
caretaker of the *Witness Blanket*. The agreement stated, "We recognize
that the Witness Blanket is not owned by any single person, and that
this agreement and any exchange of funds does not transfer legal ownership of the Witness Blanket, but formally shares responsibility for the
physical and spiritual care of the Witness Blanket."[91] Marsha Lederman,
a journalist who was called to witness, emphasized in her account, "The
work does not belong to the museum but is now its responsibility."[92]
That responsibility extended to those who embodied witness in a legal
sense alongside those charged as story keepers. The ceremony marked

the first time a Crown Corporation joined a transsystemic legal agreement of this order, drawing from both Kwakwaka'wakw traditional legal order and Canadian common law.[93]

The agreement enacted a relationship of "collaborative stewardship," in which the CMHR, Newman, and joining witnesses would become joint stewards. At the center of the agreement was the realization of the *Witness Blanket* as a living entity afforded with legal protection. Neither Newman nor the CMHR "possess" the project; rather, the installation itself is a holder of knowledge and experience.[94] The CMHR is, in turn, lodging for these beings to rest and to hold the living nature of story and people. In contrast to a typical museum "acquisition" that has long served as a colonial practice of museology, the agreement explicitly names "stewardship" as a collaborative responsibility for care. As defined by the agreement, care encompasses "respectful lodging," "respectful methods for treating and preserving," and "repair and display." These contrast with inheritance in its modern heteroproductive sense, of care as a privatized relation twinned to reproductive sexualities. Responsibility displaces notions of ownership and instead balances museum-based iterations of preservation of museum property with, according to the agreement, physical and spiritual care. Moreover, as the written and oral agreements stipulate, this is a living relationship renewed with a feast after four years in ongoing demonstration of responsibility to the past and those impacted in the present and future.

Along these lines we might imagine the *Witness Blanket* as a powerful example of regeneration grounded in practices and ritual that cannot be contained or managed by colonial grammars of resistance, much as the settler state may strive toward cleansing itself of its ongoing genocide, as if colonialism were solely in the past.[95] In his own understanding of reconciliation, Newman says, "Reconciliation means letting go of certain ways of doing things and looking for new ways that fundamentally alter the nature of relationships."[96] Newman's definition of reconciliation differs from more dominant, statist usages that celebrate incorporation—a coming together. And, moreover, his capacious definition of reconciliation enables deeper reflection: *What* relationships deserve letting go? What *new* relationships might be altered or (re)generated? As I detail in the opening of this chapter, stealing children from their families made up part of the larger process of settler resource extraction. In the context of this book, in both Canada and the United States, stealing children and forcibly detaining them in institutions served as a pretext for the celebration of vitality. Moreover, inheritance as seemingly earned and naturalized over time also depends on these relationships. Through regeneration and witnessing, "reconciliation" might imagine different ways of living. Regenerative aesthetics are rife with imagination, particularly along the lines of offering paths to inhabit the violence of colonial biopolitics in a way that might reorient, restory, and remap in gestures of transfiguration. But the process of determining difference cannot be prescribed or predicted, particularly not through colonial frames. Until settlers learn this first lesson, capacious imagining and collaborative stewardship—within and beyond the museum—cannot become realized.

CHAPTER 4

Affected Persons, Sexual Transits, and Contested Public Memories

We can't move our prison. They can build that CAFO anywhere.

—2013 Minidoka Pilgrimage participant

Names of memorial sites for violence scatter across the U.S. West, and their signage beckons drivers from highways toward desolate landscapes. Not far from now dormant lava fields and the Fort Hall Reservation, the Minidoka National Historical Site is one such memorial that I first heard of as a college student visiting Pocatello. Then, again, references to Minidoka surfaced during a visit to Heart Mountain in northwest Wyoming. Authorized as a national monument in 2001, Minidoka has been an interpretive site that preserves the lands and ruins of one of ten former wartime Japanese American detention facilities operative between 1942 and 1945 and now collaboratively stewarded by the U.S. National Park System (NPS) and the nonprofit Friends of Minidoka. In February 1942 President Franklin Roosevelt signed Executive Order 9066, calling on all Japanese Americans to be removed from their agricultural fields and homes on the West Coast and detained within incarceration centers spanning California, Idaho, Wyoming, Colorado, Arizona, Utah, and Arkansas, all in the name of national security. In the past decade, however, the site has been at the center of contested land use and food systems.

Notably, in 2012 the Supreme Court of the State of Idaho maintained a district court ruling to permit an eight thousand Animal Unit Livestock Confinement Operation (LCO)—also colloquially referred to as a CAFO (Concentrated Animal Feeding Operation)—owned by Big Sky Farms, located approximately one and a quarter miles from the

Minidoka National Historic Site.[1] The court's decision was the culmination of a roughly five-year process, after the Jerome County Board ruled in favor of permitting the LCO.[2] As petitioners in the case, Friends joined with six other entities, spanning from individual property owners, environmental preservation organizations, and the Japanese American Citizens League. From the perspective of an already precarious site, Big Sky Farms threatened Minidoka and the ongoing revitalization of its surroundings. Friends joined with the understanding that the LCO's toxic air and waste would endanger the site's ongoing regeneration, through the proximity of accumulating particulate matter, ammonia, and sulfides traveling with wind and water. Established to protect and care for the land's memory forged by the labor of family members forcibly detained, Friends argued for what they felt was a sacred relationship to the land.

The Idaho Supreme Court's decision largely centered vital procedural questions: Who among the petitioner had legitimate "standing" in the case, and what legal capacities constitute grounds for their objection? First, it's helpful to clarify standing relative to environmental controversies as a broader matter of determining who legally has access to demand accountability to institutions for environmental harm. As Phaedra C. Pezzullo and Robert Cox explain, decisions regarding who does and doesn't have standing also encompass a much longer and uneven history of constituting key terms, including *injury* or *threat,* consequentially gatekeeping the capacity to seek legal redress.[3] Standing in disputes over CAFOs, including this one, often hinge on the salience of *property* and *residence.* In his opinion Chief Justice Roger Burdick affirmed the district court's decision to limit standing but found "except for Friends of Minidoka, each appellant has standing to appeal the Board's decision."[4] Justice Burdick included property owners initially dismissed, noting two reasons for this ruling. First, standing in judicial review is wholly contingent on meeting the administrative definition of an *affected person,* a legal figure recognized within Idaho's land-use law to mean "one having a bona fide interest in real property." Second, for cases involving LCO disputes, standing must be further delimited to those with a primary *residence* within a one-mile radius of the site, though situations may call for a revision of that definition. And so his final ruling actually maintained the interest of *property* rather than *residence,* noting that from the very start Jerome County opened permit hearings "to anyone who wanted to hear it."[5] Thus, his decision determined "the right to judicial review is limited to those who had an interest in real property affected by a land use decision."[6] Friends, as caretakers but not property owners in the strictest of legal senses, would thus occupy a legal space beyond the terms mediating this dispute, particularly *affected persons*.

Simply because the court ruled as such does not mean we should limit the overarching lessons of this case to an instrumental application of land use and property law.[7] In the context of this tension between the LCO and the memorial site, the meaning and use of affected persons constitutes a symbolic and material struggle encompassing and exceeding the court's decision. Taken on its own administrative grounds, the term governs a legal capacity to protect personal residence and property in land disputes, as authorized by the structure of the Idaho Code. A large sector of the agricultural economy, CAFOs have steadily populated the landscape of southern Idaho since the 1980s, appropriating tracts of surplus and laxly regulated land. In response nuisance laws couched in the language of individual property protection have provided smaller farm operations some legal teeth to resist further development and environmental impact. In this case individual property owners joining Friends based their appeal within the sanctity of the "small family farm" to starkly contrast the "perverse" space of the CAFO, a juxtaposition that brings into relief the sexual politics of scale.

This contrast of idyllic innocence and industrial perversion implicitly routes public argument through the sexual politics of agriculture, one of the oldest forms of biopower.[8] Stripped of its technical language and the romantic imagination of animal husbandry comingling with the reproductive unit of the settler family, agriculture simply is an orchestrated governance of human, plant, and animal life to produce more life and specifically life as *capital*. In the United States agriculture is labor and capital intensive, subtended by settler legal structures of land-use regulation and citizenship-based exclusion.[9] These land-based relationships of racial capitalism intersect with the specific sexual dimensions of agriculture.[10] Friends' involvement in the case necessitates moving beyond well-treaded frames of CAFO controversies. Their dismissal enacts a form of procedural injustice, wherein those most affected by environmental decision making are rendered without legal capacity to participate.[11] As such, their procedural dismissal warrants deeper scrutiny of legal terms beyond instrumental meaning, turning toward a deeper social and ecological analysis of Minidoka's land lines.

This chapter insists on the rupture of affected persons to narrate the overlapping and conflicting relationships it encompasses—specifically, the story of energy created by racialized and sexualized violence. Spaces of confinement governed by the settler state are inseparable from the racial administration of sexuality, and so the tension between these three sites have much to offer to understandings of biopolitics and the story of sexual modernity. Recognizing the deeply social life of nature, I read the controversy as a cultural struggle over the memory of the land, specifically the underlying legal, social, and physical infrastructure enabling different modes of human and nonhuman confinement over time. As a structure of private individual land sovereignty, I read affected persons as figures born of a land line sedimented by formations of extractive racial capitalism and settler biopolitical governance. Consider this approach so to imagine *affected persons* as an inherited consequence of earlier appropriations of land from its earliest uses prior to contact, land grabs, and later appropriations of land into the public domain of the United States. The aggregation of land appropriation illuminates a region of Minidoka encompassing at least three contradictory environmental relationships: the role of detained Japanese American labor in its mid-twentieth-century cultivation, the institution of the privatized family farm emplaced by the federal sale of that land after the closure of the camps, and the later acceleration of industrial agriculture's CAFO development throughout Jerome County beginning around the 1980s.[12] It is not surprising, then, that each of these relationships come into conflict during the Big Sky controversy as a consequence of competing environmental frames.

My challenge to the strictly instrumental domain of *affected persons* matters because its administration makes sense only within a settler colonial structure that has over time demarcated how land can be used for the cultivation of capitalist value. Attending to the frames of the controversy or the cultures of interpretation that amplify a particular orientation to the world brings into relief chains of land appropriation that structure the contradictory landscape of Minidoka.[13] For industry southern Idaho is idle land, an unproductive and vast space whose latent energy should be maximized and standardized through animal operations. For individual farmers CAFOs pervert an otherwise saccharine rural agrarian imaginary, governed by the generational authority of the family farm. But for Friends Minidoka is a place cultivated and made possible by the labor and energy of their ancestors. Consequentially, the sanctity of "a bona fide interest in real property" in a region produced through the dispossession and labor of others constitutes a racial regime of energy and value, wherein the language of property protects the whiteness of an agrarian nature.[14] The success of *affected persons* to protect those with a residential or property tie enacts *one* articulation of a broader chain of land and infrastructural appropriation or the successive repurposing of land and water into new regimes of confinement and ownership.

The purpose of this chapter is to examine these land lines that surface within the dispute and to foreground contradictory energy relationships constructing and troubling affected persons. Constrained by scope and scale, my practice of tracing land lines follows appropriations of land, from the emplacement of the camp to the transfer of state land *surplus* to private ownership to the much later dispute over the siting of the LCO. My approach follows nonlinear contradictions made intelligible in the dispute over and against the curated stories Minidoka tells about its own history. In consequence we're left with a much different narrative about the region and the tension between family farms and CAFOs as sexual sites: one rooted in the ecological, energetic, and sexual transits of empire, all made possible by an array of overlapping federal and state agencies.

DETOURS: SETTLER COLONIAL METHODS

The wartime detention of Japanese Americans was largely governed by bureaucrats in the War Relocation Authority (WRA), many of whom had prior experience within the apparatus of the Department of the Interior.[15] The latter office notably managed massive swaths of federal lands throughout the western region, but prior to World War II the agency also gained expertise managing *people,* specifically Indigenous nations and their homelands. Some scholars insist administrative overlaps complicate vocabularies of settler colonialism, too often constrained by Native/settler binaries.[16] Jodi Byrd (Chickasaw), for example, argues the deeper logics of containment and expropriation in WRA internal documents and regional authorities "enjambed" Japanese Americans into histories of state spatialities of Indianness. Overlapping discourses of racism and liberal assimilation within the WRA and adjacent agencies converged "into a biopolitical assemblage justifying recursive colonialisms."[17]

But how those legal structures become an *ecological* formation has yet to be articulated; here I do so with the inflections of racialized energy through labor on the lands of Minidoka. In other words, the tension between the memorial site and the LCO begs the question of how Japanese American labor under conditions of confinement cultivated public lands later transferred to private homesteaders. This chapter then builds on Byrd's and Iyko Day's reconceptualization of settler colonialism through land, labor, and contradictory formations of racial capitalism. These relationships matter because they illuminate the complexities of land, capacity, and race as domains of sexual governance.

As such, in this chapter I argue the land lines underwriting Minidoka highlight the appropriation of land within settler colonialism as an ongoing containment to produce wealth, govern sexuality, and naturalize ethnonationalist exclusion. Most scholarship on Japanese American confinement centers on critical recovery work, drawing from wartime experience, camp life, and the multilayered negotiations of power practiced by those living behind barbed wire.[18] This scholarship certainly informs my interpretation of the pilgrimage; however, I foreground recent turns toward the explicit environmental dimensions of the camps themselves to deepen understanding that the camps made a lasting structural impression on regional land use. For example, as environmental historian Connie Chiang powerfully argues, administrators envisioned nature and land as dimensions of confinement and an experiment of progressive social engineering.[19] Minidoka's violent inheritance encompasses the residue of administrator's and labor's imprint on the land. As such, the LCO dispute illuminates how appropriation enacts settler violence in reproducing land as a sacrifice zone and simultaneously encompassing conflicting relationships of sexuality.

In what follows I trace the nonlinear environmental relationships between the lands of the Minidoka National Historical Site, the grounds of the family farm, and the mechanisms of standardized life in CAFO space. But first, here are a few caveats. This chapter is not an official nor chronological history of Minidoka camp life nor the CAFO. As a historical site in the NPS, Minidoka is already tightly curated, and so my inquiry rests with its curatorial context, which moves between oral memories, interpretive signs, maps, and photographs, in addition to repurposed infrastructure such as the guard towers, barbed wire fence, restored barracks, and a root cellar. Nor do I want to suggest the camp and CAFO are *analogous* spaces or experiences, even as the CAFO is not the first time Japanese American incarceration overlaps with structures of contained animality.[20] Rather, triangulating racial and sexual regimes of property subtending these spaces deepens understanding of their mutually constitutive relationship. More broadly, this chapter demonstrates how confinement is used to produce life in the settler nation by extracting energy from laboring bodies.

After posing an initial inquiry with Friends about the court ruling, I accepted an invitation to attend the pilgrimage. I draw from an extensive archive, including participation in and observation of the pilgrimage, conversations with attendees, archival documents, and regional newspapers. Opening with a constellation that comprises "Minidoka," I map a place that simultaneously references networks of movement. Before recounting how the pilgrimage unearths the land's transformation, I contextualize the category of affected persons as a racial regime of property that bundles infrastructure, sexual natures, and settler nationalism, countering the operation of energy and sexuality in the first two chapters. Each of these components come together over different eras of settlement and land use in the region, providing a contextual basis for reading the CAFO controversy as a paradoxical manifestation of sexual modernity rendered through bodily capacity and contested sexual normativity. Against the naturalization of private lands maintained by legal common sense, the tour reassembles intimate spaces, spaces of labor, and military order to map a "racial ecology," the historically specific relationality of racializing systems with embodied ecologies.[21] Finally, I return to the site of the CAFO to examine how public discourse constructs factory spatiality and sexualities. In these debates the figure of the family farm dominates as the grounds of sexual normalcy. Reading them both against their histories of heterosexualization, I gloss their varying relationships to sexual modernity. I highlight agrarian imaginations of propertied and proper sexuality alongside corporate structures of animal production and capacity taken to its extreme.

In the liminal space of the court decision and the ongoing uncertainty of the LCO, this chapter maps how Japanese American confinement underwrites the familial normativity of affected persons, grounded as an appeal to the sexually normative that underwrites objections to the CAFO. I've gestured toward the process of appropriation in which after the war the state made available lands viable for settlement to private individuals. While that appropriation underscores a specific relation to the dispossession of labor and energy, it doesn't tell us how a land-bound familial alliance becomes publicly salient as an appeal to the *nostalgic* form of the settler family unit. Nostalgia's rhetorical culture always intermixes with historical fictions rather than discrete origin points. And so the court dispute holds three different but overlapping domains of sexuality with land use at the center. First, the wartime population-based governance of Japanese Americans, wherein camp designs explicitly engineered forms of sexual control based on racist and nationalist theories of bodily energy and disposition; second, the state appropriation of lands giving way to the emplaced sanctity of the familial form as the *appropriate* unit to govern the sexual relations of agriculture; and, finally, the acceleration of capacity building through the standardization of animal life in the sexual space of the CAFO. Together and in conflict in public culture, each highlights the administration of sexuality through different land-based relationships. At its heart the court dispute centers sexuality as a means of adapting existing infrastructures for energetic potential through the extraction of value. However, the family farm and the LCO largely took prominence, eliding broader public attention to the sexual politics of the camp and the import of memorializing to reconstituting kinship for those whose families were forcibly detained as consequence of Executive Order 9066.

PILGRIMAGE ITINERARIES AND PERFORMING MINIDOKA

Amid a crowd of witnesses gathered in the Fine Arts Auditorium at the College of Southern Idaho, Seattle poet Larry Matsuda recollected his first tour of the ruins of Minidoka. Two hundred Japanese Americans joined with local residents and employees of the NPS and arrived to Minidoka for the annual pilgrimage. Many travelers reiterated the path of forcible migration between assembly centers in the Pacific Northwest and the desert of southern Idaho, departing from their homes in the Seattle area not far from Bainbridge Island. Others traveled after pilgrimages in other states, meeting the gathering at Minidoka that would span three days in a mix of desert and lush green agricultural fields in what is now called Idaho's Magic Valley.

Incarcerated at Minidoka as a child, Matsuda repurposed the landscape depicted by the photograph through his own vernacular cartography of place and memory. His body anchored by the podium, his voice ebbed and flowed, as if a force opposing the otherwise slow erosion of Minidoka's surroundings. Here Matsuda narrates his encounter with "ghosts of Minidoka wandering the land." His recounting of volcanic ash, basalt, and irrigated water activated somatic memory. Using an enactment and remix of bodily repertoire and photographs, Matsuda connected disparate processes of displacement and forced relocation, the stripping of temporary dwellings from isolated landscapes, and the bodily and generational residue of incarceration. As he spoke, laying claim to the psychic and bodily ruins of Executive Order 9066, a declaration that authorized the creation of "military areas" from which identifiable persons could be excluded and forcibly relocated, Matsuda's address located a complex structure of feeling tethering place and violence, inheritance and renewal. Matsuda's testimonial maps land lines of the transition between the forced extraction of labor for U.S. empire and the land's revitalization through time, nature, and cultivation. We might interpret Matsuda's memory map of dust, water, and loss as a temporal guide to the sediment and structures in the land that continue to shape somatic memory.

Regardless of our place of departure, our choreographed movements to this rural locale demanded managing long hours of travel, inevitably cut by interruptions, waiting alongside feelings of delay and desolation. Minidoka is more than a static location or cartographic space. Minidoka's past and present are constellations of movements and routes, what performance studies scholar Dwight Conquergood calls itineraries.[22] The 2013 pilgrimage to Minidoka, the tenth in its lifespan, was a performance of sacred time paying homage to generations both living and dead. Those itineraries weave together a past of anti-Asian racism in addition to racialized kinships and family formations amalgamated with soil and dust.

Spoken to me during a short break in between walking the grounds of the detention site turned memorial, the epigraph that opens this chapter crystalizes objections to the LCO for some of the attending participants at the 2013 pilgrimage. As we traveled on the bus, I listened to my *nisei,* or first generation of persons born to Japanese migrants, neighbor share a story of his experiences at Poston and Minidoka, and I later walked alongside elders recalling feelings connected to Minidoka's memory ecologies. Listening to their frame "we can't move our prison" shifts the nationalist public memory frames like "internment" or "relocation."[23] Despite the permit approval prior to the pilgrimage, the LCO's construction continued to hang in the balance, delayed again by settlement agreements.

Listening to this small-group conversation heightened attention to *labor* and their commitment to honor the sacrifice of *issei,* or those who migrated from Japan to the United States or Canada, whose bodily dispossession worked the land to create value for the state. Labor in this context means the bodily transformation of the land into its productive value. For these participants the land comprises the ruins of a sacred place. One attendee argued, "This is sacred ground moistured by those people who survived here." The LCO would certainly pose imminent and ongoing environmental harm through accumulating toxins such as ammonia in air and water. But, more to the point, participants mapped the place where kin survived as now symbolic of stolen life and labor.

Remembering labor—the value produced by dispossession—functions as a technique of memory that simultaneously rewrites kinship ties and relationships to the extractive form of state-sponsored sexual modernity. This relationship matters because it ruptures the normative definition of *affected persons* and the logics of property fetishized by the court's interpretation. Through the context of the pilgrimage, I interpret Friends as framing their relationship through stewardship and justice, in which their responsibility as historical witness is to steward and care for the land-based remains of their kin. While the pilgrimage enables connecting with and repairing relationships to the land, it also affords recomposing intimacies and kinships.

The question remains how the pilgrimage unearths Minidoka's land lines and ruptures the property articulation of affected persons. In contrast to dominant logics of affected persons that privatize attachments to the land in terms of property value and residence, the tour enacts a strategy of lived redress, naming how land was used as a site of agricultural development. The central question for this chapter is how the event of the pilgrimage makes labor and energy intelligible through photographic markers, somatic memory, and storytelling. These repurpose the landscape in ways that run counter to the legal categories and spatial designs that underwrite environmental ruin and constrain the mobilization of memory to public audiences. In short, the movement of the pilgrimage through the place of Minidoka tests ongoing infrastructural violence against the ephemeral nature of somatic memory.

As a rhetorical performance, the pilgrimage highlights *nikkei* labor to improve the land and the resistance and the resilience of those incarcerated.[24] The pilgrimage is grounded in the rhetorical structure of presence, which Pezzullo argues in relation to advocacy tours is when "people, places, processes, and things may seem more tangible" to those without direct experience, who "may be more persuaded to identify with or believe in their existence, their significance, and their consequence."[25] Tangible qualities including exposure to elements, ruins, juxtaposition, and oral memories may carry a potential for moving audiences into a position of historical witness and alignment in belief of the site's existence, significance, and consequence. The audience for this tour, therefore, splits between familial and public. Its function is to ritualize ongoing memory work amid Japanese American families and political organizations to honor the violence suffered by the first and second generation of Japanese Americans and, ideally, enact them "never again."[26] For those who do not share a familial lineage of incarceration, the pilgrimage might align beliefs, enabling hearing, seeing, feeling the land in a different register. In this case the pilgrimage denaturalizes white regimes of industrialized nature in addition to the infrastructure supporting their confinement.

The pilgrimage brings into relief constellations of racial management animating their liveliness as pilgrims move through contemporary Minidoka. By racial management I mean the administrative production of racial difference through labor, crosscut by the managerial ethos of the western region.[27] Interest in excavating ecologies of memory emerged alongside Days of Remembrance events in the late 1960s.[28] But the role of the environment and broader racist articulations of nature in administrative planning and the actual experience of camp life remains grossly understudied, with rare exception. I discuss these aspects with more depth in the following section, but remembering how administrators deliberated about the capacities of the physical environment for agricultural potential remains critical to understanding the biopolitical state's racialization of nature in addition to the use of racialized labor to develop public lands later sold to private individuals.

The question that remains is what those environmental dimensions teach us about the contradictions of sexual modernity as an extractive energy regime. In the context of the camps, detained Japanese American labor functions as an *energy reserve* for the state. We might understand energy in two ways: first, the agricultural transformation of matter into value later transferred to the public domain and after the war to private individuals; and, second, the transformation of a racialized *population* through the governance of kinship, particularly a political atmosphere of policing intermarriage and childbirth within a race-anxious nation.

Minidoka, then, is a living place of both intimacy and violence, enfolding land and story, experience and environment. Paired with memory, experiential and ecological bodies activate intimacies between self, place, and time through spatial practices of itinerate walking, observation, and reflection.[29] As a consequence, the tour disrupts the interpretation of *affected persons* as individuals with an "interest in real property." From the vantage point of the pilgrims, the frame of property elides the hold of the land on the memories of its caretakers, who have been charged with the responsibility of preserving what remains of their ancestors' capacity to survive the unbearable. In the next section I map those land lines through the racial ecology of the region.

AFFECTED PERSONS: NATIONALISM, SEXUAL NATURES, AND RACIAL REGIMES OF PROPERTY

The Idaho Supreme Court's decision to limit standing to individual property owners epitomizes how *affected persons* in the context of land use operates as a legal formation in a system of white settler dominance. Herein lies one of the critical dimensions of the term as a relationship to the environment, shifting its function from a term of art to the consequence of contradictory relationships between capital and the state.[30] The court and broader public render property and residence as seemingly natural terms, as if both relationships are exterior rather than intrinsic to the region's history of Japanese American detention. An extension of property law and a settler colonial technique of managing land and life itself, *affected persons* embodies what Brenna Bhandar calls a racial regime of colonial modernity. Property law, writes Bhandar, works as "one of the most significant orders, an amalgam of legal techniques, through which colonial appropriation of land and the fashioning of colonial subjectivities take place and are secured."[31] By extension a key aspect of unsettling the case requires asking how the legal and cultural salience of *affected persons* depends on a particular regime of racialized energy, structured by the contradictions of labor and the legal administration of Japanese Americans as "citizen-alien."[32] *Affected persons* in its strictest legal sense disavows Japanese American labor in the region's production of lands, agriculture, and water infrastructure. To better grasp how Japanese American confinement underwrites the familial normativity of affected persons, this section retraces three dimensions biopolitics in camp administration: the sexual politics of racial exclusion prior to and during World War II, the state configuration of "Japanese American" as a population, and the particular energy logics that rendered Minidoka a desirable location to WRA administrators.

Asian American studies scholars emphasize how legal mechanisms of confinement extended and shifted ongoing legal techniques of Asiatic racialization to contain Japanese migrants from the white settler social body, techniques that simultaneously governed sexuality.[33] Confinement was certainly the most extreme state form of "alien citizen" containment, wherein the WRA and many white citizens more broadly believed wartime detention to provide a spatial fix for national crisis or the constraint on mobility for those marked as "racial enemies" of the national body.[34] Once again racial animosity accompanies settler nationalism, taking the form of "yellow peril" exclusion acts, antimiscegenation laws, and antisodomy laws that cast Asians writ large as unassimilable villains.[35] Nyan Shah maps at length the heightened suspicion of public and leisure spaces for policing "crimes against nature," the term invoked to criminalize social interactions between younger white men and Asian migrants.[36] Criminalizing contact emerged from the fear that "the threats of other interloper masculinities, cast as foreign and degenerate," would contaminate "normative American masculinity."[37] These histories matter because they illuminate the racialization of crimes against nature and the specifically sexual dimensions of demarcating "alien" over and against normate, "national" sexualities. But these correlations between national identity and sexual normalcy would again surface later in administrator's arguments in favor of confinement, specifically building on existing miscegenation laws to protect property.

The entry point of World War II exacerbated and shifted political arguments in support of racially targeted social control of sexuality. Western nativism added a volatile mix to national debates about the color line, often aligning racial management of the U.S. South with western lands, particularly sites of intensive agricultural development. The anti-Blackness of lynching spectacles converged with nativist attempts to police the "blood line" of a so-called white nature. In the context of national debates about wartime incarceration, John Rankin, senator from Mississippi, vociferously argued against the perceived threat of subversion by summoning a fantasy of nature made impure through intermarriage and blood mixing. Historian John Howard emphasizes Rankin's orientation to physiological segregation, recalling how Rankin, in an alarmist screed against the removal of demographic data from blood banks, warned against "taking the labels off the blood bank...so it will not show whether it is Negro blood or white blood. This is one of the schemes of these fellows to mongrelize the nation." Rankin later expanded his warning, arguing against "either 'Jap or Negro blood [being] pumped into the veins of white Americans.'" His insistence on physiological containment also informed arguments related to camp design. In fact, while nativists propagated paranoia of California as a "breeding ground" for Japanese American and Chinese American families, Rankin argued for the sex segregation of camps to prevent "over population."[38] Thus, at the onset of the war, racialized sexualities oscillated between arguments of the "deficit" of Japanese American men's heterosexuality and the submissive nature of Japanese American women (and thus potential for social control), in addition to state desires to regulate the birth rates of Japanese Americans.

As a whole, figures like Rankin and governmental officials acting as social engineers used logics of detention as a technology of energy management, crossing bodily, regional, national, and transnational scales. Government officials remained split on the function of relocation, oscillating between positions of containment versus the potential consequences of assimilation strategies. For some containment functioned as a military necessity. Commander of the Western Defense Command, Gen. John L. DeWitt was the most popular purveyor of the argument, grounding his argument in racial logics of heredity. Citing the proximity of military operations to Japanese farms, he argued that "the Japanese race is an enemy race" and that even among second generations of U.S. citizens, "the racial strains are undiluted."[39] State governors also held this view, vociferously resisting federal appropriation of lands. Idaho's governor Chase Clark compared nikkei to a noxious weed, stating, "My only thought now is to keep Idaho for Idahoans, and not to sell it to the Japanese."[40] The assimilationist position held by Dillon Myer, the second director of the WRA, believed in opportunities for social engineering through design. Mae Ngai elaborates how these New Deal liberals imagined the camps as "'planned communities' and Americanizing projects' that would speed the assimilation of Japanese Americans through democratic self-government, schooling, work, and other rehabilitative activities."[41] Reflecting on his own grandfather's experience living at Minidoka, environmental historian Robert Hayashi links the legal apparatus of Executive Order 9066 and its physical manifestation as the "institutional architecture that signified federal control over these individuals' movements and futures."[42] Rendered through racist logics of paternalism and childhood, both positions bundled previous deployed techniques of internal and external colonial control, weaving "conservative and liberal discourses into a biopolitical assemblage."[43] In short, land and environment converged in design practice to codify strategies of racialized sexual management.

The architecture of various campsites actualized logics of energy management but overall utilized the differences of their respective landscapes. Design was a critical tool in imagining containment as a solution to national crisis at the level of population *and* land. WRA officials approved a total of ten locations, but those were selected from at least three hundred potential sites.[44] Accounts of this selection process typically remember the emphasis of distance from strategic military sites along the West Coast. But, more important, the WRA's criteria also included metrics based on the environment, soil quality for agricultural production, and proximity to federal water infrastructure. So what environmental characteristics would make Minidoka—deep in the unforgiving desert of southeastern Idaho—a suitable location?

The answer was public land in addition to the presence of existing federal infrastructure and the promised potential development of those lands with detained Japanese American labor. The WRA chose Minidoka's site on the basis of three criteria: southeastern Idaho was composed of a large tract of federal land, that tract was also suitable for holding thousands of people, and it was geographically distant from strategic military bases but proximate to irrigated farms where incarcerated people would work.[45] Those lands became "public" through previous capitalist economies and the dispossession of Indigenous lands, making possible the early nineteenth-century declaration by the U.S. Army Corps of Discovery claiming land in what would become Idaho territory.[46] The presence of water and rail infrastructure, respectively for irrigating farms and the relocation of Japanese Americans to the camps, were consequences of increased settler encroachment that extracted minerals, engineered water, and built settlements for the purpose of wealth accumulation.[47] With the labor of structural and civil engineers, private companies built larger irrigation systems and dam projects and later sold water rights to individual farmers who needed irrigated farms. Federal land surplus was made in part through a series of land acts that accelerated agricultural development by creating patents from the public domain. Foregrounding these forms of land use, albeit briefly, matters to better understand shifts between state and individual governance of land and water, and the specific arguments forwarded by the WRA that anticipate the sedimentation of affected persons as a property-bearing category.

In planning stages Minidoka was an ideal location because of its potential *value* to the state, which was already anticipating the sale of its lands to individual white farmers after the end of the war. In her groundbreaking environmental history, Chiang details the specific environmental and infrastructural logics at play in siting the camps on public lands. In fact, state officials spoke explicitly in terms of the transfer of value: from the energy expenditure of Japanese American labor to the cultivation of the land to the later benefit of individual farmers, whom they imagined to be largely veterans returning from the war. A local newspaper even described the camp's potential as a "self-liquidating project," generating value from the federal investment in the land. Along with improvements to the Milner-Gooding Canal, detainee labor invested value so that it would "be ready for occupation by white settlers"; WRA officials further pontificated detained labor would create relief for "possibly returned service men [through] a degree of cultivation...which should add materially to the tract and lighten the labor of reclamation usually attending the homesteading of desert land."[48] Read otherwise, part of the justification for wartime containment entailed a belief among administrators that Japanese American laborers would expend energy into cultivating the land to enhance its value. That value would later be transferred from the state to future individual white settlers.

This transfer is a process of racializing property, what I've previously referred to as the appropriation of land, and implicates how I've mapped sexual modernity as a set of technologies of energy and capacity building. The *potential* value of the land depended on contradictions of racial capitalism, what Lisa Lowe describes as the legal necessity of immigrant (or citizen) labor yet "alien" relationship to the national body.[49] Emerging from administrative documents, this contradiction clearly explicates the racialization of energy.

Throughout the book thus far, I have rerouted sexual modernity from its locus in a theory of individuation to point toward broader environmental relationships that make such a theory possible. Normative accounts of sexual modernity rely on an extractive web of capacity building, in which the constitution of white heterosexuality accompanies the governance of a national land base. White heterosexuality is *not* a natural category. In fact, as Susan Koshy has argued about miscegenation laws targeting Asian Americans, it is a category defined in opposition to racialized others.[50] Detained Japanese American labor created capacity for regional lands later tethered to white settler familial units. So, in the context of wartime detention, biopower as energy production is twofold: first, the administrative imagination of Japanese Americans as racially malleable and capable of transformation into a national body through the molding of camp design; and, second, the Japanese American cultivation of the land from potential to actualized value.[51] Minidoka's dual function in the mid-twentieth century is to contain *and* to make the desert landscape productive with racialized labor. The farm lottery at the camp's end would create proximity of family farms as settlers appropriated land once federally used for incarceration. In the controversy of Big Sky Farms, all of these relationships of value disappear from proceedings because they are frames unintelligible to a legal and settler imaginary premised on the protection of individual property.

The Big Sky controversy triangulates three claims to this historically appropriated land: first, by Friends as a place of Japanese American survival; second, by stewards of the family farm who find CAFOs to be a perverse mechanization of human and nonhuman labor; and, third, the CAFO system itself. When we conjoin these relations against one another, they concretize conflicting webs of racial and sexual governance. The CAFO registers as perverse because of its heavily industrialized production of bovine life, aided by ideals of standardization. At this point I want to hold off unpacking the assumptions of each of these. For now triangulating affected persons through these key sites reveals both underlying assumptions about why affected persons become such a problematic during the proceedings and illuminates what sexual norms detractors rely on for argumentative power. Legal imaginations of affected persons protect the whiteness of agrarian nature undergirding both the family farm and the CAFO.

The CAFO proceedings reveal how agricultural law depends on the common sense of property-based personhood, a kind of sovereignty made possible by state and corporate engineering. Territorializing the land through the continual passage of land acts and technologies of environmental control epitomizes the whiteness of industrialized nature as a formative energy regime. Tracing the afterlives of these relationships matters for any number of reasons, the foremost that labor remains one of the most important frames of Friends' legal objection in the Big Sky controversy. Holding these layers together, I interpret the pilgrimage in retrospect as revising in real time the time and space of confinement, its movement a tactic of spatial resistance that denaturalizes the land's history, labor, and transformation for a variety of audiences.

REASSEMBLING AFFECTED PERSONS IN THE THEATER OF MINIDOKA

To be situated as an affected person amid the environment of Minidoka is to be enveloped by an expansive openness to smellscapes, volcanic dust, and wind that come alive as vehicles of environmental violence. Dust juxtaposed to lively agricultural fields visualizes the contrast between vitality and confinement, making intelligible environmental violence as a racialized project.[52] This iteration of affected persons runs counter to its legal predecessor. Instead, affected persons can encompass a body's capacity to be affected by surrounding ecologies, a relationship that moves between violence and, potentially in this case, generativity and care. To the extent they are able, the collaborative ethic between nikkei and the NPS preserve and maintain their relationship to the land, safeguarding its legacy against white settler possessions of nature. The concept of affected persons takes on new meaning as nikkei narrate and reassemble the archive of incarceration. Feeling in time, the ecological body, woven through the North Side Canal, concrete ruins, and dirt roads, transfigures the substance of memory. The pilgrimage maps vital connections between land, bodies, and memory through verbal recollection, historical photographs, scrapbooks, and repurposed buildings. As such, one way to track the consequences of ecological feeling and memory is a memorializing form that renders present the land lines of confinement.

Following the tour's itinerary curates an experience of the land contesting the naturalization of that landscape's history. Grounded in the basalt-bearing desert, the tour locates the demarcation of boundaries, technologies of containment, labor practices, and everyday spaces. Crafted in particular for participants of the pilgrimage—including those incarcerated as children or born in the camp, along with later generations—the itineraries enliven Minidoka's emotional landscape. In what follows I detail portions of the tour. Although I cannot reproduce the tour in its entirety, the spatialities featured here illuminate the centrality of the state in crafting racialized sexualities as energy—intimate forms embedded and dispersed in land, water, and air.

RESISTING SEXUAL MODERNITY, REGENERATING INTIMATE SPACES

Earlier I elaborated how anxieties surrounding miscegenation and sexual perversion intersected in the state's decision to detain Japanese Americans as a "population." In what follows my focus on design elements marked throughout the pilgrimage elaborates extensive work within Asian American studies examining the history of sexuality from the perspective of the camps. Design codified a broader surveillance strategy to govern those incarcerated and to transform the rhythms of everyday life. However, in the space of the pilgrimage, we see these relationships reconstituted through narrative and visual practice. Memories of intimate life such as family structures, rituals, and home making become reservoirs of feeling, especially in juxtaposition to camp structures. The constitutive work performed here recomposes kinship *resistive* to the extractive regime of sexual modernity and a break in the cycles of violence composing land lines.

Pilgrims reassemble intimacies in their narration of the camp's spatial design. In partnership with the NPS, Friends preserved a barrack from Block 22. The building itself is sparse, slowing movement across the creaky floorboards. The tour guide and elders ask visitors to imagine arriving to this sparsely furnished place, to prepare to share a "home" place with several families. One elder noted how families separated the space of the barrack with curtains or dividers. Rather than enable a sense of home as a center of everyday life, barracks were used merely as sleeping quarters. Eating, bathing, or using the toilet had designated areas outside of the barracks, in part because of precarious plumbing infrastructure. Thirty-eight mess halls scattered through the blocks, providing an institutional meal system of military order, regimentation, and food rations. The lines accumulated again near lavatory and laundry buildings. Hayashi recalls how this sense of order permeated camp. Military design regimented the activities of everyday life: cooking, leisure, eating, play, sex, sleeping, bathing, and using the toilet; reshaping space, movement, and time. The militarized atmosphere facilitated a system of surveillance.[53]

The general plan for Minidoka, drawn by the architectural firm Glenn Stanton and Hollis Johnson, from Portland, Oregon, highlights how landscapes of sagebrush became grids of surveillance systems connected to broader networks of control. Depicted here, the general plan charts bodily movement through space, facilitated by block systems for living areas and the division of administrative, storage, and sewage areas (see fig. 11). Closer inspection of the plan reveals the strategic placement of eight guard towers surrounding the perimeter of the camp, located near entrances and block areas. A barbed wire fence, curved toward the interior of the camp, controlled bodily movement, constricting mobility outside of its boundary. Identification tags with assigned numbers located individual bodies within surveillance and subjugation. Each technology—from the tags pinned to bodies on the move to barbed wire, watched by the weaponized gaze of the guard tower—constitutes a network of communication linked to national surveillance.

On the day of the opening ceremony, we arrived and thumbed through thick information packets stuffed with pamphlets. Also included was an eggshell-colored identification tag, with a short string

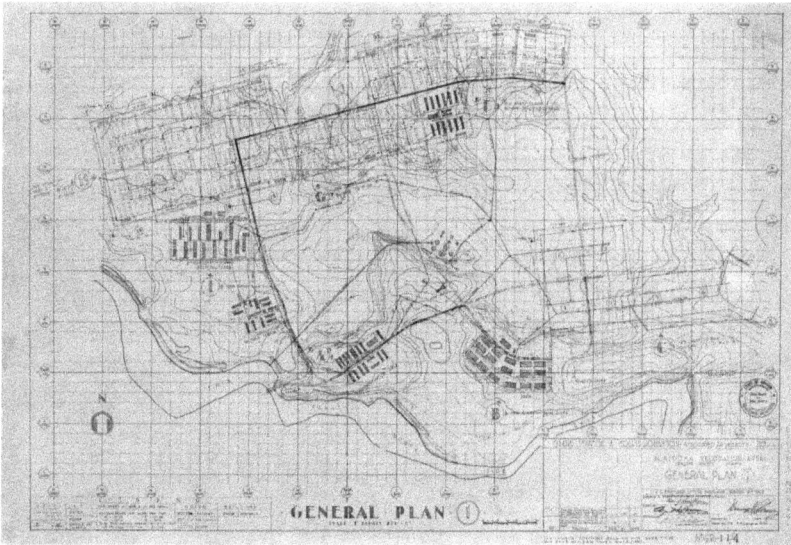

FIGURE 11. Minidoka general plans, drawn by Glenn Stanton and Hollis Johnson. Identification number 27813966, National Archives and Records Administration, Washington, DC.

and safety pin. On the label our names were written, with the details: "You are instructed to report ready to travel on." Beneath the empty box in which a date would have been written, the word, "MINIDOKA" appeared in bold black letters. Near the bottom of the tag, the instructions read, "To be retained by person to whom issued." Both the tag and the name displayed arrange a person rendered as population within the space-time of the pilgrimage. Those who had families incarcerated at Minidoka had a family number assigned as well.

The gathering carried a mood of a family reunion, unlike many of the pilgrimages to other camps such as Manzanar or Heart Mountain.[54] The 2013 tour featured pilgrims predominately displaced from Seattle, Portland, and Bainbridge Island. Because displacement affected families within a concentrated region, those incarcerated maintained regional networks during relocation and resettlement. It was not until the closing ceremony, between flag salutes and the mournful wail of a military trumpet playing "Taps" that the frame of reproductive kinship was named as a narrative structuring mechanism. In an address to the audience, one speaker argued that memories of camp life must not forget the sacrifices of those whose lives occupied the outside of biologically reproductive kinship: orphaned issei, gay and lesbian issei and nisei, and those whom never married. As Tina Takemoto has argued, surveillance systems and the organization of the barracks into discrete familial units partly explain the dearth of these narratives.[55]

The construction of kinship ties in the space of the pilgrimage constitutes a form of resistance to state-sponsored sexual modernities, in which the barracks themselves codified belief in racial containment and the surrounding lands grounded the dispossession of their labor. As caretakers of the environment where their elders survived the unbearable, their memories work as a form of repair, energized by decades of generational activism. They do not write themselves *in* to "sexual modernity"; rather, I view their memorializing as a critique of state violence.[56]

CAMPS TO FARMSTEADS: CURATING THE PUBLIC MATTER OF THE LAND

While stories conjure Minidoka back to life, permanent or temporary interpretive markers curate a timeline of the land, echoing an authoritative documentary style: "You are here. From here, you can see." These markers combined with intimate oral memory curate land lines, from dust to vibrant green and irrigated cropland. This juxtaposition visualizes archaeological time, a key rhetorical strategy to making labor perceptible. Dust jumps scale to the lungs of workers located in faraway places or distant time, including the bulldozers creating Minidoka or toward the lingering traces of nineteenth-century Japanese miners. Dust presences ghosts and inheritance. In this section I further engage the tour's interpretive strategies to guide visitors' recollection of the infrastructure that privatized the landscape of Minidoka after its closure.

After the tour bus first arrived at the historical site, we circled the perimeter to gain a sense of its expanse, pausing at times to read markers. Distinctions between private and public evaded detection until our guide mentioned that the base of the memorial site includes only a small selection of the original camp. The NPS cares for a fraction of Minidoka's former lands, but its surroundings encompass tracts of private agricultural fields and residences. As our bus circled around the camp perimeter, we encountered the border that occupied the marker between public land and private residence. The guide pointed to old, displaced barrack buildings nestled on private lands in the distance. Transformed as scrap material, barracks became barns for new homesteaders in the farmstead lottery after the war, evidence of the state's appropriation of property.

We then encountered the Herrmann family property remains, one of the few persevered buildings. A temporary and movable poster details how, after closure, the Bureau of Land Reclamation made the military veteran's family's claim to the land possible. After winning a lot in the Farmstead Lottery, the Herrmanns made their residence in Minidoka's firehouse and later built their home. The poster includes black and white documentary photos with captions reading, "What happened to the camp after the war ended." In retrospect the Herrmann story is one where individual family farms and state bodies such as the Bureau of Reclamation and WRA shape enjambed property relations between settlers and confined labor.

As we proceeded through the site, I noticed a rhythm of walking, pausing, observing, and taking photos characteristic of interpretive sites. Participants engaged these narratives through both reading and photography: creating their own images of archival photos, ruins in the ground, and building exteriors and interiors. Let's take these forms of engagement as means of generating claims to affected persons. Scholars and popular culture alike excoriate these forms of interaction, often castigated as modes of disengagement or, worse, as objectifying a place of violence.[57] These critiques depend on a sensibility of photographic technology as antithetical to the sacred. But photographic practices in situ reveal more about how we've constructed photography than what role it can play in historical witnessing. As a practice, photography functions as recording and documenting. But we could read the tens of thousands of photographs produced annually by the pilgrimage more robustly through the relationships they make possible as an archive of seeing and feeling. Situated practices of photography may create the capacity to reorient what can be seen and felt amid Minidoka's landscape.

Photographic witnessing is vital for us to establish Friends as affected persons beyond instrumental meaning. In the photograph of the Herrmann property marker, a single hand holds an iPhone and clicks a photograph (see fig. 12). I did not ask this participant what they might do with the archive of photographs created from the pilgrimage, but we could reflect how the introduction of photographic witnessing matters in making otherwise absent historical relationships present for others. This can act as a process of witnessing, connected to how one might feel moved to remember a particular moment: a piece of concrete scarred into the earth or the feeling of sunlight on the soil amid the soothing sounds of the canal.

The more permanent sign "Camp to Farmsteads," located east of

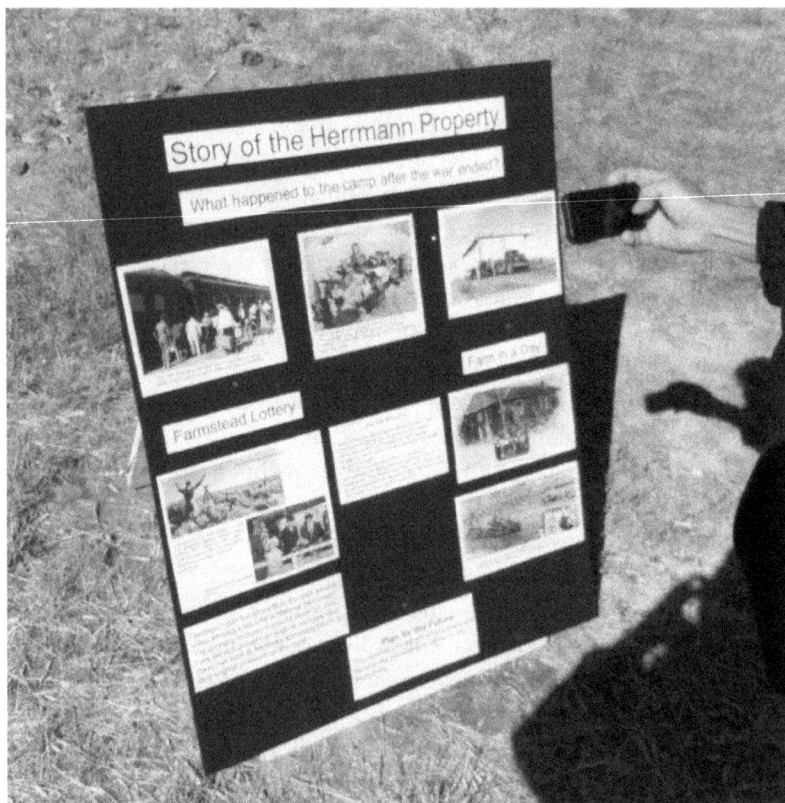

FIGURE 12. "Story of the Herrmann Property," 2013. Minidoka National Historic Site, Hunt, ID. Photo by author.

the firehouse, replicates an aesthetic strategy that arranges black-and-white photographs with textual overlay (see fig. 13). What's provocative about this sign is how it encourages spectators to orient their bodies. As a form of strategic media common to contexts such as museums, the location of the marker organizes the visual faculties of participants by turning their attention away from the public land belonging to the NPS. Instead, visitors gaze beyond the boundaries of the marker toward private farmland. The land itself marks a boundary: as one looks above and beyond "Camp to Farmsteads," pockets of brown desert soil and sagebrush fade as the horizon transforms into lush green fields below a clear cerulean sky. Positioned within the camp, spectators may witness the effects of that transformation: unkempt, still-desert landscape borders a manicured and irrigated homestead. *Cultivation* marks the

FIGURE 13. "Camp to Farmsteads," 2013. Minidoka National Historic Site, Hunt, ID. Photo by author.

boundary between idle and productive land using irrigation systems to manage the movement of water in the region. And more, the salience of "Camp to Farmstead" emerges from the permeability of private residence and the publicness of the historical site.

Also located near the farmhouse, "Dust to Cropland" asks witnesses to imagine the land as it was encountered for the first time by those incarcerated (see fig. 14). This sign reverberates the oral memories of elders who carry a lasting impression of dust storms and sagebrush. Dust is a reference point for the dislocation and trauma of leaving the plenitude of waterways located in the greenery of the Pacific Northwest. As we approached the historical site from the bus, our guide asked pilgrims to imagine encountering a different landscape of bleak dust and wind. The passenger next to me pointed to a dusty patch and said, "That sagebrush over there is probably what it looked like."

Beyond the water of the North Side Canal, Minidoka's environment left little reminders of Portland, Seattle, and Bainbridge Island. As we approached the camp, our guide asked us to "imagine that all of this is dust. It was very different from Seattle. And imagine clearing the land

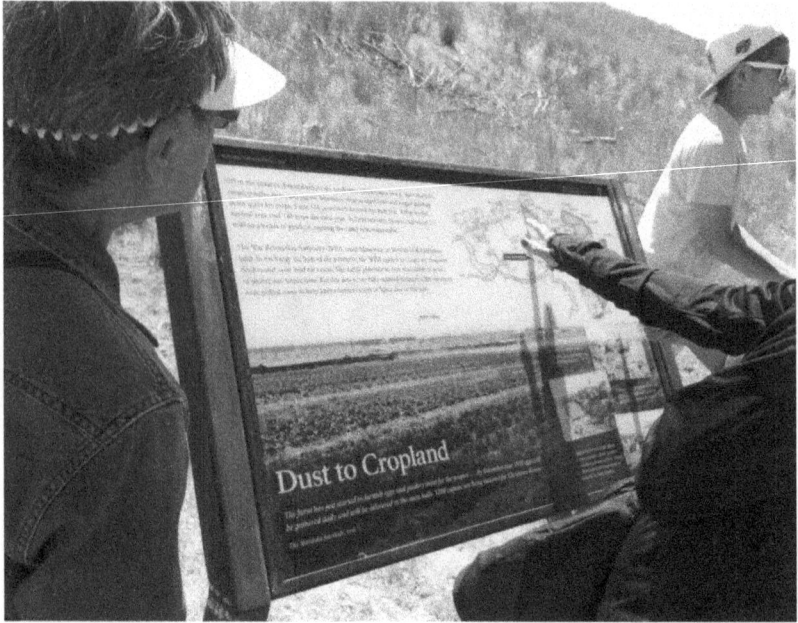

FIGURE 14. "Dust to Cropland," 2013. Minidoka National Historic Site, Hunt, ID.
Photo by author.

for the first time amidst constant dust storms." Her words made dust
agentic, weaponized fragments of minerals and metal.[58] As something
that moves and scatters in the atmosphere, dust blurred the boundaries
between human and nonhuman surroundings, moving particles of matter into mouths and eyes. Granular dust composed of volcanic basalt
blurred between natural and social worlds. In oral memories shared
by elders, dust invoked a powerful symbolic form: a condition to be
endured, overcome. In juxtaposition to dust, lush green farmlands were
evidence of issei labor. Amid the feeling issei lives were made absent,
their mark on the land became intelligible through the transformation
of dust into cropland. "*Gaman. Shikata ga nai.* Endure the unbearable
with dignity." This is the issei legacy and the racialized grounds of an
oppositional affected persons.

Technologies of containment juxtapose spaces of flow and potential
healing. The reconstructed barbed wire fence occupies a boundary with
the North Side Canal, its wire and posts pointing inward to imagined
inhabitants, its exterior facing the curvatures of the northern boundary of the canal. In both oral memories from participants and official

interpretive markers, the canal provided a soothing place. The sound of flowing water and the sight of ripples taking shape in what at times feels like the force of a river gave solace to those gathered near its boundary. According to the marker near the banks, "The North Side Canal brought solace to internees homesick for the Pacific Northwest. Here in the dry Idaho desert, the canal reminded them of familiar scenes in Oregon, Washington, and Alaska, where flowing waters were commonplace. The canal was their home tie."

The banks of the canal offered spectators a place to reflect on their experiences. I walked to the waters after the closing ceremony to meet a coparticipant from the previous day's legacy session. "What brings you to the pilgrimage?" I asked. The pilgrimage offered the creation of memory that wasn't possible otherwise, she answered. Here it felt more alive. She came to learn, to imagine what life was life in the barracks, to share with a community of persons affected by incarceration, and, most important, to heal. We stood next to the calming waters of the canal. I paused to take a photograph facing the reassembled barbed wire fence, with my back to the place where the guard tower near the entrance of the camp once stood (it would not be reconstructed until the fall of 2013). Moments later, she said, "Look at the swallows dancing on the water. They're so beautiful." I turned to watch a collective of swallows swoop down to the water, dancing alongside the ripples and then back upward. The choreography of movement was a stark contrast to the barbed wire just hundreds of feet away from the bank.

In the conjuncture of Minidoka's present and the contemporary agricultural landscape of CAFOs in southern Idaho, water has particular significance. Just as the waters of the North Side Canal offered a reminder of home in a lonely desert, its waters continue to cultivate feelings of hope. But in 2013 the ongoing process of healing hung in the balance because of the ongoing uncertainty created by Burdick's ruling. As copetitioner, the National Trust for Historic Preservation insisted Minidoka was already precarious, adding the site in 2007 to its list of "most endangered historic places." Throughout initial county hearings and first district court judicial review, Friends, farmers, and environmental organizations insisted Big Sky Farms would pollute both surface and ground waters. Their objections are supported by vast troves of research that emphasize observable flows of toxins that accumulate in water flowing beyond property boundaries. The fear is simple: CAFO's toxic streams fundamentally transform regional ecologies by introducing new contagions at a mass scale. The health effects are also real;

petitioners documented potential harms such as the exponential increase in asthma and allergies, in addition to a range of potential chemical sensitivities. Even prior to my arrival at the camp, traveling to the site delivered a glimpse of barrack-like boxes of misery, distant from the highway yet present in its seepage through every skin and respiratory surface.

Ongoing uncertainty about the LCO continued to shape how pilgrims articulated their relationship to the site and its importance in repair and care work. At the time of the 2013 pilgrimage, the process to build Big Sky Farms continued to hang in the balance, in part because of a potential settlement that would lead to a land buyout on behalf of the NPS and conservation fund.[59] Many elders seemed to express how ecological memories require *accessible* environments. Implicitly referring to the debilitating consequences of CAFOs, one elder remarked, "That discomfort was not part of our memory." Another elder, who was sixteen when she was incarcerated, said that she would not be able to return to the pilgrimage if the environment's smells became inaccessible. More, the symbolic value of the CAFO's location intensified the relation of sacrifice zone: "If this was Gettysburg or Yellowstone, this would not even be a question," one participant argued. Pilgrims resisted the planned location of the CAFO because of the unknown material risks it could pose to the site as well as how that location evidenced its cultural value: "It makes us angry and feel as if this place is insignificant." Here strangers see dust, pilgrims see inheritance, and producers see profit potential.

Although some critics might claim the linkage between smell and memory attempts to purify associations of memory, I read their resistance in the register of environmental justice. In this case a place imagined and built to once immobilize bodies marked as other now risks immobilizing recollection because of the introduction of a new system of confinement. Smell is yet another medium of violence; as Hsuan Hsu argues, "Air is simultaneously an aesthetic medium of scent and a biopolitical medium that determines life and death."[60] Here I need to clarify what I mean by air and "smell," given how profoundly hygiene and the olfactory can function to racialize space and consequentially violence. CAFOs aren't just a "foul" smell. Concentrated ammonia mixes with hydrogen sulfide and volatile organic compounds, synthesizing to become a corrosive sensory experience. The ammonia burns your nostrils, the wave of stench makes you nauseous, and the power of it all seeps everywhere.[61]

To introduce a mass scale of toxins into the landscape of Minidoka uniquely renders regeneration as healing an even more uncertain process. Healing is not a matter of a return to unmediated nature; such a sense does not exist. But confinement and toxins mark time and intensity, dispersing their matter across space. New toxins make somatic memory inaccessible and expose pilgrims to the respiratory disease of the CAFO's atmosphere. As I move forward to discuss the CAFO in particular, I highlight how the relationship to productivity and energy in sexual modernity becomes reconstituted through the standardization of animal (re)production.

CAFO SPACE: SEXUAL NATURES AND MECHANIZED "PERVERSION"

Thus far I've shown how the pilgrimage denaturalizes sexuality as a racial regime of property underwriting *affected persons*. In what remains of this chapter, I move through the key sexual frames mediated in the public tension between CAFOs and the small family farm, particularly private homesteads' critiques of mechanized sexual reproduction as a perversion of sexual natures. In public arguments private landowners asserted and contrasted "pure" and "industrial" nature as they resisted the CAFO. I can acknowledge the power "perversion" has as an argumentative strategy, even as I'm wary of how that hierarchy assumes an other (in this case, settler agrarianism) rendered as normal. I'm not convinced that "pervert" best encapsulates the violence of CAFOs *or* agrarianism; my analysis here grapples with the sexual politics of scale, to understand how this case deploys the operative logic of normal. What's striking to me is just how much CAFO systems emerge from the appropriation of earlier infrastructures of food production and labor. As Constance Gordon and Kathleen Hunt argue, emphasizing food systems traces "relations of power, capital flows...[and] biopolitical circuits that drive food's unending demand and need."[62] To grasp the regime, contemporary agriculture's energy-intensive practices must be situated within earlier systems of racial capitalism, such as wartime detention. The capitalist mechanization of life in the CAFO is profoundly structured by Anglo-American energy regimes, especially racial capitalism. The CAFO in turn is extractive human and nonhuman labor in the hyperspeed time of industrial white settler heteronormativity.

A century of long transitions in the infrastructure of animal consumption partly explains the sexual mechanics of CAFO space, even as

I would be wary to suggest they are a natural conclusion to the politics of food ecologies.[63] In fact, southern Idaho has witnessed a boom in the number of CAFOs since the farm crisis in the 1980s, many of which have pollution shopped their way to the Magic Valley before the institution of stricter regulations in 2001. In consequence farmers and ranchers with smaller operations have struggled to protect their own farms through affected persons claims in county courts. For people such as Dean Dimond, a white farmer who joined Friends to resist the permitting of Big Sky Farms, CAFOs embody perversions of an idyllic imagination, becoming "unneighborly nuisances." Dimond commented, "The dairy industry has been really good for this area. There are some that try to take care of their neighbors. But these guys just wanted to come in and build this mega facility."[64] The juxtaposition between "neighbor" and "mega" reveals implicit spatial and scalar assumptions in what makes a sustainable dairy. Dimond assumes smaller operations are better contained, obeying arbitrary confines of personal property. In contrast, CAFOs exceed their spatial boundaries, sensed through smell and a range of environmental impacts accelerating the imprint of human activity. Despite the use of abstract design to annihilate space, the spatiality of CAFOs extend far beyond the ground: their toxicity moves vertically into the air and disperses into and through bodies of water that carry toxins into new areas. Residents' statements underscore how the CAFO violates ecological limits: the CAFO cannot contain industrial odors, noise, or dust.

Adjacent to these well-evidenced environmental impacts of industrial agribusiness, residents often repeated tropes of "perversion." The Big Sky controversy leveraged a number of familiar defenses against the CAFO, including the sanctity of property. But the sexual politics of "factory" and "industrial" dominated objections, grounding arguments in the tension between pure nature and corrupting technology. Journalist Scott Weaver commented, "Over the last two decades, the vision of the dairy has morphed from an idyllic setting to an industrialized, Henry Ford–like factory—the concentrated animal feeding operation."[65] Farmers such as Marilyn Hoke narrate a sense of attenuation: "I'm not afraid of the smell of cow manure...[but] these are not dairies. They are factories."[66] Distinctions between "dairy" and "factory" become a matter of scale: factories intensify the magnitude of reproductive labor's environmental impact.[67]

At this point I want to untether the sexual politics guiding what remains unsaid in the stark distinction between idyllic nature and industrial life: the sexual mechanics of perversion. Although the public objection to "factory" indeed operates on a metaphorical register, CA-FOs *do* embody factory logics of efficiency, speed, and standardization, all borrowed from preexisting infrastructures of capitalist food production and principles of scientific management. CAFOs of all kinds standardize life to expand animal capacity, meaning "management plans" move beyond the space of the animal itself to land, water, and air.[68] CAFOs are by design land and water intensive, and, as spaces of reproductive labor, they embody entire systems of extractive violence. CAFOs are violent biopolitical spaces of "distributed reproduction."[69] Dairy CAFOs industrialize production at the scale of the global market and doing so requires mechanizing bovine reproduction to provide an ongoing supply of raw cow milk. To produce bovine milk alongside the speed and intensity of the market, humans govern the reproductive time of heifers through artificial insemination and human-animal stimulated intimacy. The process entails visceral contact and intimacy between human, animal, and machine from the extraction, preservation, and storage of semen to the stimulation of heifers to maximize the probability of fertilization, implantation, and gestation.[70] In short, the distributed reproduction of milk enacts energy extraction as human-animal labor through the standardization and speed of market time.

The modality of sexuality renders this perceived tension between nature and technology. Capitalist natures shape the spatiality, form, and legal protections underwriting both "perverse mechanization" and the "idyllic family farm." Both of these relationships to agriculture demand a sense of sexual normalcy as life-building capacity, crafted by centuries of federal and state policy within rural countrysides to produce heterosexualization.[71] Even before artificial insemination in bovine breeding took hold in the 1940s, breeding techniques have been influenced by management styles of standardization through efficiency and productivity, extensions of logics rendering life as capital.[72] Artificial insemination on the farm has become so commonplace that we neglect its place in the ongoing process of governing bovine sexuality and the human labor involved in cross-species sexual stimulation—yet another interconnection between human and nonhuman labor, sexuality, and energy.

Moreover, the CAFO system reproduces capitalist relations of production while fostering disabling conditions.[73] In Idaho, and in the United States more broadly, migrant laborers (documented and undocumented) perform highly skilled but dangerous work in compact spaces. One of those tasks include artificial insemination and sexual stimulation, necessitating workers embody animal instincts in the scene of mechanistic sexuality. Although a typical dairy cow may live up to twenty years, the heifer's market lifespan ranges up to four to five years. During that life span heifers deliver multiple calves to guarantee their ongoing supply of milk. The extraction of milk operates in the milking parlor, whose designs vary from long, elongated hallways in which heifers stand on a platform, attached to milking machines, slightly hovering above dairy workers monitoring speed and volume of milk production. Other options include the rotary milking parlor, designed to minimize time in the parlor by increasing efficiency. From birth to labor to slaughter, the space of the dairy shifts from labor-intensive to capital-intensive efficiencies, and the space of the CAFO maximizes capital by creating an ongoing supply of bovines whose bodies can be maximized until they are no longer able to work.[74] Meanwhile, human laborers are also exposed to debilitating concentrations of pathogens, ammonia, and hydrogen sulfide, all within an environment with little labor protections. Together reproductive bovine bodies and pliable workers (re)produce milk capital. Both human and nonhuman are rendered pliable yet disposable.

These processes take shape in interior and exterior spaces that remake the very ecologies of the Magic Valley to maximize productivity of the land and human and animal workers. Juxtaposing the CAFO to Minidoka as a land line insists that the "factory mentality" of industrial life emerges not in food automation but in militaristic techniques of commanding space creating the conditions to extract worker energy.[75] From a bird's-eye view, the milking parlors and feeding areas are most visible: long, narrow buildings that sit parallel to one another, resembling the layout of blocks and barracks or military-base installations, including the barracks of Minidoka. In the distance the surrounding landscape has been carefully engineered to manage waste and flow. Tracing this shift in capitalist relations of production through the specific ecology of Minidoka implicates how one interprets the argumentative grounds of "normal."

Disgust among small family farmers leaves a handful of conclusions. First, the CAFO and the small family farm entail different relationships to capital, even as they are similar spaces of sexual governance. Their distinctions between dairy and factory, neighbor and nuisance, infer that CAFOs *pervert* an aesthetic memory of animal husbandry within farm communities by shifting the speed and scale of sexual reproduction for milk-producing cows. The apparent tension between the CAFO and the small family farm do not rely on incommensurable worlds; both are sites of violence that build on each other through a sexually modern demand for capacity of life. The point worth underscoring here is that the triangulation of sites—from the camp to the small family farm to the CAFO—follows the reproduction of sexuality's entrenched entanglement through the capitalist relations of land and energy. This chapter's untangling of the CAFO controversy by tracing land lines in southeastern Idaho underscore how the protection of capitalist animality emerges through the layering of intergenerational infrastructures dedicated to spatial control, optimization, and extraction.

Read backward, federal officials imbued the administrative bureaucracy of Japanese American incarceration with militarized principles of scientific management, promoting efficiencies, standardization, and aesthetics of high modernism. I would be wary of suggesting that the twentieth-century camp and the twenty-first-century CAFO are *analogous* spaces. However, they are tethered through militaristic design and the function of energy extraction. Both incorporate the strategic function of military design, blending the high modernism of midcentury architecture with logics of concentration, efficiency, and order. Camps and CAFOs are far removed from populous areas, their locations decided based on spatial remoteness. And, finally, both spaces deploy tracking materials to surveil bodies and manage information, a software update to multiple centuries of using branding to mark property relationships of cattle and ledgers to manage the movement and confinement of human beings. These devices create uniformity, reducing life to population. The Big Sky controversy is not the only example of an environmental challenge to Japanese American historical sites, but it can teach us how carceral logics may be repurposed and reanimated into new modes of racial capitalism, justifying a deep cultural history of a singular location and broader networks.

"FOR ALL THE GOVERNMENT TOOK, I TOOK A ROCK AND LEFT A CRYSTAL IN ITS PLACE"

The historical lessons from the use of western lands for the incarceration of Japanese Americans can teach us many lessons, especially how appropriation provides a technology for the transference and reproduction of capitalist relations of energy. This chapter has foregrounded how a contest of affected persons through inheritance remaps our understanding of sexuality in justifying the camps, the active role of the environment in actualizing biopolitical logics, and, finally, the dispossession of energy and labor in making the grounds of the settler family farm. This is not to say that the incarceration of Japanese Americans is equivocal with or analogous to modern industrial agriculture. Rather, the Big Sky Farms proceedings illuminate how appropriation functions to repurpose and reproduce systems of confinement as an apparatus of energy extraction. The logic of confinement contours ongoing forms of land enclosure that delimit how a space may be used and to what extent others may have a stake in environmental decision making.

In contrast to the privatization of affected persons, the pilgrimage's performance of violent inheritance asserts Friends as affected persons in a *public* register and as an enactment of public emotionality that exceed one's status as a private, rights-bearing, property-owning citizen of the state. In spite of legal constraints on what qualifies as affected persons, performances of violent inheritance in the theater of Minidoka challenge privatized notions of residence and ownership. Performances of violent inheritance compel audiences to commemorate the physical ruins of a militarized and temporary home rather than be subjected to ongoing symbolic and literal pollution. And because violent inheritance collapses distinctions between intimate politics and public memory, the performance of affected person becomes a category entangled within intimate spaces and intimacies with the land.

The bitter irony on display during the 2013 pilgrimage is that association with a legal category that carries the historical weight of land enclosure could *protect* Minidoka from further environmental ruin. Without a residential tie to the land, Friends responds to the present injury by collaborating with nearby residents, whose own properties became possible only after the Farm Lottery at the end of the war. These emerging relationships in response to the crisis of industrial agriculture illustrate how, despite their historical structure embedded in the past, those confining relationships are not necessarily guaranteed in the future. Extractive energy regimes are remade through repurposing of the land, but *how* the land is repurposed is never known in advance.

Above and beyond, the pilgrimage is a reminder of why witnessing inheritance is an action that invites spectators to take responsibility for the historical lessons of the past by denaturalizing the architectures that order landscapes of confinement. Although the lessons of engagement will continue to circulate within the cultural production of younger generations, the landscape, with its ruins and residue, teaches much more about transitional ecology and histories of labor, privatization and shifting industrialization. To echo one of Matsuda's poems from the symposium: "For all the government took, I took a rock and left a crystal in its place." The environment of Minidoka is more than the dust of memory. It is also the ripples of hope.

CHAPTER 5

Petroculture and Intimate Atmospheres

Designed with construction beginning in the mid-twentieth century, Interstate 80 now stretches between San Francisco, California, and Tea Neck City, New Jersey. Its asphalt ridges ease against the riparian like boundaries of bioregions. More colloquially known as "80," the road connects a range of U.S. landscapes in the Rocky Mountain West: urban areas lead to prairie grasses swaying with the gusty breeze of the Midwest, in Utah the salt sucks the air dry, and elsewhere roadside attractions like the Fort Kearney bridge or Buffalo Bill Cody's ranch lure kitsch-hungry tourists. Drivers move between and amid desolation and density. It is a mediator, a tethering device that embodies the modern U.S. transcontinental imagination and, for the most part, a culture dependent on oil. I grew up in Wyoming, and driving on the road feels familiar to me—an evocative feeling place tarried between escape routes and places to linger and nestle.

The highway also is a landmark of national and bicoastal queer mobility, a mid-twentieth-century route for small-town queer dreams of moving to the Big Gay Bay or Big Apple. As a transportation culture mediator, interstates such as I-80 foster queer automobilities, including the "get out of dodge" story, circulated throughout popular culture and personal narratives alike. To speak of queer automobilities means thinking through processes of dwelling and constraints on movement, modes of self-authorship entangled within an array of technologies and surveillance networks. This is a task with promises and pitfalls, given the profound unevenness of mobility across the planet. As Aren Z. Aizura reminds us, metaphors of mobility often shape narratives of trans and queer subjectivity and parallel deep layers of colonial and extractive world making.[1] So in thinking about the question of energy's relationship to contemporary queer regional formations, queer automobilities can highlight global conditions undergirding tempos of immobility and movement as much as they might elaborate regionally specific story forms and affects.[2] This chapter interweaves queer Rocky Mountain West narratives with critical vocabulary from the energy humanities and queer studies, respectively: petroculture and sexual imaginaries.

Few North American queer theorists take seriously the cultural and technological assemblage of transportation infrastructure energized by vast petroleum cultures or the intimate nexus of oil and narratives of energized modes of sociality, particularly endless mobility.[3] In 1995 Kath Weston reflected on her time in San Francisco in the 1970s amid a cultural migration of gays and lesbians to the Bay Area.[4] Weston's objective was to think through the networks constituted by communication technologies, along with the particular sexual imaginaries forged as those networks moved in and out of place. In making sense of the great gay migration, Weston named how, at the time, part of making sense of queer life was to seek out imagined communities, the strangers in cities made real by the public circulation of narrative. These imaginaries, so often pitting the nonmetropolitan against the urban or cosmopolitan, calibrate a vision of subjectivity that depends as much on a place of arrival as it does a path traveled through vast space.[5] Weston's work always returns me to the formative power of the road. The highway or interstate, I-80 being one of many, often conjures all sorts of boring linearity, a direct conduit to a discrete place of arrival. But some never arrive, and some move back and forth in moments of brief escape from suffocating conditions. We know all too well the layers of historical violence and constraints on mobility that make movement a place of scrutiny, surveillance, and risk.[6] When we talk about movement, we should also take seriously the vast energy infrastructures that make such a social space possible.

The problem important to me is how to discern sexual imaginaries of mobility as a particular infrastructural imagination and petroculture aesthetic or the energy inflected in dimensions of contemporary queer cultures. Petrocultures, writes Imre Szeman, intertwine material infrastructures of movement powered by fossil fuel matter with the social practices, ideas, and cultures of specific energy systems.[7] The implications of this concept for queer studies are vast, at the very least offering how particular sexual imaginaries rooted in the necessity of movement need to be grounded within the energy systems that make them possible. In fact, queer automobilities seem like the *most* obvious entanglement between sexuality and the infrastructure encompassing land and energy systems. Petrocultures should matter for queer studies because petroleum and carbon byproducts literally scatter throughout queer migration stories, in all their complexity. Even under the sign "queer migration," movement varies given the national and transnational forms of stoppage, confinement, and immobilization long associated with the racialization of mobility.[8] Over the years my attempt to situate queer mobilities and constraints on that mobility have generated an array of reactions, perhaps the most haunting being the question of whether or not this work scapegoats queer people wanting to escape. So let me be clear: this chapter is not interested in a politics of castigation, nor would I rob someone of a necessary lifeline for shifting the intensity of social violence by relocating elsewhere.

Instead, I want to linger with questions of how petrocultures rooted in settler colonial structures have shaped affects of contemporary queer and trans life, their geographies, and their connections to the local, regional, and transnational. And, more to the point, I believe tracing those relationships with and against their respective land lines might afford deepening possibilities for finding more regenerative ways of living with the planet. This question is, I hope, an opening for what queer studies can do with analytics of energy, and, moreover, I hope that queer and trans narratives from one of North America's extractive capitals might illuminate for the energy and environmental humanities the necessity of confronting largely heteronormative and ciscentric modes of understanding the death grip of coal and petroleum on those who live near the front lines of extractivism.

Overall, in this chapter I argue for shifting gears to reimagine this sexual imaginary as tethered to a structure of queer living inside the infrastructures that oil made. This argument is part of a broader history that took hold in the twentieth century, what Stephanie LeMenager calls "living oil." Here I build on LeMenager's work by focusing on what living infrastructures can offer queer studies, especially queer ecology and geography. The previous chapters explore the breadth of relationships afforded by energy analytics to unearth earlier energy systems, technologies, and contexts of bodily and environmental extraction. This chapter, however, builds on the analysis of legacy infrastructure to illuminate the condensation of violent inheritance in contemporary claims to energy. From this vantage point automobility and assisted forms of movement enact incorporating practices that produce a constellation of transportation affects. These "living infrastructures," LeMenager argues, demand new ecological narratives: "decoupling human memory from the infrastructures that have sustained it may be the primary challenge for ecological narrative in the service of human species survival beyond the twenty-first century."[9]

I am not interested in hierarchies of rural or urban space so much as I am in tracing their *connections* to each other within regional and transcontinental sexual imaginaries, which illuminate a different terrain for queer ecologies and queer studies more broadly. From an environmental and especially infrastructural standpoint, *rural* and *urban* characterize intertwined spaces within supply-chain networks of extraction and commodity production—a foundational argument in the environmental humanities forwarded since at least William Cronon's *Nature's Metropolis*. Attending to the broader networks of energy systems that undergird sex as a domain of vitality production or techniques of exhaustive biopolitics shifts the possibilities for a queer studies enmeshed with contesting environmental power and precarity. As such, this chapter brings me to the intertwining of the petroculture state and the navigation of whiteness, transphobia, and homophobia. Together these overlapping hegemonies illuminate the honesty of queer living in one regional petroculture in the Rocky Mountains.

The Rocky Mountain West is an energy-intensive producer of fossil fuels, specifically coal, crude oil, and so-called natural gas. The desire to monopolize energy markets comprised central aspects of settlement, surveying, and regional development. At the time of this writing, Wyoming has dominated coal production in the United States since 1986; it is eighth in crude production, and its energy-intensive operations are second only to Louisiana's.[10] Colorado's energy economy ranks higher in crude production, coming in at fifth in the nation, and as of 2020 became the seventh-largest producer of natural gas.[11] The scale of these energy economies at times surpass everyday perception, but one is often reminded when driving past jack pumps, the apparatus for crude extraction that moves a pivoting beam up and down; refineries that break down crude into usable petroleum products; or the large, white cylindrical tanks associated with the fracking industry. With time they all take on a feeling of violent *ordinariness*, hegemonic backdrops of a landscape that illuminate just how powerfully energy systems have been incorporated into western regional culture. But even as the petroculture state constitutes a lived hegemony, we cannot lose track of the contestation of that relationship, in both everyday and exceptional ways—within and beyond the region.

Inheritance once again affords a mode of moving through energy regimes, this time rendered through story forms and metanarratives of mobility. From Marfa, Texas, Joey Russo poses the prescient question: "What does it mean to think about structures of feeling residing in a region's story forms?"[12] These are vernaculars generated by the specificity of dwelling, and, indeed, they circulate within and against a variety of cultural flows. At times regional story forms might elucidate "a certain kind of disturbance or unease, a particular type of tension."[13] But when we pair the individual story line, regional metanarratives, and the physical infrastructures underwriting modernity, feeling hits differently. Grasping at the scalar connections tethering it all, we might center the gravitational pull of feeling, so as to put into relief "how things are felt (rather than known) break apart, reinforce, build up, or bring into focus the various structuring frames of our lives."[14] The Rockies and other energy-intensive regions have many stories: this chapter traces some of these land lines through the residual presence of older energy systems sustained by the petroculture state, transfixed into the condensation of resentful settler whiteness, heteronormativity, and territoriality.

Reaching for a regional affect rooted in bodily movement, immobility and isolation, fear, and noxious plumes of extractive masculinities, this chapter's stories become mosaics of queer life under *petromodernity,* a term from the energy humanities that foregrounds the mutually constitutive relationship between modernity and the energy systems of discovery, extraction, delivery, and consumption associated with fossil fuels. Shared stories from lesbian, gay, bisexual, queer, and trans folks open windows into relational selves in which the queer ecological body lives and breathes fossil fuel extraction and accompanying social violence—those elusive feelings of structure.[15] But petroculture also exceeds the boundaries of the region; indeed, petroculture is a central aspect of the oil-soaked American century, alongside the emergence of other extractive cultures such as fracking nonrenewable hydrocarbons (which the industry calls "natural gas").[16] Overarchingly, extractive energy cultures maintain their dominance throughout the United States and Canada because we continue to inherit the path dependency of legacy infrastructure. Contestations to those relationships (such as the challenge at Standing Rock to the Dakota Access Pipeline) become targets of surveillance and criminalization. Still, despite the fact that petroculture encompasses national and global dimensions of everyday life, the risks of living in extractive centers are not shared equally. Recalling my discussion of sacrifice zones in the introduction and previous chapters, energy cultures become intense sites of environmental privilege and dispossession.[17] Thus, while the West's mineral, coal, and oil extraction may share similarities with regions such as Pennsylvania and West Virginia, my interest remains with how narratives of relational selves intersect with the cultures of *this* region, so central to the production of the particular geographies of violence I have been mapping.

I make sense of regional affects through "intimate atmospheres," what Neel Ahuja refers to as the intimacies and processes of reproduction forged by structures of environmental violence and crisis. For affect studies "atmosphere" evokes multiplicity: all at once a grasp on mood, tempo, and rhythms; the palpable registers of ambient crisis; or something more material and measurable like the combination of gases, particulate matter, and toxins encircling air required to sustain life. Bridging affect, environment, and queer studies, Ahuja's intimate atmospheres reimagines as a political necessity the relations of intimacy and reproduction in an age of planetary disaster long in the making. Queer theory's antisocial and relational work, he argues, are both a symptom and a consequence of absent ecological frameworks. As a whole, tracing intimate atmospheres attunes us to cross-species collaborations in generating intimacies alongside the contradictions "imbricated in racialized forms of carbon privilege that disperse social and biological precarity."[18] In listening to queer regional stories, I sit with stories of navigating violence and risk but also desire and longing.

To seek out these intimate atmospheres, I conducted interviews between 2012 and 2018 in Laramie, Wyoming; and Boulder, Colorado. Though both are connected to the region by highways, Laramie is on I-80 and Boulder is not. I focus on these places as nodes within the region partly because of their national significance to sexuality. Laramie, as readers might remember, became known nationally in 1998, when two white men left Matthew Shepard—a white gay college student—on a fence post to die.[19] And Boulder's queer memory landscape, as I detailed in the introduction to this book, is profoundly structured through the legacy of the sanitarium and the proselytizing of John Harvey Kellogg's lifestyle politics. Together they provide a fascinating tension around contemporary accounts of vitality, exhaustion, burnout, isolation, and transportation affects through race, gender, class, and disability. Moreover, their stories underscore how regional atmospheres are made through the networking of places through highways and other infrastructures of petroculture.

In both of these places, my interlocutors are in a transitional place in their lives, trying to make decisions about where and who they want to be, crafting in turn desires and distance. Working with liminal narratives provides a deeper understanding of the affects structured by the suffocation of the petroculture state. Still, I also recognize the limits of a small group of people, largely white settlers and college-educated students. I also chose these locations because of my own queer intimacies with them. Laramie is a small college town of approximately thirty thousand people. At the time of my initial interviews in Laramie, I met people in one of two ways. First, I leaned heavily on introductions from people in the community whom I'd known since around 2001, when I lived in Laramie as a college student, and it is a place I have visited regularly since. Second, I circulated a call for formal interviews through the email list of Spectrum, a LGBTQ student group on the flagship University of Wyoming campus. Both of these techniques relied on preexisting relationships, though I manage relationships as an "outside-insider." Moreover, my relationship with these individuals deepened over years of traveling long distance to check in if I could (nearly everyone I met was a student, making us both transitory), to catch up, and sometimes to meet new people. Although part of my initial call for participants included an interest in stories about the specificity of the Rocky Mountains in stories of queer selfhood, I also led those calls with an interest in the cultural legacy of Shepard and how the ongoing production of memory surrounding his death shapes the experiences of new generations of queer students. I also can't help but wonder how many people did not want to talk to me—insider as much as I might present—because of this framing.

I also turned to Boulder because of my own queer intimacies and friendships, a much larger location of about 106,000 people, including not only the University of Colorado flagship school but also headquarters for many natural food companies and tech industries. In 2018 I once again cast a net through my existing networks throughout the region and elected to concentrate additional interviews in Boulder, given Kellogg's legacy and the work of an outdoor nonprofit organization named Queer Nature, which was based in Boulder between 2015 and 2020.

Moving betwixt and between queer ecologies and their structuring metanarratives, this chapter assembles a mosaic of narrative interviews, examples of regenerative queer care, and my own critical memoir. Framed as tempos in contemporary petroculture, the first half of this chapter pulls together feelings of structure underwriting regional queer life, attending specifically to transportation stories structured by the perception of risk and surveillance. These stories of feeling suffocated in a conservative petro state underscore the desire to *escape* and where to *nestle,* a double movement that centers transportation affects in regional queer life. Here fluidity always is questioned *and* inevitable. Rather than discuss each place in a singular way, I interweave Boulder and Laramie to foreground thematic intimate atmospheres. In the second half I focus on conversations and the photographic work of Queer Nature to highlight a regional collective rooted in a queer sensibility of regeneration, who identify with contemporary climate and just transition movements.

Because I'm pulling patterns across a set of stories, my weaving of mosaics across these two places should not be interpreted as an attempt to generalize "queer life in the Rockies," given the limits of my interviews. Rather, this chapter forwards overlapping and conflicted *relationships:* queer erotics of place, intimacies, and imagination. In the climate emergency of the contemporary moment, the tension between these sections helps illuminate the kinds of relationships that transform violent inheritance into regenerative potential through intimate atmospheres. Drawing from Eli Clare, a "mosaic" is a method of storytelling that crafts together "swirling, multibranched patterns of histories, ideas, and feelings."[20] There's something about assembling fragments and moods that speaks to the feeling of inhabiting this landscape—where being in motion in different places feels like moving through someone else's story. It all rattles like tires over a cattle guard.

EXTRACTIVE CULTURES

In October 2012, during a week intersecting with the fourteenth anniversary of Shepard's murder, Queer Ally Week campus events, and the fervor of homecoming, I gathered with students from the campus queer advocacy group. Among ourselves I shared an anecdote with them about actions organized by the local chapter of Rising Tide North America, including a protest camp near the Powder River Basin coalfield, which was ultimately canceled out of concerns for safety. Some of their members organized across environmental and queer issues but largely seemed to silo their respective interests. Still, I wondered what these students in particular thought about the connection. Perhaps echoing the safety fears of the Powder River Basin protest camp, one white passing student with familiarity of the state frankly declared, "I would wave a rainbow flag anywhere around Laramie before I would even get close to protesting one of the mining operations."

Here again was that unspoken deep place knowledge: pockets of queer space amid deep, deep red—an insider's map of the region based on how and for whom it generated value. From this map Laramie, even with all of its racism and misogyny, could for white students feel like the "liberal college town." Speaking from their location in southeastern Wyoming, their anecdote juxtaposes a place associated in the state as more relaxed and flexible in contrast to the more "intense" zones associated with energy production. Surveillance seemed to feel a bit looser among white snowbirds, hippies, writers, and artists. But even that represented a limited space within the "hard" spaces, such as cowboy bars downtown. I read this student's declaration as a familiar kind of risk calculus. By contrast, the Powder River Basin in the northeast corner of the state could feel like brutality. Occupying a space of any visible difference rendered them as outsiders, a de facto contrarian to the life and blood of coal country.

But thinking through the realization of extractive cultures in the region necessitates different grammars of violence. Angry settler whiteness, bound to carbon intensiveness, erupts into displays of destruction amid forms of violence or disaster operative beyond perception and attention. Rob Nixon defines "slow violence" as that which "occurs gradually and out of sight, a violence of delayed destruction that is dispersed across time and space, an attritional violence that is not typically viewed as violence at all."[21] The petroculture state enables the ongoing flourishing of an industry so deeply embedded in global systems of violence, and cultural claims to inheritance shore up the political monopolization of what kinds of life fit within the bounds of the possible. For the queers I listened to, their lives are entangled in an avalanche of risk and surveillance, making it nearly impossible to distinguish the boundaries of queer and transphobic violence, whiteness, and the feelings of petroculture. Their transitional narratives of place make it possible to think through the structures animating escape and dwelling, moving beyond the individual storyline into cultural imaginaries, extractive culture, and the transportation infrastructures that make that possible.

The purpose of making explicit this connection is not to dismantle life lines of any given individual narrative. Rather, my hope is that making this connection explicit opens possibilities to understand the *histories* of that situation: expanding a moment's limits by moving elsewhere. Confronting petroculture's intersection with queer life in the extractive rich region of the Rocky Mountain West means engaging with an intense realization: fossil fuel energy infrastructures sustain the very ways of life that also diminish queer survival. From toxic masculinity to extractive capitalism, there is a bitter irony in knowing that what can destroy us fuels these movements to elsewhere; so too we also reproduce relationships of violence as we try to heal from the grief of social isolation, a refrain from Ahuja that "neo-liberal subjects (including queer subjects) are engulfed by processes linking the reproduction of the ordinary and the extermination of various life-forms and forms of life."[22] Simultaneously, critiques of individual consumption pale in comparison to structural responsibilities, particularly for Big Oil. As I turn toward tempos of petroculture, I can't help but wonder what queer ecologies might offer for regenerating our planetary imagination.

ATMOSPHERICS AND DEATH CULTS

"It really chokes you." Robert, a white gay man in his twenties at the time of our interview, recollected the pressure on his lungs from an atmosphere of homophobia and the scrutiny of growing up near the extractive intensive Powder River Basin. His phrase surfaces in memory each time that my body moves closer to the boundaries of Cheyenne, the place that I could call my "hometown," even as that word registers as a complication of families of origin, disassociation, and distinct feelings of grief, as my body's interior landscape collides with a now dysphoria producing environment. It was a new lesson in Doreen Massey's phrase: "You can never go home again."[23] In this case distance could be measured by the fumes radiating from the refinery on the south edge of town, just north of Interstate 80. Having left in 2001, returning only for fieldwork or to take care of my mother and hospice-bound father, I could still feel the refinery hitting me and creeping into my body, holding me in state of biliousness like never before. I thought of Robert, on my way through southwestern Wyoming's fracking country to Yellowstone in 2016. I passed green road signs for nonplaces invented by gas-extraction corporations, once again feeling a death grip in my body. That feeling cut against every punctuated moment of falling in love with the landscape again, letting the mountains hold me, shortened by this headache setting in. Robert, I, and some of my other interlocutors I met in my interview process are what you could call "misattuned" to this political and energy landscape that prizes extraction as "tradition" and "honest work," yoking oil, coal, and gas together as a violently masculine regional identity.[24]

Petro violence is atmospheric and intimate. *Atmosphere* connotes charged places of everyday life and social experience. The process of atmospheric attunement draws attention to "qualities, rhythms, forces and relations" that stretch between matter, sediment, and the elemental bodies of life.[25] Likewise, the above-ground relations of atmosphere also abound, to follow Ahuja, with plumes of toxic gases and noncarbon byproducts that concentrate and dissipate in bodies on the basis of proximity.[26] Defying colonial categories of animacy and divisions of ground, time intensive and violent processes convert what's below into usable energy, evacuating the sensuousness of intimacy as an analytic by negating an ultradeep attunement to the conditions of extractive world making. How then might this slow violence shape social experience: the tempos of petroculture, the violence of coal and the angry settler whiteness that regenerates its force, and the toxic white masculinity that conditions the atmosphere? Every breath catches itself, every dream seems infused by the limits of this imaginary. It is a slow and brutal force until the body feels awash in stank.

These linkages that shape a whole way of life are best understood as "petromasculinity," a term Cara Daggett offers to make sense of a violent marriage between energy systems and gendered dimensions of authoritarianism.[27] I like the term because it helps concretize modern cultures of nationalism, fascist masculinity, and the bad attachment to petroleum projects: all working, like an unconscious death drive to propel bodies and land toward their mutually assured annihilation.[28] But I also pause at this term's underpinnings. Instead of psychic calculation, what if petromasculinity is not anterior to settler colonialism or colonialisms of various kinds but a process and consequence of a particular formations of modernity? When we think in the grammars of energy regimes, we must also confront earlier systems that organize values and the production of energy: historical conditions of nation, territory, and extraction that contour the shape of its possibility.[29]

Petromasculinity (also manifest in how the scattered life of coal and natural gas gathers up force across the North American West), as I define it here, is a recent instantiation of violent white settler masculinities made possible by the histories of making oil God or king. To challenge this total dominance is to be *misattuned*, an objector who draws attention. The project of modern sexuality converges with the project of making the West, optimizing settler whiteness through land and value extraction for the purpose of cultivating a slightly differently energized corporeality. Reframing the death cults of climate crisis through its convergence with anti-Blackness and settler colonialism, Julie Sze draws from the intellectual traditions of James Baldwin and W. E. B. Du Bois to underscore conditions of violence and resistance, inheritance and regeneration. Settler whiteness, expanding on Du Bois, denotes "the ownership of the earth forever and ever." Herein lies a "death cult of whiteness, carbon addiction, and capitalism" produced through settler colonialism, in turn creating eugenic systems and economic abstraction that operate by monopolizing violence.[30] These systems work to sever all interdependencies through the auspices of ruling under the sign of sovereign individualism, driving extraction and abstract to point of extinction.

Such sovereign violence thus moves within, across, and between landscapes and bodies. Reflecting on how deeply gendered social spaces enable and constrain her mobility, Riley, a white lesbian in her thirties, revealed to me that she was a survivor of violence by a cis man. She and I met in downtown Laramie, where she resided after moving from the Bay Area to work at the university. Living with such violence, she uttered, "changes your entire orientation." That experience shaped her desires for political community in San Francisco, and, as she learned to navigate Laramie, that memory bubbles to the surface of her interior landscape, colliding with the suffocating atmosphere in her new town. In response Riley fashioned her own armor by strategically crafting a persona that fosters a feeling of safety as she cruised around town on a bicycle. She drew her hands inward toward her chest, gesturing to *"this,"* her own alchemy of dyke fashion. Riley donned a flannel overshirt, a well-worn band T-shirt underneath. *This* is a distancing mechanism: *Don't come near me.* As an academic, Riley understands how her own sense of embodiment and the experiences of violence shaped her movement throughout different spaces in the community: "A lot of my life is how can I avoid places where I think violence could happen again." Managing the space of her body intimately connected with her capacity to move throughout Laramie's masculine landscape.

Robert came to Laramie from the coal-rich landscapes of Gillette: the benefactor of a scholarship program that allowed for all in-state residents to receive free tuition. Although Robert was in the midst of his graduate program when we met, he remembered his undergraduate years as entangled in a complicated negotiation with his family after coming out in high school. Robert talked about the difficulty of creating space within his social world to identify with his Christian faith and conservative family, places of identification he could not find in dominant representations of metropolitan, bicoastal white gay masculinities. Nor did Robert find affinity with the aesthetics of a West that privileged cowboy and ranching masculinities. Because the descriptor of conservatism seemed at odds with his own desires, I asked him to describe the kind of conservatism of Gillette, Powell, and Cody. Grasping for words about his own religious upbringing with family members active in church leadership, he noted, "very staunch Christian, and that's how I was raised in the Wesleyan Church. And Gillette thrives on coal, we have the coal industry there. And so, you have the coal workers, miners. So, it's very staunch, I suppose."[31]

While Robert could perceive Laramie with Gillette in the rearview mirror, Riley lamented that, even on a socially progressive campus like the University of Wyoming, "outsider" dispositions felt unwelcome. Not long before we met in 2012, the university removed a public art sculpture created by British landscape artist Chris Drury. Public art installations scatter the open spaces of the university, but this one, named *Carbon Sink,* evoked scorn, ambivalence, or just plain confusion. Installed just south of the honors building in a hilly green space with scattered picnic tables and reading nooks below eastern cottonwoods and ponderosas, the installation included beetle-killed pine assembled like a whirlpool around ashed coal (see fig. 15). The sculpture built overwhelming connections between Wyoming's own energy culture and the loss of western forest growth from climate change–induced beetle infestations, a wellspring for public conversation. A controversy about free speech, university art, and carbon culture erupted after Marion Loomis, the president of the Wyoming Mining Association, demanded that university officials justify the presence of "conversation starting" public art that directly challenged one of the dominant funding streams to the university. As the largest sector of Wyoming's boom-and-bust economy, the oil, gas, and mineral industries use their economic influence to shape social policy, including what constitutes "free speech."[32] When the legislature threatened to pull funding, university president Thomas Buchanan requested the installation be quietly removed.

This acquiescence of university leadership to industry interests through the censorship of political speech—especially at a public

FIGURE 15. Chris Drury, *Carbon Sink*, April 2012. Laramie, Wyoming. Photo by author.

institution of higher learning—infuriated Riley. For her the *Carbon Sink* controversy was the perfect example of how the culture of the university drew stark boundaries between acceptable modes of living and those that would be censored or shunned. "That's the thing about this place," Riley lamented, "is you're not necessarily going to see a sign that says 'God Hates Fags' or 'If you're different, leave.' The *current* of...or the *undercurrent* of what is not socially acceptable in this place is *CLEAR* and *quiet*. It is just a *current* that just pervades the classrooms, it pervades the streets, and it is scary." Riley acknowledged the university certainly offered spaces for critical thought, but it remained an atmosphere dominated by the sciences: agriculture, engineering, and geology. The metaphor of undercurrent tethered what she perceived as a culture hostile to the diversity of thought to her experiences inside and outside university spaces.

That misattunement serves as sensing outsiderness, strangeness, and heightened feelings of vulnerability in encounters with strangers where scripts of heteromasculine commands over space and bodies play out. Sam, a white lesbian in her early twenties, felt this way too. As she revealed to me, a recent attack by a group of men followed her every movement in and through public spaces. A few weeks prior to the attack, Sam was in the process of trying to leave a living situation with homophobic roommates and found their hostility escalated after asking her then partner to stay with her. I won't share many details here, but Sam's attack left her shaken because of its explicit homophobia and misogyny. Atmospheres shift from secure to dangerous in a snap. "Here, there's always that really kind of dangerous undertone to everything. You feel relatively safe, and then somebody says something (or in my case you get jumped, so that's fun)," she said sarcastically. You know, there's just this undertone that is here and stays here, you have your bubble of people who are safe, but there's always the undertone." Even if hostile encounters became rare, the mental tax weighs. Sam emphasized, "But you're always thinking about it, because it does happen every once in a while. So that undertone is there because every once in a while, something happens and so you're always thinking about that happening again."

Sam's narrative exemplifies the regenerative capacities of violence. Though her story focuses on Laramie, those relationships operate throughout the region. For instance, while I was in Boulder, I met Jay, a white nonbinary person in their thirties who came of age with a complex relationship to Mormonism across various towns throughout Utah. From the beehive state Jay relocated to Boulder to complete a graduate program though still retaining relationships in Utah. Mormon settlement rituals dominated their memories of the region, and Jay reflected how so much of their education in assigned gender and whiteness operated through the church. Ruminating on their early twenties departure and entry into ex-Mormonism, Jay remembered their fourteen-year-old self participating in the Pioneer Trek. Teenage Jay went on a seven-day journey dressed in uncomfortably gendered pioneer dress in a tumultuous physical terrain soaked by ongoing heavy rains. The journey ritualized and emplaced assigned gender to enact a mythology of Mormon settlement. Adorned with a long-sleeve cotton dress, a bonnet, and a gunny sack of bare necessities, Jay remembered a group of adolescents pulling handcarts up a mountain in Wyoming. Remembering Brigham Young's declaration, "this is the place," the trek ritualized the geography of Mormon settlement, linking physical movement to prayer, song, and a "testimony meeting" to actualize individual faith. Beyond understanding how this rite of passage constituted a sense of assigned gender rooted in time and place, Jay offered a more critical reflection of the ritual's function within a broader ecology of violence. "Basically, we were colonizers. You know, I feel a lot of anger around that [trek] because it's like, cool, so you took a kid, gave them a bonnet, and you told them to walk up a mountain. You didn't tell them all the historical things that these folks did, you know?"

MISFITTING, AN OIL WELL OF LONELINESS

The narrative structure of isolation so often underwrites regional stories: living in the middle of nowhere, desolation. Sometimes the grief of loneliness rattles your insides and stillness feels less like a welcome breath from the daily grind. Fifty-mile-per-hour wind gusts and the deep freeze seep into your bones, erode fantasies of "grit." You just need to get through today, a thousand and counting todays. What solace comes from this? What place for kinship when you always feel longing for elsewhere? Longing conjures cravings for contact. Here it often feels like an inconsolable broken heart, an oil well of loneliness. The hope of escape itself becomes an escape route.

Just recently coming out as a lesbian in her midtwenties, Shana, a white woman, admitted she struggled planning for postgraduation. Wyoming's environment and her proximity to family and friends fostered connections of feeling in place. The thought of leaving felt audacious, challenging her ability to make new friendships elsewhere. But then Wyoming was full of *wanting*. Dipping her toes into the local dating scene, Shana lamented the challenges to "mee[t] people that are like me. There's a really small gay community in Wyoming. It's just hard; you get lonely after a while. So, everybody's advice is just go somewhere else."[33] But where to go? Shana reflected, "I'm not sure what I want or what I'm looking for, just a bigger place." Dreams of elsewhere in the form of density, population. Regional capitals like Omaha and Denver immediately surfaced. Closer but not far away, a wish lingered momentarily to displace felt isolation.

Woodzick, a white nonbinary young adult laughed at the contradictions of distance in dense environments. Chuckling, they said, "I mean, I come from Seattle area, where we joke culturally about the Seattle freeze." Let's get coffee or make brunch plans—it doesn't matter how you plan to connect; you'll never see that person. But, more generally, Woodzick's life in Boulder of all places felt *misfitting*.

Boulder was settled in the nineteenth century and promised health for those seeking arid climates. This memory flourishes within its well-known wellness culture that entices new thrill seekers to its contested spaces. Its juxtapositions feel enormous: nestled against the Flatiron formation, the city feels like a hideaway from the network of interstates and toll roads of the Denver metro area. Boulder is known for its city-wide investments in health and transformation culture, a sometimes-bizarre tapestry of commercial ventures, city regulations around consumption tax, and environmental justice organizations. Composed of block after block of strip malls, Boulder offers eat-in restaurants named Vitality Bowls, Thrive, or Leaf, nestled among hot yoga studios. In 2017 Google moved its $131 million-dollar campus into the periphery of downtown's Pearl Street Mall, much to the trepidation of growth-weary residents. Arapaho-language projects in the city and in nearby Rocky Mountain National Park highlight enduring presence despite ongoing structural dispossession and displacement, narrowly practiced as capital against a landscape of wealth, whiteness, and wellness. All of these contested, through organizations and collectivities, that to occupy the place of a *misfit* in this space calls to mind how bodies collide against narrowly imagined built environments. To become a misfit, as Rosemarie Garland-Thomson teaches us, is to notice "when the environment does not sustain the shape and function of the body that enters it."[34]

Performative healthism is the optimization of ableism and whiteness taken to its extreme. Saturating their movements in Boulder, Jay, Ryan, and Woodzick each feel the inaccessibility. "I'm not sure who isn't a professional cyclist," Ryan smirked. Ryan, a biracial queer woman, and I met in Boulder in 2018. Reflecting on how often she feels surveilled and a misfit, she continued, "It's super healthy, to the point where I would say my partner and I, who are both bigger bodies, just clearly don't belong here and don't get quite the same respect." Fatness is the direct opposite to optimization. Fat bodies are mired in lack: nonproductive failures in optimizing time and capital. Ryan also felt her physical disability misfitting exacerbated in the face of Boulder's culture of hiking, biking, and the pinnacle fourteener climbs. Woodzick differentiated between what they perceived as a health-conscious transformation culture and self-awareness of personal consumption. This was not health as holistic. For Woodzick, Ryan, and Jay, the fetishization of health and wellness intersected with queerness, race, and disability in volatile ways.

For Ryan in particular the whiteness of Boulder felt suffocating. A queer woman of color moving throughout white dominant spaces, Ryan felt distrust grow through experiences of exoticism. Moving from the East Coast to Colorado displaced a seamless feel for the ocular regime of a zoo. She characterized some of these puzzling looks: "Where are you from? What are you?"[35] It was a morbid fascination that rattled Ryan as she moved through her daily routine at bus stops and grocery stores and between buildings on her university campus. Navigating the world through a larger body, those routine movements provoked stares. "It's almost like people haven't seen people of color here."

That isolation may also be remade by nestling in chosen spaces of kinship. Amid the overwhelming whiteness of her community, Ryan found space to breathe with new queer and trans people of color (QT-POC) friends associated with a county leadership program. "All of us applied because we felt isolated," she reflected. "That was the first space where I realized, 'Oh, other people are actually experiencing the same thing.'" Ryan felt a strong sense of strange kinship, bonding through the weirdness of Boulder and their sense of misfitting. In Laramie Sam found community in QAN, the activist group on campus. A space of care after her attack, QAN fed her activist desires. Jay shared the memory of attending a poetry-night gathering with writers in the community who read works in progress. Enthusiastically, they recalled, "It was one of the coolest nights I've spent in almost three years here, *because it just felt fucking queer....* Just that moment where you're like, okay. You can let go of that inhale you've been holding in for so long." In that space they exhaled and felt the weight of the world and its possibilities for abundance: "So that was a moment where it was kind of this communion of the hope and the hurt and the collective memory of what it is to be a queer person, which of course, those aren't our only stories, and there are others to tell."

But not all isolation comes to a soothing end. Loneliness can feel inconsolable, even amid rites of tending to nonhuman forms of life. Processing a lost love from another life, Riley hoped to write a lover's field guide. Wildflowers and sagebrush cut against infinite blue distance. A balloon of longing would fill to its limits and later dissipate. In a voice cut with both defiance and longing, she noted, "The most important lesson I've learned is that the mountains, which I spend a lot of time in, the sky, which I adore, the landscape, does not affectively heal or solve or replace what is missing here, which is community. I do not *have* a community; I have not *found* a community." She feels daily the loss of former community rituals from her earlier life in San Francisco, an absence she framed in terms of affinity crossing feminist communities of color, class, and queerness. "The hikes are really still nice, but this place is, as I was saying earlier, very quiet. But the quiet is so deafening, the loneliness is so absolute, the solitude is, for me at this point not positive.

I haven't figured out how to cure that. I mean, I work a lot. I have an incomplete life here."

The violence of isolation generates longings for touch. I learned from each of them how touch is capacious—physical, emotional, spatial. Confronting the limits of isolation attempts to create more expansive social worlds, opening the queer environmental body into communion with unexpected moments of relief from exhaustion. I'm left wondering, How is that deep gut-aching loneliness shaped by the ongoing circulation of certain sexual imaginaries? The question that lingers at the center of these stories remains: What are the emotional pedagogies of grief, isolation, and longing for nonmetro queer folks? Particularly in the narratives from those in Idaho and Wyoming, driving out into the wilderness to recuperate a feeling of an autonomous self enacts another kind of lifeline: a familiar environmental feeling of motion as a mode of self-authorship and transformation.

AUTOMOBILITY AND RESILIENCE

"I needed to breathe—to let it all out." Robert once again lingers on my mind as I pass the green guide marker for the Vedauwoo Recreation Area. Pulling off I-80 to a rugged gravel road, I move toward 1.4 billion-year-old granite outcrops that loom against the cerulean horizon. Names of nineteenth-century settler generals like William Sherman linger alongside refuse. Prior to its incorporation into the National Forest System, it was known as Pole Mountain or Fort Francis E. Warren Target and Maneuver Reservation. Military detritus abounds and ruins: tactical weaponry, live artillery, sunken bunkers, seismograph boxes. By the mid-1930s this militarized environment became the grounds of contested authority and mixed usages: timber production, military training, grazing, recreation, and watershed for the nearby state capital.[36] At the same time bands of shirtless boys dug trenches, gravel roads, or hiking paths as laborers for the Civilian Conservation Corps, expanding Pole Mountain's usability as a recreation area. Every time I pass by those structures now the image passes of sexually charged innuendo as young men indulged the homosocial worlds of camp, remaking their bodies and the land in the terms of physical culture's demands for heteroproductivity.[37] As of the mid-twentieth century, carefully managed wilderness was made for the heteronuclear family seeking leisure spaces, further concretizing a system of sexual governance linking home and land to systems of automobility. The fantasy of autonomy created by living oil traffics in antagonisms of all sorts, especially emotions of independence. Linked to an extensive network of highways and interstates, with layered functions of land use, white Rocky Mountain queers craft their longings for escape alongside the traces of a militarized environment repurposed into outdoor recreation.

Configuring the Rocky Mountains as a strategic defense location for military outposts and engineer feasibility for the transcontinental passage of the Union Pacific Railroad, the western region is now locked into automotive dependency. Settlements grew alongside mining and rail towns, linked by networks of gravel, pavement, and concrete built through Chinese and Indigenous labor that fortified the pulse of Anglo-American modernity.[38] Chains of labor disappear amid the mythos of individual willfulness now embodied so fully in the fantasy of autonomy afforded by automobility. Bad day? Drive somewhere and scream to Bikini Kill spilling from the open windows. Want to get lost in the landscape and dream with clouds moving? Drive and let yourself go into this world in motion. Movement shifts mood. All of these are exemplars of automobility's connection to self-authorship and what Szeman calls the "fiction of surplus."[39] Thinking through regional queer culture's tether to mobility is full of antagonisms. As relayed to me, mobility is a response to chronic or acute experiences of social violence, where people try to make sense of their lives by forging queerly intimate relations in movement. Automobility in particular—the promise of white selfhood connected to unfettered movement—concretizes all the violent inheritances that made these land lines possible.

The nexus of automobility and the desire for distance create a number of antagonisms. I find this question endlessly fascinating because at least in this context I'm trying to understand how these regional *and* national bad attachments become a resource of LGBTQ identity formation in the region. It is meaningful to interrogate the powerful association to recreation and outdoors as a site of healing as inextricably bound to modern infrastructure, a kind of carbon intensive self-care. Beyond the struggle to align his sexual identity with his understanding of faith, Robert named Wyoming landscapes as part of his sense of self: "Wyoming landscapes have really become a part of who I am. In a variety of ways. Like, I don't do cowboy boots or cowboy hats. My home is not western. I live in a Victorian house. But the wide-open spaces is something that I love. The mountains. Just everything that is all around you. I can drive for thirty minutes and be totally away from town." That distance allowed Robert to feel like he could create "breaks" between managing fragmentation and a sense of self more holistically aligned with his various identities.

Maintaining the division between "out" and "not out" felt emotionally exhausting. "I need breaks," Robert told me. Bracketing intensive identity work looks like these momentary sojourns outside of town on back-country roads. Despite images of urban and coastal gayness that felt dislocated from his experiences, I asked Robert what it meant to connect with his surroundings.

Cram: Can you talk about what it means to level with someone from Wyoming? To tap into what it's like to live here?

Robert: You form a network where there is none. And you all go into it knowing each other's story because it's also yours. And that's a huge thing. If you're from Wyoming, you have an experience of the conservatism, but also the sense that place can bring you. I always knew when I was in the mountains by myself, I felt a lot more free than when I was in town. Or like Gillette. Or, I mean, my favorite thing when I'll drive between Gillette and Laramie is stopping in just a blink [inaudible] and just hanging out for a little bit. You know, 'cuz there's nobody there, it's just you. To your own thoughts and your own identity. You don't have to pretend to be anybody.

Cram: So, can you describe that feeling of freedom?

Robert: It's a break. It is a much-needed reprieve. You know, there are still things that I hide. Because I know that they don't want to hear about it. But I also got to the point where I was like, you know, get over it. And so, I need breaks. After a visit with my mom, I drove towards Centennial, stopped the car, ran, and just yelled. And I was just like, yeah, get it out. It's a break. It is...it restores sanity.

In stark contrast to modernity's energetic complex of expansive vitality, Robert narrates affective limits—feeling fed up from ongoing identity work, at the point of breaking from the suffocation of heteronormative worlds. But I'm also struck by the scale of connections. Driving into the wilderness becomes an act of *revitalization,* the ebb and flow between exhaustion and energy. Robert in turn feels autonomous, even *free.* He is not alone here, in that this environmental emotion connected to automobility is deeply characteristic of twentieth-century U.S. culture. But the antagonism here is that revitalization is not wholly autonomous—to the contrary—his movement is afforded by petrointensive energy regimes of violence that extend to the older energy systems I examined in chapter 1.

Sam remembered driving to Vedauwoo to process a fairly recent violent attack by a group of men. Coping strategies of writing through the trauma found their limit, and so she too needed to get away.

Sam: The other day I was having a rough time, and I was just like, I can't do this, I need to get out of this town; this town is *annoying.* And so, it was like eight o'clock at night, and I just left town, and I drove north and then I hit Vedauwoo, and I woke up before the sun rose and watched it rise, and then I hiked all around the Box Canyon and all that area until like one in the afternoon. It was amazing, it was just me and it was great.

Cram: Do you feel like it just gave you space?

Sam: Yeah, and I'd been having a hard time with being by myself, so that was kind of a…you're gonna be by yourself, and you're gonna have fun, and you're gonna be fine. So…and so I did."

Managing the violence of isolation meant Sam felt a deep ambivalence about her place in Laramie and life more broadly. She made sense of that trip to Vedauwoo through feelings of resolve and resilience: "You're gonna be by yourself, and you're gonna have fun, and you're gonna be fine."

Beyond individual automobility Vedauwoo seasonally transforms into a place for Wyoming pride events sponsored by state organizations. Will, a white gay man and graduate student I met in Laramie long before that first meeting referenced earlier in the chapter, emphasized the appeal of Rendezvous, the region's largest gay camping gathering. "Camping in the mountains, going to the lake, that's what Wyoming people do in their spare time. There's nothing *else* to do. And we all have, you know, we all have close associations with the mountains…. Everybody wants to go way the hell out in the middle of the wilderness and drink beer and goof around and camp." Despite his insistence that "everyone" wants to participate in a ritual of Wyoming identity, he acknowledged that in actuality the event wasn't accessible for all, only white cis gay men. He contrasted the high pressure and immense energy of comparative events like Denver Pride. Rendezvous felt like an escape that "feels very much like home." Will continued, "Walking around in the woods is something I've been doing my entire life. It's a very comfortable feeling, and soothing feeling instead of the more high-pressured feeling in Denver." And, further, Will found pleasure moving in a vehicle: "One of my favorite things to do is drive, especially in the summer or the early spring when there's lots of storms. Between here and Casper, past the windmills and when there's cloudy skies. I love to drive when there's nobody else on the road."

The purpose of thinking with these narratives is not to diagnose certain acts as "more" or "less" queer. Petromodernity is far too pervasive for that, and it is a fetish object for queer and heteronormative cultures alike. Rather, my commitments are to trace the broader ecology of queer life, identifying *how* infrastructure plays a central role in identity creation and regional culture and how intimate atmospheres are made through trying to make sense of the violence saturating one's life. These narratives highlight mobility born by desires to embody resilience through escape, resolve, and connection. They are in turn indexes of queer space making, if queer space means something like inhabiting spatialities resistant to dominant modes of reproduction: "location, movement, and identification."[40] Driving to places like Vedauwoo as a practice of self-care because it *feels* embodies the powerful incorporation of infrastructure as a mobile, disciplinary embodiment. These regional movements parallel the metronormative story, but at a different scale. Be it migration to the metropolis to find oneself or momentary escapes to the wilderness, both are queer mobilities afforded by the same underlying system. In this vein queer automobility offers an epitome of resilience narratives—a concept itself wearing thin against the decimation of planetary inhabitance.

If anything, taking stock of the invisible forms of violence and chains of labor and production that inhabit Sam's, Robert's, and Will's narratives of autonomy means confronting the limits of resilience. In their usage each desire is a mode of living queerly within the constraints of the environment they inhabit. Resilience is a limited space to dream as much as it offers a powerful mode of adapting to existing systems. Resilience portends an extractivist mentality of infinite bending until breakage. To consign queer life to resilience leaves us at a potent contradiction: landscapes provide a place of momentary healing and cultivation of desire, even as the practice of those intimacies in a petroleum-based automobility are generated through cycles of violence that make life precarious. These practices can be life lines for LGBTQ individuals, but we can also imagine other possibilities. Next I turn to my conversations with Queer Nature, a queer- and trans-led nonprofit nature-connection organization rooted in explicitly regenerative practices. The narratives here highlight a complex range of affects associated with the slow violence of extractive cultures. Regeneration, I hold, offers an antithesis to petroviolence by, first, holding accountable the petro settler state and, second, embodying a practice of queerly erotic place making. Petroculture and regeneration are two modes of organizing queer lives—the former rooted in the violence of extraction and the latter a future-oriented mode of erotic possibility.

REGENERATIVE INTIMACIES AND DECOLONIZING NATURE CONNECTION

Previously based in Boulder, Colorado, since 2015, Queer Nature was founded by Pinar and So Sinopoulos-Lloyd. Pinar is a neurodivergent enby with Wanka Quechua, Turkish, and Chinese lineages. So is a white queer Greek American who grew up connected to the northern hardwood forests of Alnobak territory (central Vermont). In their public interviews Pinar and So story the lineage of Queer Nature as a love story; for example, in an interview with *Outfront Magazine,* they note their collaboration emerged after connecting at a wilderness-based school in the Pacific Northwest.[41] Their collaboration, Pinar said, mirrors the connectivity of the more-than-human world, aligning affinity with the generative capacities of living and connected systems. Through their mission to teach others place-based skills as creative inhabitance with interspecies relations, Pinar and So materialize a desire to cultivate spaces of care and healing through ecological and situational awareness. For them teaching skills such as wildlife tracking, scout craft, or survival strategies offer a critical response to social and environmental violence, particularly for those deemed "unnatural" and "unfit." Both Pinar and So blend their own academic training into accessible ecophilosophies; Queer Nature in turn could be imagined as critically queer ecological praxis.

Queer Nature's project follows a much longer history of land-based intentional communities intersecting with LGBTQ rights, feminist, and environmental movements in the United States. In the 1970s and 1980s a rural-based "lesbian land" movement built on the energies of 1970s feminist organizing. Largely populated by women living in cities, some "back to the land" lesbians created necessary kinships with local rural women who often traded survival skills.[42] Around the same period gay men founded the Radical Faeries, a loose collective of spiritualist energy emerging from the Gay Liberation Movement. They purchased rural lands in search of "sanctuary," building on the existing "landed infrastructure" of sexual and political dissident safekeeping in the early 1970s.[43] Finally, the still operating intentional community Idyll Dandy Arts would be founded in 1993, not far from the Faerie sanctuary of Short Mountain in rural Tennessee. Although they do host long-term residents on the land, Idyll Dandy Arts is most well known for its music festivals and work parties, which draw both queer and trans people to its landscape. Residents of these spaces have produced various writings in the form of 'zines, newsletters, letters, or community magazine entries that surpass scholarly attention. However, the scholarship that does exist characterizes these as complex spaces that materialize desires for refuge and sanctuary in a heteronormative and misogynist world *and* how their largely white and cis gatekeeping also reproduced settler colonialisms and transmisogyny.[44] I don't have the ethnographic perspective to ramble through these relationships as navigated on the ground, but the history of intense exclusions they produce are but one of the kinds of inheritance some organizations explicitly choose to (or not) engage as they build and reflect on their relationships with residents, visitors, and the land itself.

In their mission Queer Nature overlaps and departs from these models. At the time of our conversation, Queer Nature did not have access to purchase land, given the relative wealth inaccessibility of land in Colorado, meaning that all of their skill shares did not parallel the enclosed sense of "sanctuary." Moreover, given this book's engagement with the natural and social ecologies of the Rocky Mountains, Queer Nature also grounds their engagement with place making in a practice of "tracking," an overarching philosophy, naturalist skill, and survival tactic they mobilize as a queer decolonial heuristic. Tracking offers another method to trace sedimentations of violence and stewardship on the land.

Grounded in their respective ancestral knowledges, Queer Nature embodies a practice of what I call "regenerative intimacies," or practices of tending to nature connection as responsive to the violence of settler colonialism. Nature connection is not neutral. Indeed, access to woods, waters, and forests is an issue of racial, sexual, migrant, and disability justice, given the historical constitution of nature connection through environmental eugenics. The pernicious challenge of violent inheritance is how to move against and beyond extractive worldviews that associate space with dominance. In what follows I draw from our conversations and their curated social media presence to interpret how they use story-telling, aesthetics, and ecological thought to image speculative environmental futures. By centering imagination, intimacy, and queer ancestral futures, Queer Nature unsettles a violent present, confronting both extractive culture and white heteronormative environmentalism. As bodies bend into kin lines of land and interspecies relations, tracking brings transformation and eros as forms of relation to the more-than-human world.

I met with Pinar and So on an unusually warm fall day in September 2018, in the midst of their preparations for a hide-tanning workshop. As Pinar left to finish errands, most of my conversation foregrounded So's perspective of their offerings and collaboration. Deep in the heart of the buzz of Pearl Street Mall, we lamented about Boulder's transformation culture. Remembering Ryan's, Jay's, and Woodzick's frustrations with fatphobia, the dominant meaning of transformation in Boulder means something akin to self-optimization through control of outdoor terrains. Fragments of this sentiment circulate in the vocabulary of outdoor culture: "conquering a mountain" or "dominating fourteeners."

For Pinar and So transformation is a concept often saturated with registers of health as capital, but they work to broaden its meaning through their own ecophilosophy. In the region Boulder is a unique place to rupture these associations. Imagine a place in which the standardization of design reflects the able and fit body, adorned with status symbols of Patagonia and Lululemon yoga pants, which pass as casual or relaxed in day to day life. To be in these spaces means to hold the inquiry of what relations have come before as an ethic of "cultural humility."[45] For example, Pinar emphasized the importance of storying the land lines of a home and crossroads known to the Ute, Apache, Comanche, Cheyenne, and Arapaho, land remapped by the 1851 Fort Laramie Treaty and later the Treaty of Fort Wise. In their offerings Queer Nature explicitly centers the land's toxic legacies—from the Sand Creek Massacre to Valmont Butte—that conjure grief to the foreground. "You can't have transformation when you bypass grief," Pinar emphasized. Here they allude to the diversion of grief that happens when settler cultures fail to acknowledge and center whole histories of land and place.

In turn Queer Nature's understanding of transformation exemplifies regenerative intimacies. Their vision holds grief as a relational form, tethering disposability of human bodies deemed unnatural to the reproduction of settler structures of ownership that shape land knowledges. In other words, they recognize we are the inheritors of a system that transforms living beings into extracted commodities. In contrast, Queer Nature offers a crucial space for LGBTQ persons seeking what it might feel like to imagine radical belonging as rooted in place.

In the absence of the ability to participate in one of Queer Nature's offerings, I want to thread pieces of our conversation in Boulder with their social media, where they curate an organizational identity, document their workshops in action, and circulate snapshots with narratives that articulate their collaborative ecophilosophies. As of mid-2021, Queer Nature has over 43,700 Instagram followers, spanning individuals; organizations with a diversity, equity, and inclusion focus toward outdoor culture; and cultural producers and advocates. As practitioners of regenerative ethics crystalized through the method of tracking, Queer Nature offers a set of practices, relationships, and concepts that model one way to redefine queer and QTPOC relationships to the environment; acknowledging intention and accountability for white queers on one hand and making space for QTPOC healing and coliberation on the other.

Queer Nature centers a praxis in which trauma and grief tether individual bodies to land, articulating an expansive notion of selfhood as enmeshed in one's environment. On February 22, 2018, Pinar posted a snapshot with their back facing the camera, inviting the spectator to inhabit a contemplative relationship with the surrounding landscape located on Yavapai, Hopi, and Western Apache territories (see fig. 16). Pinar's caption reads, "What kind of harm does living in a humancentric society do to our souls and psyches? How do we integrate our ecological community members into a conversation of co-liberation? This is integral to the movement of diversifying the outdoors." Written less as an indexical caption that might place the subject of the photograph in a historical time and place, it reads more as an invitation for reflection on accountability. Addressed to others in a largely outdoors community, Pinar notes how the cosmology of queerness, for them, is an extension of traditional ecological knowledge. They underscore that the maps that underwrite so-called public lands, such as parks, create a cultural track of settler colonialism that non-Natives must acknowledge. Pinar ends the post with the questions: "What place(s) are you accountable to? Who are your ecological community members? How do you uplift them in the Anthropocene?"

These questions inevitably surface in their offerings, in which Pinar and So emphasize the interconnections between slow and acute violence or entanglements of extractive mentalities and the disposability of queer and trans bodies. In turn Queer Nature is a trauma-informed practice

FIGURE 16. *Harm in the Anthropocene*, February 22, 2018. Photo by Queer Nature.

that confronts feelings of social isolation. So explained, "We aren't therapists necessarily, but we acknowledge that folks are coming to this space and that things could potentially be triggering around some stuff we're doing, and we're acknowledging that a lot of folks in the queer community experience higher levels of isolation and suicidality and depression or assault—and part of what we want to do is just name that and normalize all the different emotions that might come up while we're in the space that could be related to trauma, including political terror." Reflecting on the loss of a startling number of their friends who had died by suicide in the midst of the Trump administration, So insisted that nature connection is lifesaving, in multiple ways. "We feel the work of nature connection and inviting your folks to enter this process of belonging—it's lifesaving, it will save people's lives in some way even if it's just one person. And when I think about depression and suicidality and despair, I think about .... isolation from non-human people, and land."[46]

At the foundation of their ecology is the idea of situational awareness and tracking to cultivate deeper attachments, practices of a regenerative intimacy. On September 18, 2018, Queer Nature posted a side portrait of So delicately holding the golden edges of mid-autumn quaking aspen leaves (see fig. 17). With the narrow frame of the shot, So's gesture

FIGURE 17. *So with Aspen,* September 18, 2018. Photo by Queer Nature.

is akin to an embrace, enmeshed within the branches as their glance downward into their touch magnifies the accompanying narrative. So writes, "The medicine of listening spans across species. Observing ecological relationships and learning patterns in the natural world isn't just about furthering your own knowledge, it's also about witnessing for the sake of witnessing, because the wild ones are hurting, too. The land and the wild ones also witness us." So defines listening as "hearing with thoughtful attention." That form of attention, or situational awareness that emerges through the practice of tracking, offers a vital survival strategy. So outlines the contours of what witnessing through thoughtful attention might embody in practice: "Listening across species and across worlds is a visionary act and an act of deep faith. It requires the whole body. It is an act of surrender in its humility and its unknowing, and it is an act of love in its unbidden granting of trust and solidarity." In other words, listening beyond control or purely for data acquisition can function as a relational practice: holding the unknown can become one way to regenerate intimacy.

Observing connections that defy categorization centers translation as an inventional practice to generate new vocabularies or grammars that shape ecological relationality. In our conversation So connected this sensibility to a "queer decolonial lens." Speaking from their own experience as a non-Native and white settler, they said, "When I started to learn so-called survival skills and natural history, there was a point at which I realized that all these skills that focus on awareness and tracking of relationships and patterns and the articulation of more and more details, creating new language for new types of information that are there, that are existing in ecology, that all of that pointed to having to also include the human history of the land and the human ecology of the land, and that is actually part of natural history. It's not separate. It's a part of tracking as a way of knowing." For So tracking grounds them, cognitively and emotionally, as they learn about the impact that both settlers and Indigenous peoples have had on the land. They emphasized this confluence between social and environmental history often becomes invisible for white settlers. But definitions of "alteration" or "stewarding" practiced by First Nations in different bioregions also become invisible.[47] Learning how to perceive these differential relations to land becomes an essential practice for understanding one's place in space and time, learning to regenerate a more just relationship to the past, present, and future.

Tracking also generates the capacity to trace land lines through emergence, hybridity, and chimeric entanglements with what has come before. In a January 21, 2019, post, So captured a portrait of lichen growing on/into/out of moss, describing the image as "We hybrid/intersectional/intertextual/interspecies beings and communities grow out of the fuzzy foundation of all those who have come before us" (see fig. 18). The narrative accompanying the post turns toward a meditation on how tracking is fundamental to belonging: tracking encourages attention beyond the categorical, somatic, and sensory ways of knowing. But in a world in which work like Queer Natures' may often slide into the language of diversity, equity, and inclusion initiatives, So provides a caveat:

> In our contexts this does not mean belonging to just one place—it means knowing how to belong wherever you go. When you have spent time with the trees, and the songbirds, they can help ground and protect you. Belonging

FIGURE 18. *Lichen Growing On/Into/Out of Moss,* January 21, 2019. Photo by Queer Nature.

through inter-species relationship and accountability creates resilience. Belonging isn't a metaphor. Belonging isn't about staking a claim to place either—it is about respecting a place, entering with a question, and listening. Belonging can, actually, be unsettling. Skills of belonging can help you realize when you actually aren't welcome on land, or in a certain role, or occupying a particular space.

While queer folks may be poised to use their emotional survival skills as a way to be in tune with forms of grief in the natural world, So wondered aloud what possibilities arise through "creat[ing] and open[ing] a space for an erotic connection to the Earth, erotic in the sense of more than human Eros."

Audre Lorde describes "the erotic" as a form of energy for change, an energy and power otherwise misrecognized, abused, or devalued by cisheteronormative white supremacist cultures. Contrasting the merely sexual, Lorde's erotic "is the measure between the beginning of our sense of self and the chaos of our strongest feelings…a reminder of our capacity for feeling."[48] Lorde's erotic is, closely read, a concept that

FIGURE 19. *I Eat Place*, September 13, 2018. Photo by Queer Nature.

emerges from Black feminist theory and, for her, the lived experience of Black ciswomen. In his recounting for the context of transmasculinities, Daniel Coleman Chávez routes the erotic as trans possibility, grounded in "the full power of our beings and the pleasures of our existence" while simultaneously "decolonizing the violating ways we improperly understand the real difference of the other."[49] I read Chávez here through a resistance to the categorization of "crimes against nature" that resurfaces more recently through trans exclusive radical feminist discourse, that seeks to possess, not unlike property, "gender" as nature. This transing of the erotic is where I want to close, with another image of berries, a hand, an embrace, an act of trans care (to riff from Hil Malatino), a becoming otherwise, a dream, a wish.[50]

In a September 13, 2018, post, Pinar articulated this sensibility of attachment and eroticism as a practice of consuming flesh, of mutual enfolding (see fig. 19). Their hand extended with a collection of blueberries, Pinar writes, "when I step into place—I am the / Consumed / to remind myself, I delicately forage / berries / and I consume them / I eat place / a core erotic practice."

LET THIS PLACE HOLD YOU

As So and I said our thanks to each other for presence, for witness, I shared with them my own reflections about this land. As someone raised by the Rocky Mountains, a spine-like sprawl that anchored my body in its teenage years, that landscape now felt alive in the most unsettling of ways: lost loves who in passing glances struggle to place the present of each other.[51] But everything from the wind to the hum of interstates or gravel roads or the horizon point where the mouth of the sky opens to other worlds...reaches inward and shakes every layer of once dormant grief.

Perhaps I learned to smell the blood in the soil as my world of western memory cracked open as if the Yellowstone Caldera erupted, imperceptible to public view beneath its sapphire waters. That regional memory tour only a few years into a decade of my father and us living with his Alzheimer's, my father's memory would fade: of his family's farm life near Neebo Junction to Sand Draw, to Riverton as the new oil fields in Wyoming began to occupy a mythic status in everyday life. Despite warning, he chose the oil fields instead of farming, and so my life lines were written with his. As his memory languished, so did the chosen name of his wayward child. Feeling an urgency for witness, I looked at So and recounted a hike in Chautauqua mere weeks before the end of his life. Moving each foot upward the Flatiron, I could feel my lungs expand to the borders of my body, into the layers and layers of grief. Expansion itself felt healing, breathing my body and self back into being. When we return to landscapes throughout our lives, we may not be able to go home again, but something moves, touches, electrifies, and unsettles. In response So's last words were a lasting gift: "Let this place hold you."

Infrastructures of Feeling and Queer Collaborative Stewardship

So's directive to let this place hold me opened a litany of questions. "Hold" implies an action that cuts so intimately between care and violent possession, and that tension in meaning gestures toward different modes of world making. Of course, in So's refrain the relationality shifts so that, in contrast to settler possession, my own healing necessitated vulnerability. Holding becomes conditional on an action of inviting movement or passage.[1] Thus this invitation became more of a meditation to consider what might *move* in the gesture of *being held*. There is, as Kim TallBear (Sisseton Wahpeton Oyate) argues, a structural link between settler spatialities of possession and intimate relationality.[2] The only livable future imaginable is a decolonized one—centered by the relations of "land back," or the return of lands to Indigenous systems of stewardship, sovereignty, and decision making.[3] Possession is a whole way of life, seeding toxicity into every relation. Part of making sexual modernity, as I have argued throughout, is a core belief in energy as a relationship to actualization, necessitating environmental orders that materialized those values and relationships. Moreover, this book has modeled how tracing land lines, in the North American West or elsewhere, maps the intersection of sexuality's convergence with practices of energy extraction.

Mapping relationships of energy—particularly through vitality and exhaustion—matter more than any particular energy form, because the challenge before us is actually contesting systems of environmental privilege and injustice that have long structured the making of the modern world.[4] In pointing toward the possibilities of regeneration, we must reconsider a deeper web of relations to map eroticism and the queer environmental body. TallBear poses this challenge as part of decolonial praxis: "In small moments of possibility, can we resist naming 'sex' between persons and 'sexuality' as nameable objects? Can such disaggregation help us decolonize the ways in which we engage other bodies intimately—whether those are human bodies, bodies of water or land, the bodies of other living beings, and the vitality of our ancestors and other beings no longer or not yet embodied? By focusing on actual states of relation—on being in good relation-with, making kin—and with less monitoring and regulation of categories, might that spur more just interactions?"[5]

In turning to the past, meditating on "let this place hold me" meant lingering on what conditions might afford that possibility for all relations. This isn't an uncomplicated gesture. For instance, Scott Lauria Morgensen details in depth the ways queer land projects in North America such as the Radical Faeries have both appropriated indigeneity and negotiated their racialized non-Native inheritance with Two Spirit members.[6] The lesson here is that any gesture toward collaborative stewardship, of imagining a different world, cannot be prescriptive; it is a task that must be routed through ongoing, situated process. Collaborative stewardship, as I imagine it, is fundamentally a practice of kin making and relational justice. Asking these questions is a beginning but cannot replace the more complicated task of confronting ecological imaginations that leave the structure of settler colonialism unquestioned and seamless, even in queer ecological imaginations.

The project of imagination is central to remaking relationalities of regenerative potential.[7] For too long voices like Edward Abbey, John Muir, and Aldo Leopold have dominated our ecological imagination and leave a violent white supremacist legacy for environmentalists. As representatives of their broader social context, their relationalities come with deep consequence: land grounded in xenophobia, ethnonationalism, misogyny, and eugenic whiteness through a hold on "wilderness."[8] Justice work has required an ongoing confrontation to the divisiveness of whiteness, as the first Black president of the Sierra Club, Aaron Mair, has argued relative to his organization's own work of transformation and accountability.[9] What kind of ecological imaginations will provide a space to dream for a future amid rising fascism and white supremacy and their intersections with gender and sexual politics? With the intensification of planetary violence and fascism, various kinds of trans-antagonism (an array of both conservative and liberal hostilities toward trans people) are on the rise among the mainstream, particularly in the United States and United Kingdom. While their expressions vary, an ecological politics grounded in a belief of gender as "natural" holds them together, particularly an imagination of a "pure" white suprem-acist femininity. Sadly, for both academic and mainstream audiences, the necropolitics of transantagonism rarely maps onto what could be a more expansive vision of environmental issues that interrogates the whiteness of gendered "nature."

In this book I have tried to hold a tension between regenerative vio-lence and a more affirmative regeneration grounded in queer and decolo-nial thought. This agonism could map otherwise on the tension between environmental communication as a discipline of both crisis and care.[10] Amid the crisis of the present, queer and trans ecological imaginations such as Queer Nature provide some respite.[11] Queer Nature responds to the presence of the past in all relations, simultaneously dwelling in a decolonial ancestral imagination that abides in the political poten-tial of eroticism. Eroticism can articulate an environmental politics of care. Practices of care, argues Phaedra C. Pezzullo, work to "not only prevent harm" but to honor "human and nonhuman interconnections, interdependence, biodiversity, and system limits."[12] I've shown how the violence of sexual modernity leaves residual traces within the bioregion of the North American West, enumerating the vexed processes of engag-ing with those land lines. Other modalities of care might be models of stewardship by Queer Nature, imagined as an erotic practice, unteth-ered from desires of possessive attachment.

Just as violent inheritance embodies recursive relations, binding in-frastructural and ecological violence, they are met with varying prac-tices of resistance. On April 15, 2019, climate organizers in Laramie, Wyoming, gathered at the commons area known as Prexy's Pasture at the University of Wyoming. Approximately fifty people (significant for a climate event in Wyoming) participated in Carbon Sink Lives!, a rec-reation of Chris Drury's incendiary installation. Climate witnesses from the front lines testified to the audience, such as a survivor of the fires in Paradise, California, that left the earth ablaze. A Native American student read a letter from the president of Oglala Sioux Nation doc-umenting displacement and crop loss from devastating floods across the Midwest in 2019.[13] In the heart of oil and gas country, fire, water, and carbon were conjured as elements of despair, death agents of the

Capitalocene. After these testimonials participants lay their bodies on a black plastic sheet divided by white spiraled lines. In this re-creation, community members reconstituted beetle-killed pine logs, materializing a vortex in human form. As a reimagined and embodied protest, the parallel emphasized humans as part of the natural world and forecasted human extinction.

Throughout the book I've argued for queer studies, energy, and environmental humanities scholars to revisit "sexual modernity" as entangled in an extractive energy regime that demands vital energy and exhausts racialized populations. Our world is one already witness to many apocalypses. Writing in the midst of climate catastrophe as this book goes to press in 2021, ending with the resurgence of *Carbon Sink* feels especially apt, because the original piece illuminated "what goes around comes around." My approach throughout relies on how contesting inheritance often comes directly into friction with different domains of sexual modernity—from vitality, intimacies, childhood, labor, and land. The focus on inheritance follows the ecological ruins of this energy regime and what forms of responsibility emerge in the present. For settlers structures of dominance insist on *naturalizing* these relationships, creating seamlessness where there is friction. My task has been driven by a desire to untether connections that have been forced into being through violence. What can be done with those traces is a political question as much as an emotional and imaginative one.

Hence, the big question that opened this book: What does it mean to route sexuality through the social ecologies of modernity's relationship to energy?[14] Asking how sexual modernity reproduces over time is but one critical opening to the energy systems that emerge through social formations. In turn the necessary interdisciplinary inquiry of this book amplifies ongoing questions in the environmental humanities and cultural studies about the crisis of disciplinarity. Although cultural studies has long embraced what might be a strange orientation to "discipline" (strangeness does not have to be a negatively charged word), the future of the humanities now rests on forging a deeper intimacy between two stories: the "natural" and the "human."[15] As these two frames of knowing press together in ways that make or break disciplinary boundaries, the queer occupies a restless flâneurery, zipping through cruising grounds because it never properly belonged to either from the start. To close this book, I want tread through with speculative thinking that crystallizes the main lines of the book, providing frames to reorient care, imagination, and queer environmental futures.

INFRASTRUCTURES OF FEELING

Let's return briefly to why Riley was so incensed by the removal of Drury's original installation of *Carbon Sink*. The placement of beetle-killed pine with ash on a university campus made visible relationships that may otherwise seep into the background of its audiences' everyday perception. *Carbon Sink* collapsed vast distance and temporal registers to move audiences to an understanding of emergency, a feeling that may linger in the atmosphere yet never reach a point of discrete articulation. For Riley *Carbon Sink* embodied dissent, and its removal constituted a form of violence. This violence carried an atmospheric and ambient quality as much as a register of specificity. For Riley the removal of *Carbon Sink* and her attendant rage spoke to a feeling of structure that values conformity. Interpreting her anger as such, we might understand these expressions in a negative valence relative to a popular argument that infrastructures serve as metrics of life making.[16] Amid so much infrastructural violence in this book and in the contemporary world, this foundational assumption of infrastructure begs critical revision. Infrastructure modulates life and death and conjures unbelonging—a necropolitical vision of the world that has always been a part of its making. Taken to the extreme, Riley's anger might otherwise be interpreted as such: How does resistance to residual infrastructural violence necessitate remaking the extractive vision of the modern world?

When Raymond Williams initially theorized "structures of feeling," he sought to understand the difference of emergent generations in the complexity of cultural process. Structures of feeling gather "the always moving substance of the past" with uneven "lived relationships." From his own situated and limited geography, he believed residual and emergent forms always existed in tension to one another. The residual differed from the "archaic" and ebbed and flowed in relation to the present, at times creating possibilities for its "revival."[17] Williams's tendency to favor the emergent as more politically progressive illuminates the cultural, intellectual, and political context in which he was writing, as was clear in the more well-known critics of his concept. For my purposes Williams was predominantly interested in a question of culture as "incorporation"—how do lived meanings, practices, and values attached to a multiplicity of generations with their own structures of feeling become *incorporated* into the broader cultural process?

This problem of incorporation is partly infrastructural. Williams didn't use the language of infrastructure to conceptualize structures of feeling, but he did consider the broader "ambience" of situated feeling.[18] Structures of feeling, in turn, implicitly offer a geographic account of affect, rooted within specific knowable communities.[19] As his debates with Stuart Hall and E. P. Thompson make clear, this approach has profound limits. I approach those limits as a way of acknowledging the constant multiplicity of structures of feeling at any given time, often to excess and in conflict. Culture, is, as he knew, a struggle over tradition and dominance. The aesthetic life of infrastructure necessitates thinking more critically about the conservative impulses of residual culture, especially outside the selective tradition. This book highlights the affective and political possibilities of *sedimentation,* fragments hardened through time and gravity but malleable and erosive. *Infrastructures of feeling* locate an ongoing struggle of the residual, particularly along the lines of marginalized environmental memories occluded from "tradition" from the start.

The residual matters, especially in settler colonial structures, where some residual surfaces amid ongoing extractive projects. Consider, for example, the way affected persons depend so much on narrating the transformation of the land to contest claims that naturalize white settlements. As a term, *infrastructures of feeling* offers a more precise account of environmental affect, turning toward standards, values, technologies, and historical contexts that shape the conditions for feeling. These inevitably lead us to accounts of infrastructural struggle, be it about land, technologies that facilitate movement, or extract energy. Now more than ever we need accounts of struggles over infrastructural violence to denaturalize the mainstreaming of white supremacist "blood and soil" rhetorics witnessed again in the twenty-first century. Infrastructures of feeling return to the ecological body as an archive: its openness that collects sedimentation of historical traces, an ecosomatics that tethers modernity to flesh. How, then, do we work to untether?

IMAGINING QUEER COLLABORATIVE STEWARDSHIP

One of the orientations of this book is to work consciously against the ease of academic extraction, magnified in historical experiences that are not my own. This requires grounding inquiry in a place of accountability and care. As a white settler, I benefit from the modern project of making land an infrastructure for the maximization of productivity and wealth accumulation, something clear to me from having come of age in the western region. But I do not inherit the specific trauma of histories such as residential schools or Japanese American incarceration. Academic extraction stories scatter the landscape of higher education. So one way of thinking about accountability is to ask, "Why am I drawn toward these histories, stories, and ways of thinking about ecological relationality?" A necessity of field-based research means always negotiating assumptions of power, especially the possibility of doing harm to others. D. Soyini Madison has described the open process of interview-based research as an "ethics of accountability," and I would agree this tenet is magnified when engaging with archives of violence, even in the absence of direct interviews.[20] One answer to this question is a matter of proximity: to account for western lands in their full complexity requires meeting up with their disparate histories of violence. As more evidence accumulates to document the intermingling of colonialism and the climate crisis, those who occupy settler colonial terrains face an important question: In these times how will you mobilize for a power shift in intimate and infrastructural terms?[21]

During the life of this book, collaboration can be interpreted as a "method" in addition to a relationship observed in the field. As a method, collaboration necessitates moving away from notions of interview research as "giving voice to the voiceless"—an often colonizing orientation that also presumes opacity is not always desirable. To the contrary, sometimes opacity is a survival mechanism. For instance, I have chosen *not* to include a complete demystification of queer survival skills nor take advantage of intracommunity debates when I am not a member (topics such as energy sovereignty, the politics of reconciliation, the vexed politics of patriotism in World War II remembrance). At the same time there have been times I wished this project could have been more *deeply* collaborative. This ultimately would have required writing a different book, one unconstrained by the scarcity of time and financial support for extensive travel in the field. Sadly, the contemporary settler academy celebrates interdisciplinarity as an empty signifier but rarely creates infrastructures for humanistic inquiry or stymies creativity by policing disciplinary boundaries. And so this book has tried to model in some way what addressing the settler problem might look like—on a personal level and as a matter of academic inquiry. This model is a relationship to proximity, a careful kind of stewardship that relates to the kinds of collaboration operative in the sites covered in this book. For me this has meant a different relationship to what Audra Simpson (Kahnawake Mohawk) calls an "ethnographic refusal."[22] This accounts for why I have largely traced administrative histories as they interface with land, embodied memories with that land, and the promises and pitfalls of memory sites to model different imaginations of accountability. As a white settler, I've turned that gaze inward and outward, trying to trace a map of sexual modernity's reproduction over time and space through formative infrastructures. Ecology—interdependence and relation—has become a way of life, always tracking sedimentation lessons. To me an explicitly *queer* ecology models a different kind of queer politics routed not through liberal imagination but through an ecological imagination. Building on existing work that mobilizes queer ecologies as a framework attuned to tropes of *naturalization* in regimes of sexuality, whiteness, and energy, this book works toward a praxis that displaces a violent history of managerialism for the regenerative work of care.

What do I mean by "collaborative stewardship?" When used in the world of resource management, collaborative stewardship often signals agreements to mainstream traditional ecological knowledge within governmental agencies, often referred to as "co-management."[23] "Resource management" is one of many ways federal and state governments have eroded Indigenous sovereignty, and so any project of collaboration may be fraught from the start because managerialism assumes particular protocol, regimes of knowledge, and practice. In the context of the *Witness Blanket,* collaborative stewardship bridges both notions of "possession" and protocol. Neither the Canadian Museum for Human Rights nor Carey Newman "possess" the material of the *Witness Blanket,* negating the relationship of colonial acquisition. As a resting place, the *Witness Blanket* also defies colonial logics of animate and nonanimate, delineating how the collaborative stewardship model creates accountability for care, an agreement to be renewed in the future. Although the collaborative stewardship agreement discussed in chapter 3 encompasses a museum "acquisitions" agreement, its larger principles might plant seeds for how to practice in other contexts.

In this way collaborative stewardship is not a prescriptive framework. Instead, it must always be a grounded, situated foundation for determining everything from protocol for decision making, cultural perspectives of animate life, and honor for self-determination. We might ask similar questions of each chapter. How did a history of affected persons enable and constrain collaborative stewardship in the case against the Concentrated Animal Feeding Operation? How could the American Heritage Center manage their legacy collections in a way to properly situate Grace Raymond Hebard's papers and auspicious absences, such as her lack of attention to Black settlements?[24] Why were there so few collaborations between queer and environmental organizers at the time of my interviews? I do not have any answers for these questions; they are instead probing of the conditions that shaped and continue to contour these particular sites.

But, much like demands for "reconciliation," collaboration also poses risks rather than offer a magical cure-all. In the context of engaging the historical tensions between environmentalism and environmental justice movements, Pezzullo and Ronald Sandler highlight the possibilities and pitfalls of mutual collaboration. Historically, these movements share mutual interests and yet have also worked in tension to each other. For example, they echo Robert Bullard's insistence that the "conservation/preservation movement, really reflects the larger society. And society is racist." To imagine environmental futures, any history of environmentalism or environmental thought must take account of its eugenic underpinnings. In turn Pezzullo and Sandler frame collaboration as a kind of relationship that at times necessitates working together and at other times working apart.[25] Although grounded in actually existing tensions between two movements, theirs is a model that does not collapse difference into a rubric of inclusion. This collapse of difference into sameness has long governed mainstream queer politics, consequentially deepening precarity for those who live outside of structures of palatable sexuality such as compulsory monogamy, respectable forms of labor, or proper uses of space.[26]

In contemplating what a queerly embodied collaborative stewardship might entail, one example comes from the work of Queer Nature. In their writings and teachings, "steward" offers something akin to the eros of TallBear's intimate relationality with bodies of various forms, shapes, intensities, and flows. This eros is one premised by relationships of care rather than the managerialism that has governed structures of settlement throughout the North American West. Kyle Powys Whyte (Potawatomi), for example, argues that, for some Indigenous people, the "Anthropocene" already feels apocalyptic. Reflecting on examples of collaborative projects, Whyte illuminates conservation as "not only about whether to conserve or let go of certain species" but rather about grounding practices on "what relationships between humans and certain plants and animals we should focus on in response to the challenges we face." One of those challenges is the ongoing violence of settler colonialism, creating conditions for collaboration that "seek to find ways to reconcile—as much as that makes sense—with settler societies so that Indigenous and settler conservation can share responsibilities and hold each other accountable."[27] Whyte offers a way of orienting stewardship as a model of care rather than as managerialism, while simultaneously resisting a totalistic fantasy of reconciliation and collaboration. Collaborative stewardship is about deepening and refusing to live on the surface of myth and the stories we tell. The whole point of myth is to never notice the roots jutting from the ground.

A queerly embodied collaborative stewardship resists a scarcity framework of settler modernity in favor of abundance. One dimension of western modernity was the calculated shrinking of what forms of life are possible or valuable. But to embrace abundance in the time of the Capitalocene requires ongoing tending, cultivation, and care. During the long process of writing this book, places outside of the North American West supported my inquiry and found me slowly sinking into all the different ways to be held by a landscape. Being held can be a place of learning and feeling abundance. Just as we center care as an ecological relation, learning to be cared for may open pathways of healing.

In the final months of writing this book in 2021, I returned to one of the formative landscapes of my young queer life, deep in the Medicine Bow National Forest in southeastern Wyoming. For weeks on end in the drought and heat-ridden summer of 2020, pockets of the forest burned and smoke traveled hundreds of miles and lingered in the atmosphere as far east as Iowa. Standing again before the crystal edges of Lake Marie, I found myself wanting to be next to this place not because I wanted to recall memories but because this fire-surviving place compelled me to learn a different kind of connection, a different relation and kinship. I know this place will burn again. But I hear the sound of the water moving with the wind and songbirds; the smell of cedar and pine sap overwhelms me in a way I can't really describe. I did not realize it at the time, but all these relations were kin to me as a child trying to survive this petro state called Wyoming. And so I have learned to take these feelings with me, moving elsewhere. I feel it when I walk through the woods in Iowa. Even amid these "natural" enclosures, my body passes pockets of worlds of weird nature. Aged bark supports tiny tendrils of green moss. In my small summer garden bed, I delicately tickle tomato flowers to assist pollinators. Or, at Schoodic Point in Maine, I see pools of molten magma cooled into granite, fragmenting and forming around newer magma flow. I feel it here too, listening to the tides swell. My lungs work to align with the rhythm of the waves pushing and pulling, an azure embrace. "Blue is a color of longing"; tides lick barnacles gripping volcanic remains.[28] I feel something in my body release.

Notes

1. Patent 545866 was filed by Frederick in 1916. Patent 101881 was filed by Nancy in 1928.

2. TallBear, "Making Love and Relations," 155–64; Morgensen, *Spaces between Us;* Rifkin, *Indians Become Straight.*

3. These details are based on a short nonfiction story written by my father in 2009.

4. This is a vast literature, but highlights include Engels, *Origin of the Family;* Spillers, "Mama's Baby, Papa's Maybe"; and Butler, "Merely Cultural." In particular, Butler argues that the reproduction of human life itself is made contingent by virtue of the normative reproduction of gender, making desire and the "regulation of sexuality...systematically tied to the *mode of production* proper to the functioning of political economy" (40). See also S. Lewis, *Full Surrogacy Now.*

INTRODUCTION

1. John Harvey Kellogg, "Why We Are Cripples," January 7, 1897, box 3, Kellogg Papers.

2. Kellogg, "Physical Basis of Faith," January 8, 1897, box 3, Kellogg Papers.

3. "Brief History."

4. *Colorado Sanitarium Bulletin,* 1902, Sanitarium Collection, 6, 8.

5. Foucault, *History of Sexuality,* 23–24.

6. Kahan, *Book of Minor Perverts,* 2.

7. Throughout this book I draw from Puar's work on capacity, which she defines closely to "ability." My focus is capacity as an environmental concept, produced through friction and networked across places. Puar gestures toward environmental racism as a reason to theorize capacity as consistently modulat-

ed, but she does not develop an environmental framework. See *Right to Maim*. My use of innervation and enervation also emphasizes the energy politics of capacity and debility, but a full discussion is outside of the scope of this book. I have made a decision to foreground scholarship with a long resonance in environmental justice, along with environmental history attentive to environmental violence.

8. Szeman and Wenzel, "What Do We Talk About?," 506.

9. Szeman and Boyer, *Energy Humanities;* LeMenager, *Living Oil;* Wilson, Carlson, and Szeman, *Petroculture.*

10. Foucault, *History of Sexuality,* 36–37 (emphasis mine).

11. Chen, *Animacies;* Luciano, *Arranging Grief;* Luciano and Chen, "Introduction."

12. Here I am responding to the claim that Foucault never talked about energy; see Szeman, "Conclusion," 454–55.

13. See Niblett, "Energy Regimes"; on capacity, see Puar, *Right to Maim,* 19.

14. Podobnik, "Sustainable Energy Regime"; Niblett, "Energy Regimes."

15. Indeed, this work builds on efforts to think about energy more expansively, specifically as relationships of power, labor, emotion, and more. Notably, however, sexuality remains absent. For the environmental humanities broadly, see LeMenager, *Living Oil;* Moore, *Capitalism,* 205; and Podobnik, "Sustainable Energy Regime." For energy communication, see de Onís, *Energy Islands;* Schneider and Peeples, "Energy Covenant"; Schneider et al, *Under Pressure;* Endres et al, "Communicating Energy"; Endres, "Wasteland to Waste Site"; and Endres, "Rhetoric of Nuclear Colonialism."

16. This statement summarizes much of my inspiration in the energy humanities, see particularly Daggett, *Birth of Energy;* Szeman and Boyer, *Energy Humanities;* and LeMenager, *Living Oil.*

17. Morgensen, "Theorising Gender," 10.

18. Podobnik, "Sustainable Energy Regime"; Niblett, "Energy Regime."

19. Cronon, *Nature's Metropolis.* Cronon's work has deeply influenced my thinking about place as networked through infrastructures of various sorts, shaping the production of commodities. See also C. Johnson, *Just Queer Folks.*

20. Park and Pellow, *Slums of Aspen.*

21. I am influenced here by performance studies scholarship centering the body in environmental communication, including Conquergood, "Rethinking Ethnography"; Conquergood, "Ethnography, Rhetoric, Performance"; Madison, *Acts of Activism;* Pezzullo, *Toxic Tourism;* McKinnon et al., *Text + Field;* and Middleton et al., *Participatory Critical Rhetoric.* The foundational tenet of environmental communication is that words such as *nature* and environment are mediated by systems of representation and thought, rendering these keywords as profoundly cultural, bound up in human histories and hierarchies. How nature and environment are culturally imagined ultimately shape affordances for relationships or use-value. See Oravec, "John Muir"; and Cox, "Nature's 'Crisis Disciplines." Within cultural studies, see Williams, *Keywords,* 219–24; and Pezzullo, "Overture."

22. Bullard, *Dumping in Dixie;* Voyles, *Wastelanding.* This also implicitly

references a vast literature beyond the scope of this project related to atomic landscapes and the Cold War.

23. Park and Pellow, *Slums of Aspen*, 4.

24. Moore, *Capitalism*. Moore's refusal of the "nature/culture" binary can be interpreted as a different kind of materialism that sees "modernity in nature" and focuses on the "relations that co-produce manifold configurations of humanity-in-nature, organisms and environments, life and land, water and air" (5). Moore's insistence on resisting a singular story of the "human" in "Anthropocenic" language and movement toward relations of capital is also helpful. However, Moore also neglects sexuality as an important force, even as sexuality studies has long been interested in processes of capitalism.

25. These characteristics summarize a massive literature about the resilience of the western myth. In addition to Slotkin's work mentioned earlier, I am drawn toward the following exemplars in this tradition: Solnit, *Savage Dreams;* R. Nash, *Wilderness;* H. Smith, *Virgin Land;* Marx, *Machine in the Garden;* Limerick, *Legacy of Conquest;* and LeMenager, *Manifest and Other Destinies*. Most intellectual histories date the emergence of "New Western History" in the 1990s, through the work of Patricia Limerick, William Cronon, Richard White, and Donald Worster. "New western" historiography emerged in contrast to older paradigms, as a consequence of a debate about the West as a frontier-constituted "process" versus a defined geographic place and region. What counts as "the West" is a product of historical forces, as the category is a mobile and porous boundary. Rejecting Frederick Jackson Turner's influence, the new western historiography defined the U.S. West as a "place of conquest" (Limerick, *Legacy of Conquest*), whose continuities of violence continue to shape contemporary life in the region, in addition to the region's place in a global energy infrastructure. Of course, additional subfields influence how scholars understand a western past and present. These influences include the study of borderlands as informed by the work of Chicana feminism and Native American and Indigenous studies scholars, including Gloria Anzaldúa, Cherríe Moraga, Ned Blackhawk (Western Shoshone), Vine Deloria Jr. (Standing Rock Sioux), and Beatrice Medicine (Sihasapa and Minneconjou Lakota). My own commitment is to understand the spatial production of the "North American West" as both idea and physical geography in a context of political struggle, a framework that inevitably limits my archive in addition to what spaces and histories are included therein. Foundational Indigenous scholarship rooted in histories of the Great Basin include Blackhawk, *Violence over the Land;* and V. Deloria, *Custer Died*.

26. Here I am referencing Ferguson's *Aberrations in Black*. Specifically, he writes, "Queer of color analysis presumes that liberal ideology occludes the intersecting saliency of race, gender, sexuality, and class in forming social practices. Approaching ideologies of transparency as formations that have worked to conceal those intersections means that queer of color analysis has to debunk the idea that race, class, gender, and sexuality are discrete formations, insulated from one another. As queer of color critique challenges ideologies of discreteness, it attempts to disturb the idea that racial and national formations are obviously disconnected" (4). In communication studies these moves away from

"discrete formations" and the flatness of uptakes of intersectionality are best challenged by Yep's "Toward Thick(er) Intersectionalities."

27. On the connection between work and energy, see Daggett, *Birth of Energy*, especially chap. 1.

28. K. Chávez, *Borders of AIDS*, 5–9.

29. Foucault, *History of Sexuality*, 54.

30. There are certain exceptions to this, particularly in terms of "nature." Of course, queer ecologies, and particularly the work of Seymour, Luciano, Alaimo, and others, do this work. Energy, however, is largely an absent analytic.

31. Though Foucault identifies biopower as both spatial *and* temporal, his brief attention to eugenics eclipses a more robust account of scientific racism in the deployment of biopower through colonial projects, a task taken up by postcolonial scholars such as Ann Stoler. For scholars of settler colonialism, biopower provides one vocabulary to map "geopower," a meeting up of federal doctrines and policies that have tethered the regulation of Indigenous identities, kinships, and land. Thus, although Foucault fundamentally miscalculates scientific racism and colonialism in his theorization of biopolitics, critics have simultaneously read with and against him to reframe western modernity as a fundamentally settler colonial epistemological structure.

32. Coviello, *Tomorrow's Parties*, 4–8.

33. LaFleur, *Natural History of Sexuality*. LaFleur's argument is that the primacy of *subjectivity* as the premise driving a history of sexuality occludes the critical place of eighteenth century.

34. Terry, *American Obsession*, 11.

35. LaFleur and Schuller, "Introduction," 603–4. LaFleur and Schuller write, "Biopolitical frameworks have much to offer as we analyze how capitalism and its need for land, raw materials, and labor intersects with racializing, gendering, and eroticizing structures" (604).

36. I am basing my thinking here on some formative texts in queer studies, including, among others, Somerville, *Queering the Color Line*; Snorton, *Black on Both Sides*; and Duggan, *Sapphic Slashers*.

37. Roediger and Esch, *Production of Difference*. Under the influence of Lamarckianism, heredity was a way of thinking about latent forms of energy inherited and transmitted over generations. See Schuller, *Biopolitics of Feeling*, 5; and Duggan, *Sapphic Slashers*, 156–71.

38. Kahan, *Book of Minor Perverts*.

39. Bederman, *Manliness and Civilization*, 27. See also Carter, *Heart of Whiteness*, 12.

40. S. Hall, *Fateful Triangle*.

41. Stern, *Eugenic Nation*.

42. I discuss this with more depth in chapter 4, but here let me be clear that "racializing" indigeneity speaks to the colonial relationship. See Kauanui, "Structure, Not an Event"; and TallBear, *Native American DNA*.

43. Byrd, *Transit of Empire*, chap. 6.

44. I am drawing on a large literature here, explicitly related to settler colonial studies (which is distinct from Indigenous studies). See Byrd, *Transit of Empire*; C. Anderson, *"Métis"*; Day, *Alien Capital*; Goeman, *Mark My Words*;

Goldstein, "Toward a Genealogy"; Kauanui, "Structure, Not an Event"; Rowe and Tuck, "Settler Colonialism"; and Simpson, "Settlement's Secret." Finally, Wolfe's "Settler Colonialism," is, as he admits, overly cited. Kauanui's essay "Structure, Not an Event" provides an excellent interpretation of these citations, which often displace long-standing Indigenous critiques of settler colonialism and its difference, tensions, or overlaps with other forms of colonialism.

45. Byrd, *Transit of Empire.*

46. Byrd, "Variations under Domestication."

47. Sandilands, "Queer Life," 310.

48. Sandilands and Erickson, "Introduction," 5.

49. Luciano's *chronobiopolitics,* or "the sexual arrangement of the time of life," works against a number of pitfalls she identifies in Foucault's approach to biopower. Whereas Foucault's attention to "sex" often privileges reprosexual practices, Luciano treats sex as a speculative category, opening for environmental histories of sexuality what might "count" as sex outside of "sexuality." *Arranging Grief,* 11; here Luciano discusses Foucault's *History of Sexuality.*

50. Greyser, *On Sympathetic Grounds,* 15; Rifkin, "Indigenizing Agamben."

51. Larkin, "The Politics and Poetics"; Edwards, "Infrastructure and Modernity"; Bowker and Starr, *Sorting Things Out;* Supp-Montgomerie, *Medium Was the Mission.* In sexuality studies infrastructure shifts between implicit to explicit. Gray's *Out in the Country* uses infrastructure to question the "infrastructure of visibility" produced by metropolitan environments for LGBTQ youth. Gray examines the possibilities and constraints for LGBTQ youth in the rural United States who work with a precarious overlap of public and private infrastructure in their capacity to shape terms of belonging (89, 116, 128). Rosenberg develops "people as infrastructure" in "Youth as Infrastructure"; Wilson shifts beyond "sexuality" as a category of analysis toward "intimacies" and the infrastructure of intimacy. In rhetoric and communication studies, Greene argues for a spatial materialism that traces a "governing apparatus [that] polices a population, space, and/or object by articulating an ensemble of human technologies into a functioning network of power to improve public welfare." "Another Materialist Rhetoric," 22.

52. A. Wilson, "Infrastructure of Intimacy," 249.

53. Nishime and Williams, "Introduction," 4–6.

54. Rifkin, *Indians Become Straight,* 6.

55. R. White, *Railroaded,* 144. See also Packer and Robertson, *Thinking with James Carey.*

56. Wells, *Car Country,* xii.

57. LeMenager, *Living Oil,* 104.

58. Byrd, *Transit of Empire,* 190. An exemplar, Byrd notes the limits to thinking of Agamben's "state of exception" as emerging in war-era confinement of Japanese Americans.

59. Edwards, "Infrastructure and Modernity."

60. For example, Towns argues that Blackness has operated as an extension of "man," radically rereading how infrastructure requires extracted Blackness to bring the modern world into being. See "Black Media Philosophy." Consider alongside this Hartman's argument that the flesh of enslaved Black women

constituted the commodities of the plantation as carceral landscape, producing natal alienation in turn troubling the intelligibility of western demarcations of gender. "Belly of the World," 168.

61. Gilmore, *Golden Gulag,* 28, 26.

62. Nixon underscores the need to supplant the violence of fast capitalism and compression with a "slow violence" of delayed consequences. *Slow Violence,* 8.

63. Massey, *For Space.*

64. Goeman, "Land as Life," 72–73.

65. A wealth of scholarship exists in this regard, specific both to North America and to the geographic mapping of intimacy through colonial practices, transnationalism, and more. See A. Wilson, "Intimacy"; Ballantyne and Burton, *Moving Subjects;* Stoler, *Carnal Knowledge;* and Stoler, *Haunted by Empire.*

66. Williams, *Marxism and Literature,* 132.

67. Williams, *Long Revolution,* 69.

68. Grossberg, "Affect's Future," 310.

69. Luciano, *Arranging Grief;* Chen, *Animacies;* Schuller, *Biopolitics of Feeling.*

70. In their debates Stuart Hall called attention to the limits of Williams's profound attempt to understand his own Welsh sense of place relative to something of a "border country." The limits of "structure of feeling," Hall notes, reside in William's emplacement within the knowable communities of the Welsh countryside. "Culture, Community, Nation."

71. As a rhetorical practice of cultural production, myth encompasses a powerful resource of cultural memory. Slotkin's foundational study illuminates the mobilization of key archetypes in the resurgence of threats posed to the integrity of coherent nationalism, grounding myth as a resource of nation formation. This is what we can call "regenerative violence," a symbolic and material process that dramatizes moral consciousness, consequentially reinscribing old myths into extensions of national territory. Western myth, writes Slotkin, turns the matter of land and bodies into "abstract[ions]...reduced to deeply encoded set of symbols, 'icons,' keywords,' or historical clichés." *Gunfighter Nation,* 5.

72. Williams, *Marxism and Literature,* 110.

73. Singh, *No Archive,* 29.

74. Connerton, *How Societies Remember,* 72.

75. Hirsch and Smith, "Feminism and Cultural Memory," 5.

76. Singh, *No Archive,* 29. On the importance of the nonhuman, see Alaimo, *Bodily Natures.*

77. Most of this scholarship celebrates the nation in positive terms, often grounding memory as a site of civic or national identity. I have a pessimistic orientation toward both nation and citizenship as grounds for thinking about the politics of memory. Still, this literature illustrates how memory is a central site of citizenship production. See Dickinson, Blair, and Ott, *Places of Public Memory;* Morris, *Queering Public Address;* Dunn, *Queerly Remembered;* Rand, *Reclaiming Queer;* Phillips, *Framing Public Memory;* D. Taylor, *Archive and the Repertoire;* and Lynch, *Origins of Bioethics.* See also S. Hall, "Whose Heritage"; and Williams, *Marxism and Literature,* 115–16.

78. L. Simpson, *As We Have Always*, 3.
79. Klein, *This Changes Everything*, 424.
80. Haraway, *Staying with the Trouble*, 31.
81. I am drawing on a body of rhetoric and communication scholarship that traces the significance of communication forms prior to their recording or textualization, often amid publics or communities beyond what Hubbs calls the "narrating class" in *Rednecks*.
82. Greyser, *On Sympathetic Grounds*, 2.
83. P. Deloria, *Playing Indian*, 106.
84. LeMenager, *Living Oil*, 17.

CHAPTER 1. CARTOGRAPHIES OF SEXUAL MODERNITY

1. Owen Wister, journal of world's fair, June 16, 1893, collection 00290, folder 4, box 2, Wister Papers, 3.
2. Wister.
3. Scholars in American studies and queer studies more recently tend to cast *rural* and *urban* as binaries. My approach understands them as embedded in an interconnected network. This approach to systems of extraction and production has shaped the environmental humanities at least since Cronon's *Nature's Metropolis*. Consequentially, it makes little sense to reference one without the other or how energy is made through their connection and by whom.
4. On the breadth of neurasthenia as a category (I limit my scope here to work in the history of medicine and cultural histories of gender, race, and sexuality), see Schuster, *Neurasthenic Nation;* Carter, *Heart of Whiteness;* Bederman; *Manliness and Civilization;* Seitler, "Unnatural Selection"; and Fleissner, *Woman, Compulsion, Modernity.* On Wister and Mitchell in particular, see Will, "Nervous Origins"; and Bold, *Frontier Club*, 59–60.
5. Mitchell, *Wear and Tear.*
6. This definition of networks (i.e., networked communication) is common in communication studies. See Supp-Montgomerie, *Medium Was the Mission,* 17; and Kang, *Igniting the Internet.*
7. Kahan, *Book of Minor Perverts,* 46.
8. Fleissner's *Woman, Compulsion, Modernity* notes that the same modernity instilling fears of "demasculinization" à la Teddy Roosevelt juxtaposed new emerging freedoms for white women in North America. Fleissner associates repositories of "sentimental, therapeutic, indeed nostalgic culture in the 1890s" with the era's manly men (17). Moreover, neurasthenia's gendered dimensions highlight how the constitution of gender also intersects with the arguments I'm making about vitality. Fleissner writes, "If the neurasthenic is the individual whose stalled life trajectory threatens to stall the trajectory of history, in America in particular, this tended to mean that girls were not 'becoming women,' and boys were not 'becoming men.' And thus loomed the prospect of a populace without a future, for history's unfolding depended, as Teddy Roosevelt argued, on male action and female maternity" (58). On the linking of reproductive motherhood to the nation, see Fixmer-Oraiz, *Homeland Maternity.*
9. Cronon's *Nature's Metropolis* is a model of "commodity regionalism,"

scholarship that does not study places as discretely bound but as *networked* through commodity markets. As a whole, he traces shifts in the relationships between places by following specific forms of life transformed into commodities: agriculture, meat, grain, lumber, and prairie. His approach is driven by a theory of value derived from the "usefulness" of nature, in which soil, and abundance of forests, and "stored sunshine" constitute elaborate energy chains. Of this value he writes, "Although plants might convert the sun's energy into useable carbohydrates, and animals might then concentrate that stored energy in their flesh, they all finally drew their sustenance from the light of the nearest star. The abundance that fueled Chicago's hinterland economy thus consisted largely of stored sunshine: this was the wealth of nature, and no human labor could create the value it contained" (149–50).

10. Boag, *Re-dressing America's Frontier Past*, chap. 5.

11. Carter, *Heart of Whiteness*, 45.

12. Stern, *Eugenic Nation*, 144–45.

13. Indeed, neurasthenia was a deeply gendered discourse and deserves sustained inquiry, and much of that work has already been done. In feminist criticism (particularly in the 1970s and 1980s), the recovery of texts such as Gilman's *Yellow Wallpaper* enabled critiques of medical misogyny, using as an example Mitchell's gendered distinction of the "west cure," and the "rest cure." Gilman was the most vocal of Mitchell's patients, and she described her homestay under Mitchell's care after treatment at a Philadelphia sanatorium as "mental torture and agony." Schuster, "Personalizing Illness," 719. Whereas the camp cure postulated that rigorous western environments could generate friction capable of restoring energy within masculine bodies, practices of rest, at least for Gilman, emphasized immobility and inaccessibility to technologies of recording or writing. In "Unnatural Selection" Seitler refers to Gilman's *Yellow Wallpaper* as a "feminist regeneration narrative," as a contrast to her novel *The Crux* (63). The latter novel is a story of a group of women who relocate to Colorado. A full synopsis of the novel is beyond the scope of my purposes here, but Seitler's interpretation of Gilman's eugenic feminism, or construction of a feminism *through* eugenics, is helpful here, especially as those come into connection in chapter 2 of this book.

14. Cronon, *Nature's Metropolis*.

15. N. Harris, *Cultural Excursions*, 117.

16. For example, one of the landmark texts that engages gender and environment through metaphor is Kolodny's *The Lay of the Land*. Even Boag's *Re-dressing America's Frontier Past* treats land and movement largely metaphorically.

17. Kellogg, "Darkest Chicago," August 27, 1897, Chicago Medical Missionary School (and Working Men's Home and Medical Mission), 1891–1907, box 12, Kellogg Papers.

18. Beard, *American Nervousness*, vi.

19. Schuller, *Biopolitics of Feeling*, 10–11.

20. L. Nash, *Inescapable Ecologies*, 33. Nash argues that health is a missing frame in the environmental history of the West. Further, she argues that modern, enclosed body is a forgetting of other ways of knowing the body.

21. Beard, *American Nervousness*, 96, 100.
22. Mitchell, *Wear and Tear*, 3, 4.
23. Mitchell, 5.
24. Mitchell, 14.
25. Here I am drawing largely on Schuller's *Biopolitics of Feeling* to interpret sex as a technology of securing race (60–61).
26. Mitchell, *Wear and Tear*, 28.
27. Beard, *American Nervousness*, 171.
28. Beard, 265; Beard and Rockwell, *Sexual Neurasthenia*.
29. Beard and Rockwell, *Sexual Neurasthenia*, 25–26.
30. Beard and Rockwell, 31, 16.
31. Beard and Rockwell, 105–6.
32. Rockwell, *Medical and Surgical Uses*, 197, 198, 470.
33. Beard and Rockwell, *Sexual Neurasthenia*, 93.
34. Beard and Rockwell, 106–7.
35. Freud, "Autobiographical Study," 15.
36. Wister, journal, July 8, 1885, collection 00290, folder 1, box 1, Wister Papers, 5.
37. Mitchell, *Nurse and Patient*, 45.
38. Nash, *Inescapable Ecologies*, 27–33. For an example of the characteristics of medical climatology, see Solly's address to the Twelfth Annual Meeting of the American Climatological Association, printed as "Principles of Medical Climatology."
39. Mitchell, *Nurse and Patient*, 57.
40. Mitchell, 57, 60.
41. Watts, *Rough Rider*, 128.
42. P. Deloria, *Playing Indian*. See also Bederman on the broader cultural context of various beliefs about somatic forms of masculinity and racial dominance, in *Manliness and Civilization*.
43. Watts, *Rough Rider*, 130.
44. On this transition, see Buell, "Short History"; and LeMenager, *Living Oil*.
45. Luciano and Chen, "Introduction," 191; Puar, *Right to Maim*; Haraway, "Manifesto for Cyborgs"; Sandilands, "Some 'F' Words," 446; Rosenberg, *4-H Harvest*, 14. On life as "management," see J. Bennett, *Managing Diabetes*.
46. Turner, *Frontier in American History*.
47. In addition to those cited by Cronon, *Nature's Metropolis*, 459n1, I would include Trachtenberg, *Incorporation of America*, 208–34; Rydell, *World's a Fair*; N. Harris, *Cultural Excursions*; Hinsley and Wilcox, *Coming of Age*; and Maddux, *Practicing Citizenship*.
48. Wilson, *Dr. John Harvey Kellogg*, 51–53.
49. Schwartz, "Dr. John Harvey Kellogg," 6.
50. Wilson, *Dr. John Harvey Kellogg*, 53; Schwartz, "Dr. John Harvey Kellogg," 6.
51. Wilson, *Dr. John Harvey Kellogg*, 53, 55.
52. Schwartz, "Dr. John Harvey Kellogg," 11–12.
53. Kellogg, "Darkest Chicago."

54. N. Harris, *Cultural Excursions,* 117, 118.

55. "Sanitarium and Hospital Exhibits."

56. Kellogg lectured and assembled numerous pamphlets on "healthful dress," wherein he reinforced a believed connection between muscle tightness and "rightful" health; these include "On the Hygiene of Dress," "The Evils of Conventional Dress," "Women's Dress," and "How to Dress Hygienically."

57. "Sanitarium and Hospital Exhibits," 13–14.

58. LaFleur, *Natural History of Sexuality,* chap. 5; Lyons, *Sex among the Rabble;* Gilfoyle, *City of Eros;* Shah, *Contagious Divides.*

59. N. Harris, *Cultural Excursions,* 114.

60. Larson, *White City.*

61. N. Harris, *Cultural Excursions,* 115.

62. Draper, "White City," xii.

63. Burnham, *Final Official Report,* 33–36, 5.

64. Bolotin and Laing, *Chicago World's Fair,* 60–61.

65. Berlant, *Queen of America,* 27 (with thanks to Colin Johnson).

66. Douglass, preface to *Reason Why,* 1.

67. Carpenter, "Frederick Jackson Turner," 121, 122.

68. Cronon, *Nature's Metropolis,* 47.

69. Slotkin, *Gunfighter Nation,* 69.

70. Luciano, *Arranging Grief,* 6, 9.

71. Burnham, *Book of Builders.* Cited in De Wit, "Building an Illusion," 68.

72. De Wit, "Building an Illusion," 68–69.

73. The spectacle of spaces such as the Anthropology Building and the Midway at the 1893 fair and future exhibitions has been excoriated by a number of disciplines, including a more self-reflexive anthropology. On the creation of visual cultures and the rhetoric of display in particular, see Garland-Thomson, *Freakery.*

74. Hinsley and Wilcox, *Coming of Age.*

75. Bauer, *Hirschfeld Archives,* 21, 25.

76. Handy, *Official Directory,* 61.

CHAPTER 2. SETTLER INTIMACIES AND THE SOCIAL LIFE OF THE ARCHIVE

1. Those maps consequentially demarcated allotments for private claims between homesteaders, miners, and ranchers. Mackey, *Inventing History,* 8.

2. Hebard's papers underscore her process of collecting and why she believed certain items held value, but her published books also center a sentimental style. Throughout this chapter I use her materials from Hebard Papers.

3. For a nationalist interpretation of her speeches, see T. Lewis, "Marking America's Progress."

4. In particular, I'm referring to letters to Michelet regarding the care of Agnes Wergeland's materials and her 1928 bibliography of curated materials, framed by "Here in the West, the Dreams of the East Come True" and "Finest Hope Is Finest Memory," both part of Hebard's papers at the AHC.

5. Greyser, *On Sympathetic Grounds,* 3–4.

6. Throughout the book *indigeneity* is an analytic. As such, it affords tracing the varied forces under colonialisms (settler and otherwise) that displace and replace relationships to land. My primary influence here is P. Deloria's *Playing Indian*, which examines the desire to replace (to *consume*) as a structure of U.S. identity. Arvin defines indigeneity as "the historical and contemporary effects of colonial and anticolonial demands and desires related to a certain land or territory and the various displacements of that place's original or longtime inhabitants." "Analytics of Indigeneity," 121.

7. Scharff, *Twenty Thousand Roads*, 94.

8. See Kent's critical engagement with Lillian Faderman and Carroll Smith-Rosenberg as earlier theorists of women's sentimental culture and female friendship, highlighting how their determinist approach often limits historical understanding. See also VanHaitsma, *Queering Romantic Engagement*.

9. Those who have published about Hebard from a "contribution" perspective include Scharff, "Independent and Feminine Life." I'm also pointing to an intellectual move in gender history and communication studies that privileges "contribution" frameworks. My approach differs in that my interest is how gender, sexuality, race, and disability are "meaningful categories" (to riff from Scott's subtitle, "A Useful Category," in "Gender") in producing the settler colonial nation.

10. Cram, "Archival Ambience," 112.

11. Coviello's notion of "earliness," in addition to Kent's historicization of sentimental culture that refuses a teleological certainty, animates my reading. See Coviello, *Tomorrow's Parties*, 211n24; and Kent, *Making Girls into Women*.

12. Predock, "American Heritage Center."

13. Predock.

14. See, among others, Burton, *Archive Stories;* Morris, "Archival Turn"; Morris, "Archival Queer"; Steedman, *Dust;* Rawson, "Rhetorical Power"; VanHaitsma, "Archival Absence"; Finnegan, "Picture"; and Stuckey, "Presidential Secrecy."

15. Rawson, "Accessing Transgender," 128–30. As someone grounded in rhetorical studies, I am thinking specifically of the work inspired by Morris's edited collection, *Queering Public Address*. Or, in the words of Marshall, Murphy, and Tortorici, "archives become legible as such through its facilitation of systems and practices that press sexuality and gender into some form of signification (usually language)." "Queering Archives," 4.

16. Steedman, *Dust*, 75.

17. This spatiality of "wanted" as the proxemics of object and capture comes from R. Hall's *Wanted*.

18. *Oxford English Dictionary*, s.v. "heritage," accessed October 20, 2020, https://www-oed-com.proxy.lib.uiowa.edu/view/Entry/86230?rskey=eUSOfe&result=1&isAdvanced=false.

19. Burton, "Thinking beyond the Boundaries," 66.

20. This summary is premised on Steedman's reading of Derrida and Foucault relative to the archive as "a way of seeing, or a way of knowing; the archive as a symbol or form of power" (*Dust*, 2). Steedman cites Burton to describe archival absence (5).

21. Steedman, *Dust*, 69, 81, 83.

22. Marshall, Murphy, and Tortorici, "Queering Archives," 3.

23. For example, DeVun and McClure note how the circulation of historical materials in archival spaces gives way to modes of disobedience, writing, "Archival objects circulate in ways that parallel yet differ from their previous uses....Instead of being a catalog of dead objects, the archive may foster an afterlife, and it may recirculate. And such circulation inextricably depends on bodies." "Archives Behaving Badly," 122.

24. Sedgwick, *Tendencies*, xii.

25. Van Nuys, *Americanizing the West*, 10.

26. Hebard, "History and Romance of Wyoming," 1928, folder 4, box 71 (F24), Hebard Papers.

27. Goeman, *Mark My Words*.

28. Appel, Anand, and Gupta, "Temporality," 18.

29. With the "production of space," I am drawing from an array of perspectives, predominately Greyser, *On Sympathetic Grounds*; Lefebvre, *Production of Space*; Shome, "Space Matters"; and N. Smith, *Uneven Development*.

30. Hebard, "Pilot," 467.

31. Sacajawea's name is spelled in a variety of ways, a testament to attempts by largely Anglo-American historians and mythmakers to invent her hagiography. I spell her name "Sacajawea" because, following Finley, it is the most widely used version. It is nearly impossible to speak of a historically "authentic" Sacajawea because she is largely a mythic figure spoken for by white anthropologists. See "Violence, Genocide, and Captivity," 191.

32. Heffernan and Medlicot, "Feminine Atlas," 114.

33. Hebard, "Pilot," 472.

34. Schuller, *Biopolitics of Feeling*, 103.

35. On "eating," see Schneider, "Modest Proposal."

36. Critics include Mackey, *Inventing History*; and Van Nuys, *Americanizing the West*.

37. Settler hagiography as reanimation serves as a powerful illustration of critiques of the "new materialism" that elide still-living Indigenous ontologies of animacy but also may forgo a deeper tracing of animacy's embeddedness in slow or fast violence. Confronting critiques by TallBear and Kyla Wazana Thompkins, Greyser writes in *On Sympathetic Grounds*, "One challenge, then, for new materialism, is to distinguish between forms and functions of animacy, and between the violence animate and sourcing of nature" (35).

38. Dye, *Conquest*, 290.

39. TallBear, *Native American DNA*, 35. TallBear underscores a pregenetic-era scientific racism that "delineates biophysical markers of races to categorize individuals and their body parts within those categories" (35).

40. To be clear, I use *race* and *indigeneity* as overlapping yet distinct social relations, following arguments by TallBear, Byrd, and Arvin. TallBear argues that Indigenous peoples have been racialized within the milieu of the United States (and other imperial centers). Race, in her words, has been imposed on Indigenous nations (*Native American DNA*, 32). Race is a meaningful category in that it helps to locate and map racializing processes. Even so, indigeneity is

a relation to ancestral lands and waters, and sovereignty (32–33). In *Transit of Empire* Byrd warns against the racializing discourses of inclusion and exclusion that often underwrite claims to justice in arguments against racial dominance (xxiii).

41. Green, "Pocahontas Perplex"; Finley, "Violence, Genocide, and Captivity"; Arvin, Tuck, and Morrill, "Decolonizing Feminism."

42. Green, "Pocahontas Perplex."

43. Finley, "Violence, Genocide, and Captivity."

44. Arvin, Tuck, and Morrill, "Decolonizing Feminism," 19.

45. Van Nuys, *Americanizing the West,* is perhaps the only in-depth academic account of Hebard's role as a regional agent. I draw "regional accent" from Greene and Kuswa, "Arab Spring to Athens."

46. Van Nuys, *Americanizing the West,* 6; Mackey, *Inventing History,* 43.

47. Hebard, "Exclude the Ninety-Seven," 14, 15.

48. Department of the Interior, "Immigrant Education Letter, No. 3," n.d., box 15, Hebard Papers.

49. Department of the Interior, "Syllabus of Tentative Course in Elementary Civics for Immigrants," n.d., box 15, Hebard Papers.

50. June Etta Downey, "Immigration Tests at Ellis Island: Scale of Psychology in Immigration," 1916, box 15, Hebard Papers.

51. Uhrbrock, "June Etta Downey," 351 (emphasis mine).

52. Baynton, *Defectives in the Land,* 47.

53. Morgensen, *Spaces between Us,* 42.

54. Scharff, *Twenty Thousand Roads,* 114.

55. Clifford, *Lone Voyagers,* 3, 30.

56. Van Nuys, *Americanizing the West,* 33–69.

57. Scharff, "Independent and Feminine Life." With "white women's right" I'm marking how whiteness was implicit rather than explicit in Hebard's writing and activism.

58. Kent, *Making Girls into Women,* 6.

59. American Heritage Center reference archivist, e-mail message to author, September 19, 2012.

60. Grace Raymond Hebard and Maren Michelet, correspondence, February 16, 1927; July 21, 1927; September 7, 1927; and November 8, 1929, folder 7, box 40, Hebard Papers.

61. Grace Raymond Hebard to Hon. William Michelet and I. Michelet, March 24, 1932, folder 7, box 40, Hebard Papers.

62. Belle K. Middlekauff to Grace Raymond Hebard, March 20, 1933, folder 7, box 40, Hebard Papers.

63. Hebard to Middlekauff, March 24, 1933, folder 7, box 40, Hebard Papers.

64. "Norske Kvinder, 1914–1924," folders 1–2, box 47, Hebard Papers.

65. Hebard to Middlekauff, April 17, 1933, folder 32, box 34, Hebard Papers. This letter is archived with materials related to the memorial of June Etta Downey, a close friend of both Hebard's and Wergeland's.

66. Middlekauff to Hebard, April 20, 1933, folder 7, box 40, Hebard Papers.

67. Muñoz, "Ephemera as Evidence," 6. On the rhetorical treatment of evidence, see Morris, "Hard Evidence."

68. Scharff, *Twenty Thousand Roads*, 102.

69. Michelet, *Agnes Mathilde Wergeland.*

70. Agnes Mathilde Wergeland, "Thy Hand," September 17, 1904, collection 400012, box 4, Wergeland Papers.

71. I extend Newman's argument that evolutionary categories of race permeated the discourse of the women's suffrage movement. *White Women's Rights*, 8.

72. Newman, *White Women's Rights*, 8.

73. Wergeland, "Thy Hand."

74. This represents a view of photography as mechanical reproduction, one that reproduces an external and objective reality. By contrast, the argument that I'm making regarding the affective economy of photography depends on an orientation to photography as performance and participatory. Cram, Loehwing, Lucaites, "Civic Sights"; Cram, "Angie Was Our Sister"; Hariman and Lucaites, *Public Image.*

75. Edwards and Hart, "Introduction," especially 3–6.

76. Lugones, "Toward a Decolonial Feminism," 747, 753.

77. Cited in Wanzer-Serrano, *New Young Lords*, 181.

78. One of the most important concepts to "structures of feeling" is the notion of "culture." Williams traces the regenerative characteristics of structure by periodizing. However, he notes the transference between "culture as it is lived" and culture as it is documented as a central site of tension. *Long Revolution*, 68–71.

CHAPTER 3. CHILDHOOD AND SETTLER AESTHETICS OF VIOLENCE

1. This conversation is expansive; in communication studies I am thinking of Dickinson, Blair, and Ott, *Places of Public Memory;* Dickinson, Ott, and Aoki, "Spaces of Remembering"; T. Bennett, *Birth of the Museum;* and Lehrer, Milton, and Patterson, *Curating Difficult Knowledge.*

2. Lehrer, "Canadian Museum," 1205.

3. P. Deloria, *Playing Indian*, 106.

4. Stockton, *Queer Child;* Bernstein, *Racial Innocence.*

5. Foucault, *History of Sexuality*, 103–5.

6. These debates are largely represented by Berlant, *Queen of America;* Edelman, *No Future;* and Muñoz, *Cruising Utopia.*

7. Kauanui, *Paradoxes of Hawaiian Sovereignty*, 23, 9.

8. Foucault, *History of Sexuality;* Stoler, *Education of Desire*, 35 (emphasis mine).

9. Cole Harris, *Making Native Space*, 269.

10. On challenges to Agamben's exclusion of indigeneity from the state of exception and situated biopolitics within settler colonial genealogies, see Byrd, *Transit of Empire;* Rifkin, "Indigenizing Agamben"; Rifkin, "Geo into Bio"; Morgensen, "Biopolitics of Settler Colonialism"; Morgensen, *Spaces between*

Us; Stoler, *Education of Desire,* 93; and Kauanui, *Paradoxes of Hawaiian Sovereignty.*

11. Morgensen, "Biopolitics of Settler Colonialism," 56.

12. Here I'm drawing on a central idea of the relationship between museology and space: that even as sexuality is not *explicit,* all museums—especially when they are sites of contestation—can teach us about the politics of sexuality. See Tyburczy, *Sex Museums.*

13. Kauanui, "Structure, Not an Event." Here I need to be clear that this chapter, and this book as a whole, seeks to contribute to *settler colonial* studies rather than *Indigenous studies.* In her essay reflecting on the uptake of Wolfe's account—which often includes the bypassing of Native American and Indigenous studies theorizing of settler colonialism—Kauanui insists the two are not the same thing, and I agree. Settler colonial studies is a form of power analysis that traces the geographically specific histories of colonialism, its legal regimes, and overlaps and distinctions with forms of colonialism such as franchise colonialism. Settler colonial studies also maintains its roots in Indigenous theorizing, and Indigenous peoples will endure any formation of settler structural violence.

14. See TallBear, *Native American DNA,* 32; and Byrd, *Transit of Empire,* xxiii.

15. Lawrence, "Regulation of Native Identity," 7.

16. In North American queer studies, I'm drawing from scholarship that examines the mutually constitutive relationship of settler colonialism and colonial (or modern) sexuality. See Morgensen, *Spaces between Us;* Rifkin, *Indians Become Straight;* Kauanui, *Paradoxes of Hawaiian Sovereignty;* Driskill et al., *Queer Indigenous Studies;* and Rifkin, Justice, and Schneider, "Sexuality, Nationality, Indigeneity."

17. Mack and Na'puti, "Our Bodies."

18. A. Simpson, "Whither Settler Colonialism," 439.

19. Newman and Hudson, *Picking Up the Pieces.* Newman and Hudson define "intergenerational survivor" as "a descendant of a residential school Survivor who is in some way affected by the experience of the survivor." A survivor refers to an "Indigenous person who endured the residential school system and all the effects and trauma of that experience" (159). To be clear I am using these terms in the specific context of residential school redress conversations rather than more widely circulating discourses about "survivors" of sexual assault.

20. Newman and Hudson, 155.

21. Reciprocity is a powerful contrast to how I've conceptualized inheritance as a settler logic of intergenerational kinship as a property logic. Reciprocity entails mapping the power structure of colonial societies and their power exchange (TallBear, "Making Love and Relations") or the reciprocal relationships between human and nonhuman (Brooks and Brooks, "Reciprocity Principle"; Todd, "Classroom to River's Edge"). Extractivism is fundamentally nonreciprocal because it's logic to *extract* without renewal—extractivism is the quintessential ideology of capital.

22. Tuck, "Suspending Damage," 409.

23. "Secretary Haaland."

24. Cited in Regan, *Unsettling the Settler Within,* 11n15.

25. As early as 1620, religious institutions took an active role in the use of boarding schools as conversion techniques to control indigenous children within the territory currently known as Canada. Henderson and Wakeham, *Reconciling Canada,* 299; Miller, *Shingwauk's Vision.*

26. Henderson and Wakeham, *Reconciling Canada,* 299; Milloy, *National Crime.*

27. Cole Harris, *Making Native Space,* 270.

28. Ryerson, *Report on Industrial Schools,* 73–74.

29. Ryerson, 73.

30. Razack, *Dying from Improvement,* 18.

31. Lawrence, "Regulation of Native Identity," 7.

32. Woolford, *Benevolent Experiment,* 68; Woolford, Benvenuto, and Hinton, *Colonial Genocide.*

33. Woolford, *Benevolent Experiment,* 68.

34. Davin, *Report on Industrial Schools,* 2, 10 (emphasis mine).

35. I discuss the coloniality of the gender and sex system in chapter 2; for a gloss, see Lugones, "Heterosexualism."

36. Carr, "*Atopoi* of the Modern," 112.

37. Milloy, *National Crime,* 30, as quoted in Carr "*Atopoi* of the Modern," 117.

38. Woolford, *Benevolent Experiment,* 225.

39. Henderson and Wakeham, *Reconciling Canada,* 304.

40. Rollo, "Feral Children," 63. On the "abstraction" of childhood, see Bernstein, *Racial Innocence,* 2.

41. Bagot Commission, *Report on the Affairs.*

42. Cole Harris, *Making Native Space,* 8, 33.

43. Dewar, "Profound Silences"; Llewellyn, "Dealing with the Legacy"; Million, "Telling Secrets"; Hulan, "Just Allotment of Memory"; Rymhs, *From the Iron House.*

44. *Honouring the Truth,* 1.

45. A. Simpson, "Whither Settler Colonialism," 438–39.

46. Museums Act (S.C. 1990 c. 3).

47. Gough, "Peacekeeping, Peace, Memory," 65–66, 69.

48. Kauanui, *Paradoxes of Hawaiian Sovereignty.*

49. Specifically, I am drawing on Coulthard's critique of colonial "recognition" discourses in *Red Skin, White Masks.*

50. "Archeology Report."

51. Lecce, McArthur, and Schafer, Introduction to *Fragile Freedoms,* 2–3.

52. "Archeology Report."

53. Tomiak et al., "Introduction," 2. This argument parallels much of the collection's essays engaging Winnipeg.

54. O'Brien, *Firsting and Lasting.*

55. Todd, "Classroom to River's Edge," 91, cited in Brown, "Experiments," 140.

56. One of the most powerful ways of marking that colonial violence in the rivers includes several monuments to women who disappeared and their bodies later recovered in the rivers themselves. Missing Indigenous women and femi-

cide more broadly have spurned some national inquiries. In Winnipeg, on these rivers, the most notable case included the recovery of Tina Fontaine in 2014. See Dorries, "Welcome to Winnipeg."

57. Alvarez, *Immersions in Cultural Difference*, 144–45, 137, 138.

58. In *Immersions in Cultural Difference* Alvarez includes an account of traveling to Shoal Lake territory for their immersive "dark tour," which she describes as an "infrastructural time capsule" (141). Alvarez uses "dark tour," a term recognized by performance and tourist studies scholars to describe the type of rituals or scenes that tourists enter when they seek out spaces related to violence, death, or otherwise negative historical or contemporary experience.

59. Hatherly, "First Nations."

60. Annable, "Protesters Heard Throughout."

61. "Tribe Called Red."

62. Tuck and Yang's critique of settler innocence is helpful to highlight the function of the CMHR relative to so-called reconciliation. Their argument is that the uptake of "decolonization" discourses in various domains (but especially pedagogical spaces) produces "settler innocence" through the evasion of accountability for Indigenous land repatriation. Critics of reconciliation in Canada often point to the ways Canada attempts to leverage a position of "restoration" while simultaneously forward newer extractive projects such as the Tar Sands or Trans Mountain Pipeline that efface sovereignty and directly harm Indigenous peoples. "Decolonization."

63. Stickler, quoted in Alvarez, *Immersions in Cultural Difference*, 157–58.

64. Predock, "Canadian Museum."

65. Tyburczy, *Sex Museums*, 6.

66. "Structure."

67. Bozikovic, "Canadian Museum."

68. "Structure."

69. Appelbaum, "Architecture of Information."

70. Alvarez, *Immersions in Cultural Difference*, 140.

71. This bridges the long-standing pedagogical function of the modern museum and technologies of immersion. T. Bennett, *Birth of the Museum*.

72. Dhamoon, "Re-presenting Genocide."

73. "They Need to Know."

74. Busby, Muller, and Woolford, "Human Rights Museum," 14.

75. The scope of this chapter cannot address the TRC proceedings, nor the ways even the TRC mandates became frustrated by cover-ups. See Troian, "Indian Residential Schools"; and Rhiannon Johnson, "Ottawa Has Spent $3.2M."

76. Levin, "Museum about Rights."

77. Na'puti, "Archipelagic Rhetoric," 5. Na'puti builds from Goeman, "(Re)Mapping Indigenous Presence."

78. Newman and Hudson, *Picking Up the Pieces*, 7.

79. The CMHR and Newman signed an agreement of "collaborative stewardship" in 2019, three years after my tour recounted here. Rather than center how the agreement shifts a critical interpretation of the CMHR as a whole (which can be determined only through time and public engagement), this anal-

ysis remains important in narrating a moment within the museum's relationship to the project.

80. Newman and Hudson, *Picking Up the Pieces,* 7.

81. Baggins, "Witness Blanket."

82. Newman and Hudson, *Picking Up the Pieces,* 29–30, 31.

83. The instantiation of bathrooms divided into binary sex is one of the most powerful illustrations of where gender and sex systems and architecture are coconstitutive. The modern bathroom and desires to segregate along gender lines operate as a technology of racialized hygiene. In this case the bathroom signs preserved by the *Witness Blanket* can be interpreted as alluding to a colonial gender and sex system. For more on the history of the bathroom, see Bendickson, *Culture of Flushing;* Cavanagh, *Queering Bathrooms;* and West, *Transforming Citizenships,* especially the chapter about People in Search of Safe and Accessible Restrooms (PISSAR).

84. Newman and Hudson, *Picking Up the Pieces,* 56–57.

85. Newman and Hudson, 124, 131.

86. Barker, "Introduction," 7.

87. Manson, "Witness Blanket."

88. L. Simpson, *Dancing,* 22–23, 16.

89. L. Simpson, 23.

90. Threlfall, "Indigenous Oral Ceremony."

91. Rebecca Johnson, "Implementing Indigenous Law."

92. Lederman, "Witness Blanket."

93. Rebecca Johnson, "Implementing Indigenous Law."

94. This is based on the annotation of the agreement, made public by Rebecca Johnson's "Implementing Indigenous Law."

95. In their introduction to *Settler City Limits,* Tomiak and colleagues make an analytic distinction between "resistance" and "resurgence." The former "tends to react to and engage the settler state," whereas the latter describes "ways of being that centre on what L. Simpson refers to as the 'Indigenous inside.'" These include practices such as "reconnecting to homelands, cultural practices, and communities." In short, resistance orients toward the state and resurgence is a practice of Indigenous cultural affirmation and ongoing survivance (7–8).

96. Newman, quoted in Threlfall, "Indigenous Oral Ceremony."

CHAPTER 4. AFFECTED PERSONS, SEXUAL TRANSITS,
AND CONTESTED PUBLIC MEMORIES

1. Friends of Minidoka v. Jerome County, No. 38113, 2011 Idaho Supreme Court Records and Briefs 3074 (May 27, 2011). Notably, LCO is the legal term used in Jerome County's Zoning Ordinance, defined as "an animal operation functioning within a defined contiguous area of land that is typically larger than the Animal Confinement Site, but in no event smaller, and where the animal unit to total land ratio is greater than two units per one acre, or seventy-five units per parcel, and where livestock are fed, maintained and confined forth-five days or more within a twelve-month period." "Livestock Confinement Operations."

Another regulatory term in the ordinance, "animal unit" refers to "one thousand pounds of Bovidae (cattle, bison, goats, sheep." Throughout this chapter I use LCO to adhere to the specificity of the case and the ordinance. I also use the language of CAFOs relative to the scholarship on factory farming and because the Environmental Protection Agency defines a CAFO as larger than one thousand animal units.

2. Prior to the initial permitting the board actually denied the permit on the basis of a lack of a nutrition-management plan.

3. Pezzullo and Cox, *Environmental Communication,* 289. Notably, they detail the breadth of standing in environmental controversies, underscoring communicative dimensions in the legal sphere's intersection with environmental justice struggles.

4. Jerome County Bd. of Com'rs, 153 Idaho 298 (2012).

5. See the "Local Land Use Planning" chapter of Jerome County's zoning ordinance procedure. When I need to refer to the legal meaning of *affected persons,* I italicize the concept; otherwise, its nonitalicized use marks how the concept also is defined by a broader struggle over meaning. With thanks to my colleagues at the University of Iowa's College of Law, especially Jason Rantanen.

6. *Jerome County Bd. of Com'rs,* 153 Idaho 298.

7. Indeed, if delimited to a strict instrumental meaning, *affected persons* operates as a term of art in administrative law, in addition to its specific property and residential meaning in the context of Idaho land use law. However, in rupturing the term's instrumental meaning, I am guided by well-established scholarship in cultural studies that approaches the law as a rhetorical technique of governance, wherein the meaning of rhetoric is the biopolitical modulation of life and capacity. See J. White, "Law as Rhetoric"; Coombe, "Contingent Articulations"; West, *Transforming Citizenships;* and Vats, *Color of Creatorship.*

8. Rosenberg, *4-H Harvest,* 11.

9. Lowe, *Immigrant Acts,* 8–10.

10. C. Johnson, *Just Queer Folks,* 30.

11. As environmental justice advocates and scholars have long argued, procedural inequity is a prominent practice of environmental racism. See Bullard, "Environmental Justice," 156.

12. The scope of this chapter prevents me from fully detailing the different types of extractive relationships (such as mining) and the strategic development of the land into the public domain through federal land acts. For a more in-depth account of this history to the particular context of Japanese American detention at Minidoka, see Hayashi, *Haunted by Waters,* 7.

13. Pezzullo and Cox, *Environmental Communication,* 65.

14. This linkage between whiteness and property, initially formulated by Cheryl Harris, extends to settler modernity, its normative relational forms, and racialization of intimacy. "Whiteness as Property." See also Eng, *Feeling of Kinship,* 5–6; and Vats, *Color of Creatorship.* For an extension on the relational and geographic forms of racialized kinship, see Kaplan, "Manifest Domesticity"; and Lowe, *Intimacies of Four Continents.*

15. Byrd, *Transit of Empire,* 185; Drinnon, *Keeper of Concentration Camps.*

16. See Byrd, *Transit of Empire;* Day, *Alien Capital.*

17. Byrd, *Transit of Empire*, 187.

18. See, among others, Murray, *Historical Memories;* Takezawa, *Breaking the Silence;* McKay, "Gender Justice and Reconciliation"; Creef, *Imaging Japanese America;* and Ono, "Re/Membering Spectators."

19. Chiang, *Nature behind Barbed Wire.*

20. In *Haunted by Waters* Hayashi documents two examples in which Japanese Americans were confined in places typically used to house animals. First, one assembly center in Portland was on the grounds of the North Portland International Livestock Exposition (75). Second, during incarceration Japanese American laborers in Burley were housed in stables (89).

21. Nishime and Williams, "Why Racial Ecologies?," 4.

22. Conquergood, "Performance Studies," 145.

23. The issuance of Executive Order 9066 is often cited as the legal institution of the exclusion of Japanese Americans (nisei) and first-generation Japanese migrants not eligible for citizenship (issei). Panelists at the Civil Liberties Symposium reframed the centralization of this institutional moment, also characterized by some participants in the pilgrimage as "white history, not Japanese American history." Order 9066 authorized the forced relocation of persons of Japanese descent living within the borders of the United States. Although the broader discourse and literature characterizes the camps as "internment camps" or "relocation centers," here I use the words "incarceration centers." The pilgrimage I attended highlighted the politics of naming the environments in which nisei lived during World War II and elected to use "incarceration" or "concentration" as descriptions of the camps. See Japanese American Citizens League, *Power of Words.* The pamphlet was distributed during the pilgrimage cites; see Okamura, "American Concentration Camps."

24. By *nikkei* I mean an encompassing term of Japanese migrants spanning generations. Generations present herein include *issei* (first-generation Japanese migrants), *nisei* (second generation born in the United States), *sansei* (third generation, or grandchildren of issei), and *yonsei* (fourth generation, born to *sansei*).

25. Pezzullo, *Toxic Tourism,* 9; Gordon, Pezzullo, and Gabrieloff-Parish, "Food Justice Advocacy Tours."

26. "What We Do."

27. This definition is grounded in Lowe, *Immigrant Acts,* 27–28: "In the history of the United States, capital has maximized its profits not through rendering labor 'abstract' but precisely through the social production of 'difference,' of restrictive particularity and illegitimacy marked by race, nation, geographical origins, and gender." See also Roediger and Esch, *Production of Difference.*

28. Nakanishi, "Surviving Democracy's 'Mistake,'" 55.

29. D. Taylor, *Archive and the Repertoire,* 19.

30. Lowe, *Immigrant Acts,* 10–20.

31. Bhandar, *Colonial Lives of Property,* 25.

32. Lowe, *Immigrant Acts,* 10–11.

33. See Lowe; Eng, *Feelings of Kinship;* Ngai, *Impossible Subjects;* Chuh, *Imagine Otherwise;* Pascoe, *What Comes Naturally.*

34. Ngai, *Impossible Subjects,* 175.

35. Chuh, *Imagine Otherwise*, 63.

36. Shah, "Oriental Depravity," 704. See also Shah, *Stranger Intimacy.*

37. Shah, "Oriental Depravity," 704. See also Shah, *Contagious Divides.*

38. Rankin, quoted in Howard, *Concentration Camps*, 62, 63.

39. DeWitt, quoted in Ngai, *Impossible Subjects*, 176.

40. Clark, quoted in Hayashi, *Haunted by Waters*, 76.

41. Ngai, *Impossible Subjects*, 177. See also Eng, *Feelings of Kinship*, 182.

42. Hayashi, *Haunted by Waters*, 82.

43. Byrd, *Transit of Empire*, 187.

44. Chiang, *Nature behind Barbed Wire*, 40.

45. Meger, *Minidoka Internment National Monument*, 34–35.

46. In 1863 the federal government signed a treaty that would create Fort Hall Reservation. On the ongoing consequences of allotment, see Ruppel, *Unearthing Indian Land.*

47. Meger, *Minidoka Internment National Monument*, 11; Hayashi, *Haunted by Waters*, 18–19.

48. Chiang, *Nature behind Barbed Wire*, 47.

49. Lowe, *Immigrant Acts*, 8.

50. Koshy, *Sexual Naturalization*, 13.

51. On racial malleability, see Lee, *Exquisite Corpse.*

52. Hsu, "Naturalist Smellscapes," 790; see also Chen, *Animacies;* and Dillon and Sze, "Police Power."

53. Hayashi, *Haunted by Waters*, 81.

54. This observation was made during the final day of the pilgrimage by one of the board members. The regional proximity of the camp attributed to the family feel. Other pilgrimages, such as Manzanar, feature participatory archaeological digs.

55. Takemoto, "Looking for Jiro Onuma," 245.

56. Lowe, *Immigrant Acts*, 6–7.

57. On these tensions in the construction of photography, see Azoulay, *Civil Imagination.*

58. Parrika, *Geology of Media*, 84.

59. Ujiiye, "Potential Buyout."

60. Hsu, "Naturalist Smellscapes," 790.

61. The health effects of CAFOs have been well documented; see Pezzullo and Hunt, "Agribusiness Futurism," 404.

62. Gordon and Hunt, "Reform, Justice, and Sovereignty," 9.

63. See Cronon, *Nature's Metropolis*, especially 220–24.

64. Dimond, quoted in Weaver, "Cow Country."

65. Weaver, "Cow Country."

66. Hoke, quoted in Steubner, "Raising a Stink." Notably, one of the limits of the newspaper archive I use is a lack of mention of these dairy owners' and residents' race or ethnicity as a broader discussion of race and agriculture. I have tried to mark these when possible.

67. See Marx, *Machine in the Garden.*

68. Blanchette, *Porkopolis*, 19.

69. Murphy, "Distributed Reproduction."

70. Rosenberg, "How Meat Changed Sex," 485.

71. Rosenberg, *4-H Harvest,* 14; See also C. Johnson, *Just Queer Folks.* Practices of animal sexual governance hinge on what Rosenberg calls the agricultural exemption for bestiality, a category of human-animal intimacy that signals premodern sexualities. Rosenberg, "How Meat Changed Sex," 475.

72. Orland, "Turbo-Cows," 168.

73. Lowe, *Immigrant Acts,* 21.

74. See S. Taylor, *Beasts of Burden,* on the biopolitics of CAFO systems and their implication for disability and environmental justice.

75. To Blanchette's credit, he argues in *Porkopolis* that food assembly often builds from previous existing labor infrastructures (see, for example, his discussion on page 27 regarding Henry Ford's claim that the car assembly line mimicked the meat-packing disassembly line). But military or military aesthetics are largely absent from his discussion of standardization and industrial aesthetics on page 105.

CHAPTER 5. PETROCULTURE AND INTIMATE ATMOSPHERES

1. Aizura, *Mobile Subjects.*

2. This is the task of a new mobilities paradigm; Sheller describes the paradigm that "delineates the context in which both sedentary and nomadic accounts of the social world operate, and it questions how that context is itself mobilized, or performed, through ongoing socio-technical and cultural practices." "New Mobilities Paradigm," 6.

3. I am drawing on key works from the energy humanities, specifically, Wilson, Carlson, and Szeman, *Petrocultures;* Szeman and Boyer, *Energy Humanities;* and Wenzel, "Read for Oil."

4. Weston, "Big City," 253.

5. Weston's work prompted closer engagement with nonmetropolitan spaces to denaturalize this imaginary on one hand and to recover nonmetropolitan LGBTQ experiences on the other. One of the moves inspired by Weston's work was the conceptualization of "metronormativity," this time through conflations of "urban" and "visible," contextualized by the wake of the hate crimes of the 1990s. See Halberstam, *Queer Time and Place,* 36–37. The point I'm emphasizing in my reworking of Weston is an understanding of the fundamental indeterminacy of the rural-urban migration story, consistently shifting at different moments. We should trace *more* narratives about queer migrations rather than rely on a single structuring device, given the ongoing shifts structuring spaces of all kinds: rural, urban, and suburban. I think Tongson's *Relocations* is particularly thoughtful in this regard, in ways that consider living infrastructure (although Tongson does not use that word) in the generation of environmental and infrastructural intimacies in Southern California (7–10).

6. Towns, "Geographies of Pain."

7. Szeman, "Conjunctures."

8. See also K. Chávez, *Queer Migration Politics;* Flores, *Deportable and Disposable.*

9. LeMenager, *Living Oil,* 17, 104.

10. "Wyoming State Profile."

11. "Colorado State Profile."

12. Russo, "Time Gets Strange," 110.

13. Williams, *Politics and Letters*, 168.

14. Engle and Wong, "Introduction," 6.

15. This chapter draws from ten narrative interviews with self-identified lesbian, gay, bisexual, trans, and queer (LGBTQ) persons who resided in the Rocky Mountain West region between 1990 and 2018. Rather than share their anecdotes in the spirit of revealing truths of a so-called authentic representation of what life is like for Rocky Mountain queers and trans folks, I'm interested in how we might understand these as constructed narratives of a relational self.

16. LeMenager, *Living Oil*.

17. For a conceptualization and illustration of "environmental privilege," see Park and Pellow, *Slums of Aspen*; Pezzullo, *Toxic Tourism*; De Onís, *Energy Islands*; Gordon and Hunt, "Reform, Justice, and Sovereignty."

18. Ahuja, "Intimate Atmospheres," 367.

19. Relative to LGBTQ life, many outside of Laramie understandably associate the town with the murder of Matthew Shepard. This association is a consequence of ritual remembrance and the positioning of Shepard's biography and social identity within national debates about bias crimes. When I initially imagined this project, the national obsession with his death was something of a root of this project, in part because I was a student activist on the University of Wyoming campus between 2001 and 2006. In 1999, a year after his murder, I participated in a high school summer institute hosted by the Honors College, and one of the educational experiences included interviewing people in Laramie. As a then high school sophomore, here is where I first met LGBTQ campus leadership. My lack of engagement with Shepard's memory here is intentional given the scope of the chapter and because his memory often overdetermines textures of queer life in Wyoming and the West. Saying this is not mutually exclusive with saying that Laramie (and Wyoming more broadly) are structured through the same settler hetero whiteness as the rest of the United States. The purpose of queer geography is to understand how queerness and queer culture are situational—meaning that its articulation in a given place will be (in some ways) place dependent. See Cram, "(Dis)Locating Queer Citizenship."

20. Clare, *Brilliant Imperfection*, xv.

21. Nixon, *Slow Violence*, 2.

22. Ahuja, "Intimate Atmospheres," 367.

23. Massey, *For Space*, 124.

24. Ahmed, "Not in the Mood."

25. Stewart, "Atmospheric Attunements," 445–46.

26. Ahuja, "Intimate Atmospheres," 370

27. Daggett, "Petro-masculinity."

28. On oil as a destructive attachment, see LeMenager, *Living Oil*, 11.

29. Drawing from Buell, "Short History."

30. Sze, *Environmental Justice*, 100, 101.

31. Robert, interview with the author, October 18, 2012. All later quotes come from the same interview.

32. Lockwood, *Behind the Carbon Curtain.*

33. Shana, interview with the author, October 17, 2012. All later quotes come from the same interview.

34. Garland-Thomson, "Misfits," 594.

35. Ryan, interview with the author, September 26, 2018. All later quotes come from the same interview.

36. Fort Francis E. Warren Target and Maneuver Reservation (Pole Mountain), Historic Map Collection. The military decommissioned this area in 1954.

37. C. Johnson, *Just Queer Folks,* 129–57.

38. Karuka, *Empire's Tracks.*

39. Urry, "'System' of Automobility"; Urry, "Inhabiting the Car"; Szeman, "Literature and Energy Futures."

40. Halberstam, *Queer Time and Place,* 1.

41. Dooley, "Making the Outdoors."

42. Schweighofer, "Rethinking the Closet," 236.

43. Morgensen, *Spaces between Us,* 127, 133.

44. Schweighofer, "Land of One's Own"; Luis, *Herlands;* Morgensen, *Spaces between Us,* 132.

45. "Queer Nature."

46. So Sinopoulos-Lloyd, interview with the author, September 24, 2018. All later quotes come from the same interview.

47. M. Anderson, *Tending the Wild;* Whyte, "Our Ancestor's Dystopia Now."

48. Lorde, *Sister Outsider.*

49. D. Chávez, "Transmasculine Insurgency," 62.

50. Malatino, *Trans Care.*

51. My thanks to Pinar for introducing me to the phrase "raised by a landscape."

CONCLUSION

1. *Oxford English Dictionary,* s.v. "hold," accessed October 20, 2020, https://www-oed-com.proxy.lib.uiowa.edu/view/Entry/87683?rskey=xLQcto&result=1&isAdvanced=false.

2. TallBear, "Making Love and Relations," 146.

3. By "land back" I'm referring to a decentralized call for the "return of Indigenous lands to Indigenous hands." See Longman et al, "Letter."

4. The point I emphasize here comes from the energy humanities generally and particularly from Moore's central argument in *Capitalism* (172): that mapping uneven relations of production and capital in the making of the modern world should take precedence over the reification of specific energy *resources,* particularly for humanities scholars. This argument is especially important in resisting "green capitalism," global struggles over mineral extraction for new capitalist energy regimes.

5. TallBear, "Making Love and Relations," 161.

6. Morgensen, *Spaces between Us,* chap. 4.

7. Pezzullo and de Onís, "Rethinking Rhetorical Field Methods," 108.

8. On a history of the eugenic thought of these early conservationists, see Spence, *Dispossessing the Wilderness;* and Powell, *Vanishing America.* On resistance to these ideas in Black Freedom movements of the twentieth century, see McCammack, *Landscapes of Hope;* and Ruffin, *Black on Earth.*

9. Mair, "Today's Fight."

10. Pezzullo, "Environment," 10–11; Cox, "Nature's 'Crisis Disciplines.'"

11. Seymour, *Strange Natures.*

12. Pezzullo, "Environment," 11; Pezzullo, "Introduction."

13. I was not present; these accounts are re-created in Achs, "UW Community."

14. This once again is inspired by LeMenager's *Living Oil.*

15. Chakrabarty, "Climate of History," 201.

16. In particular, I'm referencing Edwards, "Infrastructure and Modernity."

17. Williams, *Marxism and Literature,* 128, 130, 122.

18. Williams's engagement with infrastructure is perhaps more evident in his novels, especially *Border Country.*

19. Williams, *Country and the City,* 165–81.

20. Madison, *Critical Ethnography,* 8.

21. Pezzullo, "There Is No Planet B"; De Onís, *Energy Islands.*

22. Simpson, quoted in TallBear, *Native American DNA,* 9.

23. Ross et al., *Indigenous Peoples.*

24. Empire was a community situated on the border of Wyoming and Nebraska, composed of Black refugees from North Carolina who migrated west after the Civil War. Empire remained small, and the town had largely disappeared by the 1930s because of ongoing white supremacist violence. See North, "Museum Exhibit."

25. Cited in Pezzullo and Sandler, "Conclusion," 310–12.

26. On systems of sexual regulation, see Rubin, *Deviations,* 137–81. For a spatial approach to these questions in terms of policing and gentrification, see Hanhardt, *Safe Space.*

27. Whyte, "Our Ancestors' Dystopia Now," 207, 210.

28. For the phrase "blue is the color of longing," I'm borrowing from Solnit, *Field Guide.*

Bibliography

ARCHIVAL AND MANUSCRIPT SOURCES

Hebard, Grace Raymond. Papers. 1829–1947. American Heritage Center. University of Wyoming, Laramie.

Historic Map Collection. American Heritage Center. University of Wyoming, Laramie.

Kellogg, John Harvey. Papers. 1832–1965. Bentley Historical Library, University of Michigan, Ann Arbor.

Sanitarium Collection. Carnegie Library for Local History, Boulder, CO.

Wergeland, Agnes Mathilde. Papers. 1882–1916. American Heritage Center. University of Wyoming, Laramie.

Wister, Owen. Papers. 1866–1892. American Heritage Center. University of Wyoming, Laramie.

BOOKS AND ARTICLES

Achs, Jordan. "UW Community, Laramie Residents Recreate Carbon Sink Installation to Protest Climate Change." *Laramie Boomerang*, April 16, 2019.

Ahmed, Sara. "Not in the Mood." *New Formations: A Journal of Culture/Theory/Politics* 82 (2014): 13–28.

Ahuja, Neel. "Intimate Atmospheres: Queer Theory in an Age of Extinctions." *GLQ* 21 (2015): 365–85.

Aizura, Aren Z. *Mobile Subjects: Transnational Imaginaries of Gender Reassignment*. Durham: Duke University Press, 2018.

Alaimo, Stacy. *Bodily Natures: Science, Environment, and the Material Self*. Bloomington: Indiana University Press, 2010.

Alvarez, Natalie. *Immersions in Cultural Difference: Tourism, War, Performance*. Ann Arbor: University of Michigan Press, 2018.

Anderson, Chris. *"Métis": Race, Recognition, and the Struggle for Indigenous Peoplehood*. Vancouver: University of British Columbia Press, 2014.

Anderson, M. Kat. *Tending the Wild: Native American Knowledge and the Management of California's Natural Resources*. Berkeley: University of California Press, 2005.

Annable, Kristin. "Protesters Heard throughout Museum's Opening." *Winnipeg Sun*, September 19, 2014.

Appel, Hannah, Nikhil Anand, and Akhil Gupta. "Temporality, Politics, and the Promise of Infrastructure." In *The Promise of Infrastructure*, edited by Nikhil Anand, Akhil Gupta, and Hannah Appel, 1–38. Durham: Duke University Press, 2018.

Appelbaum, Ralph. "Designing an 'Architecture of Information': The United States Holocaust Memorial Museum." *Curator: The Museum Journal* 38 (1992): 87–94.

"Archeology Report Criticizes Human Rights Museum." *CBC News*, December 19, 2011.

Arvin, Maile. "Analytics of Indigeneity." In Teves, Smith, and Raheja, *Native Studies Keywords*, 119–29.

Arvin, Maile, Eve Tuck, and Angie Morrill. "Decolonizing Feminism: Challenging Connections between Settler Colonialism and Heteropatriarchy." *Feminist Formations* 25 (2013): 8–34.

Azoulay, Ariella. *Civil Imagination: A Political Ontology of Photography*. London: Verso, 2012.

Baggins, Boho. "Witness Blanket by Carey Newman." YouTube video, 1:24:11. May 29, 2015. https://www.youtube.com/watch?v=L8BPPSc2_Uk&t=1809s.

Bagot Commission. *Report on the Affairs of the Indians in Canada*. Indian Residential School. 1845. https://collections.irshdc.ubc.ca/index.php/Detail/objects/9431#:~:text=Under%20a%20commission%20oled%20by,prior%20to%20Confederation%20in%201867.

Ballantyne, Tony, and Antoinette M. Burton, eds. *Moving Subjects: Gender, Mobility, and Intimacy in an Age of Global Empire*. Urbana: University of Illinois Press, 2009.

Barker, Joanne. "Introduction: Critically Sovereign." In *Critically Sovereign: Indigenous Gender, Sexuality, and Feminist Studies*, edited by Joanne Barker, 1–44. Durham: Duke University Press, 2017.

Bauer, Heike. *The Hirschfeld Archives: Violence, Death, and Modern Queer Culture*. Philadelphia: Temple University Press, 2017.

Baynton, Douglas C. *Defectives in the Land: Disability and Immigration in the Age of Eugenics*. Chicago: University of Chicago Press, 2016.

Beard, George Miller. *American Nervousness: Its Causes and Consequences*. New York: Putnam's Sons, 1881.

Beard, George Miller, and Alphonso David Rockwell. *Sexual Neurasthenia: Its Hygiene, Causes, Symptoms, and Treatment*. New York: Treat, 1884.

Bederman, Gail. *Manliness and Civilization: A Cultural History of Gender and*

Race in the United States, 1880–1917. Chicago: University of Chicago Press, 1995.

Bendickson, Jamie. *The Culture of Flushing: The Social and Legal History of Sewage.* Vancouver: University of British Columbia Press, 2007.

Bennett, Jeffrey A. *Managing Diabetes: The Cultural Politics of Disease.* New York: New York University Press, 2019.

Bennett, Tony. *The Birth of the Museum: History, Theory, Politics.* London: Routledge, 1995.

Berlant, Lauren. *The Queen of America Goes to Washington City.* Durham: Duke University Press, 1997.

Bernstein, Robin. *Racial Innocence: Performing American Childhood from Slavery to Civil Rights.* New York: New York University Press, 2011.

Bhandar, Brenna. *Colonial Lives of Property: Law, Land, and Racial Regimes of Ownership.* Durham: Duke University Press, 2018.

Blackhawk, Ned. *Violence over the Land: Indians and Empires in the Early American West.* Cambridge, MA: Harvard University Press, 2006.

Blanchette, Alex. *Porkopolis: American Animality, Standardized Life, and the Factory Farm.* Durham: Duke University Press, 2020.

Boag, Peter. *Re-dressing America's Frontier Past.* Berkeley: University of California Press, 2011.

Bold, Christine. *The Frontier Club: Popular Westerns and Cultural Power, 1880–1924.* Oxford: Oxford University Press, 2013.

Bolotin, Norman, and Christine Laing. *The Chicago World's Fair of 1893: The World's Columbian Exposition.* Washington, DC: Preservation, 1992.

Bowker, Geoffrey C., and Susan Leigh Starr. *Sorting Things Out: Classification and Its Consequences.* Cambridge, MA: MIT Press, 1999.

Bozikovic, Alex. "Canadian Museum for Human Rights: An Anticipated Work of Architecture, but Not One of Our Best." *Globe and Mail,* September 26, 2014.

"Brief History: Boulder, Colorado Sanitarium." Boulder Library. Accessed October 11, 2021. https://boulderlibrary.org/cpdfs/328-145-18.pdf.

Brooks, Lisa, and Cassandra Brooks. "The Reciprocity Principle and Traditional Ecological Knowledge: Understanding the Significance of Indigenous Protest on the Presumpscot River." *International Journal of Critical Indigenous Studies* 3 (2010):11–28.

Brown, Nicholas. "Experiments in Regional Settler Colonization: Pursuing Justice and Producing Scale through the Montana Study." In Dorries et al., *Settler City Limits,* 118–50.

Buell, Frederick. "A Short History of Oil Cultures, or The Marriage of Catastrophe and Exuberance." *Journal of American Studies* 46 (2012): 273–93.

Bullard, Robert D. *Dumping in Dixie: Race, Class, and Environmental Quality.* New York: Routledge, 1990.

———. "Environmental Justice in the 21st Century: Race Still Matters." *Phylon* 49 (2001): 151–71.

Burnham, Daniel H. *The Final Official Report of the Director of Works of the World's Columbian Exposition.* Vol. 1. New York: Garland, 1989.

Burnham, Daniel H., and Francis D. Millet. *The World's Columbian Exposition: The Book of the Builders.* Chicago: Columbian Memorial, 1894.

Burton, Antoinette, ed. *Archive Stories: Facts, Fictions, and the Writing of History.* Durham: Duke University Press, 2005.

———. "Thinking beyond the Boundaries: Empire, Feminism and the Domains of History." *Social History* 26 (2001): 60–71.

Busby, Karen, Adam Muller, and Andrew Woolford. "The Idea of a Human Rights Museum." In *The Idea of a Human Rights Museum,* edited by Karen Busby, Adam Muller, and Andrew Woolford. Manitoba: University of Manitoba Press, 2015.

Butler, Judith. "Merely Cultural." *New Left Review* 1, no. 227 (January–February 1998): 33–44. https://newleftreview.org/issues/i227/articles/judith-butler-merely-cultural.

Byrd, Jodi. *The Transit of Empire: Indigenous Critiques of Colonialism.* Minneapolis: University of Minnesota Press, 2011.

———. "'Variations under Domestication': Indigeneity and the Subject of Dispossession." *Social Text* 36 (2018): 129–30.

Carpenter, Ronald H. "Frederick Jackson Turner and the Rhetorical Impact of the Frontier Thesis." *Quarterly Journal of Speech* 63 (1977): 117–29.

Carr, Geoffrey. "*Atopoi* of the Modern: Revisiting the Place of the Indian Residential School." *ESC: English Studies in Canada* 35 (2009): 109–35.

Carter, Julian B. *The Heart of Whiteness: Normal Sexuality and Race in America, 1880–1940.* Durham: Duke University Press, 2007.

Cavanagh, Sheila L. *Queering Bathrooms: Gender, Sexuality, and the Hygiene Imagination.* Toronto: University of Toronto Press, 2010.

Chaddock, Charles Gilbert. "Translator's Preface." In *Psychopathia Sexualis: With Especial Reference to Contrary Sexual Instinct,* edited by Richard von Krafft-Ebing, vii–ix. Translated by Charles Gilbert Chaddock. Philadelphia: Davis, 1893.

Chakrabarty, Dipesh. "The Climate of History: Four Theses." *Critical Inquiry* 35 (2009): 197–222.

Chávez, Daniel Coleman. "Transmasculine Insurgency: Masculinity and Dissidence in Feminist Movements in México." *Trans Studies Quarterly* 3, nos. 1–2 (2016): 58–64.

Chávez, Karma R. *The Borders of AIDS: Race, Quarantine and Resistance.* Seattle: University of Washington Press, 2021.

———. *Queer Migration Politics: Activist Rhetoric and Coalitional Possibilities.* Urbana: University of Illinois Press, 2013.

Chen, Mel Y. *Animacies: Biopolitics, Racial Mattering, and Queer Affect.* Durham: Duke University Press, 2012.

Chiang, Connie Y. *Nature behind Barbed Wire: An Environmental History of the Japanese American Incarceration.* Oxford: Oxford University Press, 2018.

Chuh, Kandice. *Imagine Otherwise: On Asian Americanist Critique.* Durham: Duke University Press, 2003.

Clare, Eli. *Brilliant Imperfection: Grappling with Cure.* Durham: Duke University Press, 2017.

Clifford, Geraldine Jonçich, ed. *Lone Voyagers: Academic Women in Coeducational Universities, 1870–1937.* New York: Feminist Press at the City University of New York, 1989.

"Colorado State Profile and Energy Estimates." U.S. Energy Information Administration. Accessed July 3, 2021. https://www.eia.gov/state/?sid=CO.

Connerton, Paul. *How Societies Remember.* Cambridge: Cambridge University Press, 1989.

Conquergood, Dwight. "Ethnography, Rhetoric, Performance." *Quarterly Journal of Speech* 78, no. 1 (1992): 80–97.

———. "Performance Studies: Interventions and Radical Research." *Drama Review* 46, no. 2 (2002): 145–56.

———. "Rethinking Ethnography: Towards a Critical Cultural Politics." *Communication Monographs* 58 (1991): 179–94.

Coombe, Rosemary. "Contingent Articulations: A Critical Cultural Studies of Law." In *Law in the Domains of Culture,* edited by Austin Sarat and Thomas Kearns, 21–64. Ann Arbor: University of Michigan Press, 1998.

Coulthard, Glen Sean. *Red Skins, White Masks: Rejecting the Colonial Politics of Recognition.* Minneapolis: University of Minnesota Press, 2014.

Coviello, Peter. *Tomorrow's Parties: Sex and the Untimely in Nineteenth-Century America.* New York: New York University Press, 2013.

Cox, J. Robert. "Nature's 'Crises Disciplines': Does Environmental Communication Have an Ethical Duty." *Environmental Communication* 1 (2007): 5–20.

Cram, E. "'Angie Was Our Sister': Witnessing the Trans-formation of Disgust in the Citizenry of Photography." *Quarterly Journal of Speech* 98 (2012): 411–38.

———. "Archival Ambiance and Sensory Memory: Generating Queer Intimacies in the Settler Colonial Archive." *Communication and Critical/Cultural Studies* 13 (2016): 109–29.

———. "(Dis)Locating Queer Citizenship: Imaging Rurality in Matthew Shepard's Memory." In Gray, Johnson, and Gilley, *Queering the Countryside,* 267–89.

Cram, E, Melanie Loehwing, and John Louis Lucaites. "Civic Sights: Theorizing Deliberative and Photographic Publicity in the Visual Public Sphere." *Philosophy and Rhetoric* 49 (2016): 227–53.

Creef, Elena Tajima. *Imaging Japanese America: The Visual Construction of Citizenship, Nation, and the Body.* New York: New York University Press, 2004.

Cronon, William. *Nature's Metropolis: Chicago and the Great West.* New York: Norton, 1991.

Daggett, Cara. *The Birth of Energy: Fossil Fuels, Thermodynamics, and the Politics of Work.* Durham: Duke University Press, 2019.

———. "Petro-masculinity: Fossil Fuels and Authoritarian Desire." *Millennium: Journal of International Studies* 47 (2018): 25–44.

Davin, Nicholas Flood. *Report on Industrial Schools for Indians and Half-Breeds.* Indian Residential School. 1879. https://collections.irshdc.ubc.ca/index.php/Detail/objects/9427.

Day, Iyko. *Alien Capital: Asian Racialization and the Logic of Settler Colonial Capitalism.* Durham: Duke University Press, 2016

Deloria, Philip J. *Playing Indian.* New Haven: Yale University Press, 1998.

Deloria, Vine, Jr. *Custer Died for Your Sins.* Norman: University of Oklahoma Press, 1988.

De Onís, Catalina. *Energy Islands: Metaphors of Power, Extractivism, and Justice in Puerto Rico.* Berkeley: University of California Press, 2021.

DeVun, Leah, and Michael Jay McClure. "Archives Behaving Badly." *Radical History Review* 120 (2014): 121–30.

Dewar, Jonathan. "From Profound Silences to Ethical Practices: Aboriginal Writing and Reconciliation." In *The Oxford Handbook of Canadian Literature,* edited by Cynthia Sugars, 150–69. Oxford: Oxford University Press, 2016.

De Wit, Wim. "Building an Illusion: The Design of the World's Columbian Exposition." In *Grand Illusions: Chicago World's Fair of 1893,* edited by Neil Harris, Wim de Wit, James Gilbert, and Robert W. Rydell, 41–98. Chicago: Chicago Historical Society, 1993.

Dhamoon, Rita Kaur. "Re-presenting Genocide: The Canadian Museum of Human Rights and Settler Colonial Power." *Journal of Race, Ethnicity, and Politics* 1 (2016): 5–30.

Dickinson, Greg, Carole Blair, and Brian L. Ott, eds. *Places of Public Memory: The Rhetoric of Museums and Memorials.* Tuscaloosa: University of Alabama Press, 2010.

Dickenson, Greg, Brian L. Ott, and Eric Aoki. "Spaces of Remembering and Forgetting: The Reverent Eye/I at the Plains Indian Museum." *Communication and Critical/Cultural Studies* 3 (2006): 27–47.

Dillon, Lindsey, and Julie Sze. "Police Power and Particulate Matters: Environmental Justice and the Spatialities of In/Securities in US Cities." *English Language Notes* 1, no. 54 (2016): 13–23.

Dooley, Kate. "Making the Outdoors LGBTQ Friendly with Boulder's Queer Nature." *OutFront Magazine,* January 16, 2019.

Dorries, Heather. "'Welcome to Winnipeg': Making Settler Colonial Urban Space in 'Canada's Most Racist City.'" In Dorries et al., *Settler City Limits,* 25–43.

Dorries, Heather, Robert Henry, David Hugill, Tyler McCreary, and Julie Tomiak, eds. *Settler City Limits: Indigenous Resurgence and Colonial Violence in the Urban Prairie West.* East Lansing: Michigan State University Press, 2019.

Douglass, Frederick. Preface to *The Reason Why the Colored American Is Not in the World's Columbian Exposition.* Chicago: Wells, 1893.

Draper, Joan E. "The White City and Its Interpreters: Historians, Critics, and the Chicago World's Columbian Exposition of 1893." In Burnham, *Final Official Report.*

Drinnon, Richard. *Keeper of Concentration Camps: Dillon S. Myer and American Racism.* Berkeley: University of California Press, 1987.

Driskill, Qwo-Li, Chris Finley, Brian Joseph Gilley, and Scott Lauria Morgensen, eds. *Queer Indigenous Studies: Critical Interventions in Theory, Politics, and Literature.* Tucson: University of Arizona Press, 2011.

Duggan, Lisa. *Sapphic Slashers: Sex, Violence, and American Modernity.* Durham: Duke University Press, 2000.

Dunn, Thomas R. *Queerly Remembered: Rhetorics for Representing the GLBTQ Past.* Columbia: University of South Carolina Press, 2016.

Dye, Eva Emery. *The Conquest: The True Story of Lewis and Clark.* New York: Grossett and Dunlap, 1922.

Edelman, Lee. *No Future: Queer Theory and the Death Drive.* Durham: Duke University Press, 2004.

Edwards, Elizabeth, and Janice Hart. "Introduction: Photographs as Objects." In *Photographs, Objects, Histories: On the Materiality of Images,* edited by Elizabeth Edwards and Janice Hart, 1–15. London: Routledge, 2004.

Edwards, Paul N. "Infrastructure and Modernity: Force, Time, and Social Organization in the History of Sociotechnical Systems." In *Modernity and Technology,* edited by Thomas J. Misa, Philip Brey, and Andrew Feenberg, 185–225. Cambridge, MA: MIT Press, 2003.

Endres, Danielle. "From Wasteland to Waste Site: The Role of Discourse in Nuclear Power's Environmental Injustices." *Local Environment* 14 (2009): 917–37.

———. "The Rhetoric of Nuclear Colonialism: Rhetorical Exclusion of American Indian Arguments in the Yucca Mountain Nuclear Waste Siting Decision." *Communication and Critical/Cultural Studies* 6 (2009): 39–60.

Endres, Danielle E., Brian Cozen, Joshua Trey Barnett, Megan O'Byrne, and Tarla Rai Peterson. "Communicating Energy in a Climate (of) Crisis." In *Communication Yearbook 40,* edited by Elisia L. Cohen, 419–47. New York: Routledge, 2016.

Eng, David. *The Feeling of Kinship: Queer Liberalism and the Racialization of Intimacy.* Durham: Duke University Press, 2010.

Engels, Frederick. *The Origin of the Family, Private Property, and the State.* Translated by Ernest Untermann. Chicago: Kerr, 1909.

Engle, Karen, and Yoke-Sum Wong, eds. *Feelings of Structure: Explorations of Affect.* Montreal: McGill Queen's University Press, 2018.

———. "Introduction: Thinking Feeling." In Engle and Wong, *Feelings of Structure,* 3–11.

Ferguson, Roderick A. *Aberrations in Black: Toward a Queer of Color Critique.* Minneapolis: University of Minnesota, 2004.

Finley, Chris. "Violence, Genocide, and Captivity: Exploring Cultural Representations of Sacajawea as Universal Mother of Conquest." *American Indian Culture and Research Journal* 35, no. 4 (2011): 191–208.

Finnegan, Cara A. "What Is This a Picture Of? Some Thoughts on Images and Archives." *Rhetoric and Public Affairs* 9 (2006): 116–23.

Fixmer-Oraiz, Natalie. *Homeland Maternity: US Security Culture and the New Reproductive Regime.* Urbana: University of Illinois Press, 2019.

Fleissner, Jennifer. *Women, Compulsion, Modernity: The Moment of American Naturalism.* Chicago: University of Chicago Press, 2004.

Flores, Lisa A. *Deportable and Disposable: Public Rhetoric and the Making of the "Illegal" Immigrant.* University Park: Pennsylvania State University Press, 2021.

Foucault, Michel. *The History of Sexuality.* Vol. 1. New York: Vintage Books, 1990.

Freud, Sigmund. "An Autobiographical Study." In *The Freud Reader,* edited by Peter Gay, 3–44. New York: Norton, 1989.

Garland-Thomson, Rosemarie, ed. *Freakery: Cultural Spectacles of the Extraordinary Body.* New York: New York University Press, 1996

———. "Misfits: A Feminist Materialist Disability Concept." *Hypatia: A Journal of Feminist Philosophy* 26 (2011): 591–609.

Gilfoyle, Timothy J. *City of Eros: New York City, Prostitution, and the Commercialization of Sex, 1790–1920.* New York: Norton, 1992.

Gilman, Charlotte Perkins. *The Yellow Wallpaper.* London: Virago, 1981.

Gilmore, Ruth Wilson. *Golden Gulag: Prisons, Surplus, Crisis, and Opposition in Globalizing California.* Berkeley: University of California Press, 2007.

Goeman, Mishuana. "Land as Life: Unsettling the Logics of Containment." In Teves, Smith, and Raheja, *Native Studies Keywords,* 71–89.

———. *Mark My Words: Native Women Mapping Our Nations.* Minneapolis: University of Minnesota Press, 2013.

———. "(Re)Mapping Indigenous Presence on the Land in Native Women's Literature." *American Quarterly* 60 (2008): 295–302.

Goldstein, Alyosha. "Toward a Genealogy of the U.S. Colonial Present." In *Formations of United States Colonialism,* edited by Alyosha Goldstein, 1–30. Durham: Duke University Press, 2014.

Gordon, Constance, and Kathleen P. Hunt. "Reform, Justice, and Sovereignty: A Food Systems Agenda for Environmental Communication." *Environmental Communication* 13, no. 1 (2019): 9–22.

Gordon, Constance, Phaedra C. Pezzullo, and Michelle Gabrieloff-Parish. "Food Justice Advocacy Tours: Remapping Rooted, Regenerative Relationships through Denver's 'Planting Just Seeds.'" In *The Rhetoric of Social Movements: Networks, Power, and New Media,* edited by Nathan Crick, 299–316. New York: Routledge, 2020.

Gough, Paul. "Peacekeeping, Peace, Memory: Reflections on the Peacekeeping Monument in Ottawa." *Canadian Military History* 11 (2002): 65–74.

Gray, Mary L. *Out in the Country: Youth, Media, and Queer Visibility in Rural America.* New York: New York University Press, 2009.

Gray, Mary L., Colin R. Johnson, and Brian J. Gilley, eds. *Queering the Countryside: New Frontiers in Queer Studies.* New York: New York University Press, 2016.

Green, Rayna. "The Pocahontas Perplex: The Image of Indian Women in American Culture." *Massachusetts Review* 16 (1975): 698–714.

Greene, Ronald Walter. "Another Materialist Rhetoric." *Critical Studies in Mass Communication* 15 (1998): 21–40.

Greene, Ronald Walter, and Kevin Douglas Kuswa. "'From the Arab Spring to Athens, from Occupy Wall Street to Moscow': Regional Accents and the Rhetorical Cartography of Power." *Rhetoric Society Quarterly* 42 (2012): 271–88.

Greyser, Naomi. *On Sympathetic Grounds: Race, Gender, and Affective Geog-*

raphies in Nineteenth-Century North America. Oxford: Oxford University Press, 2018.

Grossberg, Lawrence. "Affect's Future: Rediscovering the Virtual in the Actual." In *The Affect Theory Reader*, edited by Melissa Gregg and Gregory J. Seigworth, 309–38. Durham: Duke University Press, 2010.

Halberstam, Jack. *In a Queer Time and Place: Transgender Bodies, Subcultural Lives*. New York: New York University Press, 2005.

Hall, Rachel. *Wanted: The Outlaw in American Visual Culture*. Charlottesville: University of Virginia Press, 2009.

Hall, Stuart. "Culture, Community, Nation." *Cultural Studies* 7 (1993): 349–63.

———. *The Fateful Triangle: Race, Ethnicity, Nation*. Cambridge, MA: Harvard University Press, 2017.

———. "Whose Heritage? Un-settling 'the Heritage,' Re-imagining the Post-nation." *Third Text* 13 (1999): 3–13.

Handy, Moses P, ed. *The Official Directory of the World's Columbian Exposition*. Chicago: Conkey, 1893.

Hanhardt, Christina. *Safe Space: Gay Neighborhood History and the Politics of Violence*. Durham: Duke University Press, 2013.

Haraway, Donna. "Manifesto for Cyborgs: Science, Technology, and Socialist Feminism in the 1980s." *Socialist Review* 80 (1985): 65–108.

———. *Staying with the Trouble: Making Kin in the Chthulucene*. Durham: Duke University Press, 2016.

Hariman, Robert, and John Louis Lucaites. *The Public Image: Photography and Civic Spectatorship*. Chicago: University of Chicago Press, 2016.

Harris, Cheryl I. "Whiteness as Property." *Harvard Law Review* 106 (1993): 1707–92.

Harris, Cole. *Making Native Space: Colonialism, Resistance, and Reserves in British Columbia*. Vancouver: University of British Columbia Press, 2003.

Harris, Neil. *Cultural Excursions: Marketing Appetites and Cultural Tastes in Modern America*. Chicago: University of Chicago Press, 1990.

Hartman, Saidiya. "The Belly of the World: A Note on Black Women's Labors." *Souls: A Critical Journal of Black Politics, Culture, and Society* 18 (2016): 166–73.

Hatherly, Dana. "First Nations Launch Human Rights Violation Museum on CMHR Grounds." *Manitoban*, September 23, 2014.

Hayashi, Robert. *Haunted by Waters: A Journey through Race and Place in the American West*. Iowa City: University of Iowa Press, 2007.

Hebard, Grace Raymond. "Pilot of First White Men to Cross the American Continent: Identification of the Indian Girl Who Led the Lewis and Clark Expedition over the Rocky Mountains in the Unparalleled Journey into the Mysteries of the Western World." *Journal of American History*, July–September 1907, 465–84.

———. "Why We Exclude the Ninety-Seven." *Woman Citizen*, June 18, 1921, 14–16.

Heffernan, Michael, and Carol Medlicot. "A Feminine Atlas? Sacajawea, the Suffragettes, and the Commemorative Landscape in the American West,

1904–1910." *Gender, Place, and Culture: A Journal of Feminist Geography* 9, no. 2 (2002): 109–31.

Heise, Ursula K., Jon Christensen, and Michelle Niemann, eds. *The Routledge Companion to the Environmental Humanities.* London: Routledge, 2017.

Henderson, Jennifer, and Pauline Wakeham, eds. *Reconciling Canada: Critical Perspectives on the Culture of Redress.* Toronto: University of Toronto Press, 2013.

Hinsley, Curtis M., and David R. Wilcox. *Coming of Age in Chicago: The 1983 World's Chicago Fair and the Coalescence of Anthropology.* Lincoln: University of Nebraska Press, 2016.

Hirsch, Marianne, and Valerie Smith. "Feminism and Cultural Memory: An Introduction." *Signs* 28 (2002): 1–19.

Honouring the Truth, Reconciling for the Future: Summary of the Final Report of the Truth and Reconciliation Commission of Canada. Winnipeg: Truth and Reconciliation Commission of Canada, 2015.

Howard, John. *Concentration Camps on the Home Front: Japanese Americans in the House of Jim Crow.* Chicago: University of Chicago Press, 2008.

"How Can a Structure Support Human Rights?" Canadian Museum for Human Rights. Accessed October 26, 2020. https://humanrights.ca/about/architecture.

Hsu, Hsuan. "Naturalist Smellscapes and Environmental Justice." *American Literature* 88 (2016): 787–814.

Hubbs, Nadine. *Rednecks, Queers, and Country Music.* Berkeley: University of California Press, 2014.

Hulan, Renée. "A Just Allotment of Memory: Witnessing First Nations Testimony in Isabelle Knockwood's *Out of the Depths.*" *Journal of Canadian Studies* 46, no. 1 (2012): 53–74.

Japanese American Citizens League. *The Power of Words.* Seattle, n.d.

Johnson, Colin R. *Just Queer Folks: Gender and Sexuality in Rural America.* Philadelphia: Temple University Press, 2013.

Johnson, Rebecca. "Implementing Indigenous Law in Agreements: Learning from 'An Agreement concerning the Stewardship of the Witness Blanket." Reconciliation Syllabus. January 31, 2020. https://reconciliationsyllabus.wordpress.com/2020/01/31/implementing-indigenous-law-in-agreements-learning-from-an-agreement-concerning-the-stewardship-of-the-witness-blanket/.

Johnson, Rhiannon. "Ottawa Has Spent $3.2M Fighting St. Anne's Residential School Survivors in Court since 2013." *CBC News,* November 20, 2020.

Kahan, Benjamin. *The Book of Minor Perverts: Sexology, Etiology, and the Emergences of Sexuality.* Chicago: University of Chicago Press, 2019.

Kang, Jiyeon. *Igniting the Internet: Youth and Activism in Postauthoritarianism South Korea.* Honolulu: University of Hawai'i Press, 2016.

Kaplan, Amy. "Manifest Domesticity." *American Literature* 70 (1998): 581–606.

Karuka, Manu. *Empire's Tracks: Indigenous Nations, Chinese Workers, and the Transcontinental Railroad.* Berkeley: University of California Press, 2019.

Kauanui, J. Kēhaulani. *Paradoxes of Hawaiian Sovereignty: Land, Sex, and the Colonial Politics of State Nationalism.* Durham: Duke University Press, 2018.

———. "'A Structure, Not an Event': Settler Colonialism and Enduring Indigeneity." *Lateral* 5 (2016). https://csalateral.org/issue/5-1/forum-alt-humanities-settler-colonialism-enduring-indigeneity-kauanui/.

Kent, Kathryn. *Making Girls into Women: American Women's Writing and the Rise of Lesbian Identity.* Durham: Duke University Press, 2003.

Klein, Naomi. *This Changes Everything: Capitalism vs the Climate.* New York: Simon and Schuster Books, 2014.

Kolodny, Annette. *The Lay of the Land: Metaphor as Experience and History in American Life and Letters.* Chapel Hill: University of North Carolina Press, 1975.

Koshy, Susan. *Sexual Naturalization: Asian Americans and Miscegenation.* Stanford: Stanford University Press, 2005.

LaFleur, Greta. *The Natural History of Sexuality in Early America.* Baltimore: Johns Hopkins Press, 2018.

LaFleur, Greta, and Kyla Schuller. "Introduction: Technologies of Life and Architectures of Death in Early America." *American Quarterly* 71 (2019): 603–24.

Larkin, Brian. "The Politics and Poetics of Infrastructure." *Annual Review of Anthropology* 42, no. 1 (2013): 327–43.

Larson, Erik. *Devil in the White City: Murder, Magic, and Madness at the Fair That Changed America.* New York: Vintage Books, 2003.

Lawrence, Bonita. "Gender, Race, and the Regulation of Native Identity in Canada and the United States: An Overview." *Hypatia* 18 (2003): 3–31.

Lecce, Steven, Neil McArthur, and Arthur Schafer. Introduction to *Fragile Freedoms: The Global Struggle for Human Rights,* edited by Steven Lecce, Neil McArthur, and Arthur Schafer, 1–22. Oxford: Oxford University Press, 2017.

Lederman, Marsha. "The Witness Blanket, an Installation of Residential School Artifacts, Makes Canadian Legal History." *Globe and Mail,* October 21, 2019.

Lee, Rachel C. *The Exquisite Corpse of Asian America: Biopolitics, Biosociality, and Posthuman Ecologies.* New York: New York University Press, 2014.

Lefebvre, Henri. *The Production of Space.* Translated by Donald Nicholson-Smith. Malden, MA: Blackwell, 1984.

Lehrer, Erica. "Thinking through the Canadian Museum for Human Rights." *American Quarterly* 67, no. 4 (2015): 1195–216.

Lehrer, Erica, Cynthia E. Milton, and Monica Eileen Patterson, eds. *Curating Difficult Knowledge: Violent Pasts in Public Places.* New York: Palgrave Macmillan, 2011.

LeMenager, Stephanie. *Living Oil: Petroleum Culture in the American Century.* Oxford: Oxford University Press, 2014.

———. *Manifest and Other Destinies: Territorial Fictions of the Nineteenth-Century United States.* Lincoln: University of Nebraska Press, 2008.

Levin, Dan. "A Museum about Rights, and a Legacy of Uncomfortable Truths." *New York Times,* October 5, 2016.

Lewis, Sophie. *Full Surrogacy Now: Feminism against Family*. London: Verso, 2019.

Lewis, Tiffany. "Marking America's Progress in the West: Grace Raymond Hebard's Domestication of Wyoming, Women's Rights, and Western Expansion." *Cultural Studies ↔Critical Methodologies* 13 (2013): 47–57.

Limerick, Patricia. *The Legacy of Conquest: The Unbroken Past of the American West*. London: Norton, 1987.

———. *Something in the Soil: Legacies and Reckoning in the New West*. London: Norton, 2000.

"Livestock Confinement Operations." Jerome County, Idaho. Accessed December 18, 2021. https://www.jeromecountyid.us/DocumentCenter/View/133/Chapter-13-PDF.

Llewellyn, Jennifer J. "Dealing with the Legacy of Native Residential School Abuse in Canada: Litigation, ADR, and Restorative Justice." *University of Toronto Law Journal* 52, no. 3 (2002): 253–300.

"Local Land Use Planning." *State Government and State Affairs*. Accessed December 18, 2021. https://legislature.idaho.gov/wp-content/uploads/statutes-rules/idstat/Title67/T67CH65.pdf.

Lockwood, Jeff. *Behind the Carbon Curtain: The Energy Industry, Political Censorship, and Free Speech*. Albuquerque: University of New Mexico Press, 2017.

Longman, Nickita, Emily Riddle, Alex Wilson, and Saima Desai. "Letter from the Land Back Editorial Collective." *Briarpatch*, September 10, 2020.

Lorde, Audre. *Sister Outsider: Essays and Speeches*. New York: Crossing, 1984.

Lowe, Lisa. *Immigrant Acts: On Asian American Cultural Politics*. Durham: Duke University Press, 1996.

———. *The Intimacies of Four Continents*. Durham: Duke University Press, 2015.

Luciano, Dana. *Arranging Grief: Sacred Time and the Body in Nineteenth-Century America*. New York: New York University Press, 2017.

Luciano, Dana, and Mel Y. Chen. "Introduction: Has the Queer Ever Been Human?" *GLQ* 21 (2015): 183–207.

Lugones, María "Heterosexualism and the Colonial/Modern Gender System." *Hypatia* 22 (2007): 186–209.

———. "Toward a Decolonial Feminism." *Hypatia* 25, no. 4 (2010): 742–59.

Luis, Keridwen N. *Herlands: Exploring the Women's Land Movement in the United States*. Minneapolis: University of Minnesota Press, 2018.

Lynch, John A. *The Origins of Bioethics: Remembering When Medicine Went Wrong*. East Lansing: Michigan State University Press, 2019.

Lyons, Clare A. *Sex among the Rabble: An Intimate History of Gender and Power in the Age of Revolution, Philadelphia, 1730–1830*. Chapel Hill: University of North Carolina Press, 2012.

Mack, Ashley Noel, and Tiara R. Na'puti. "'Our Bodies Are Not *Terra Nullius*': Building a Decolonial Feminist Resistance to Gendered Violence." *Women's Studies in Communication* 3 (2019): 347–70.

Mackey, Mike. *Inventing History in the American West: The Romance and Myths of Grace Raymond Hebard*. Powell, WY: Western History, 2005.

Maddux, Kristy. *Practicing Citizenship: Women's Rhetoric at the 1893 Chicago World's Fair.* University Park: Pennsylvania State University Press, 2019.

Madison, D. Soyini. *Acts of Activism: Human Rights as Radical Performance.* Cambridge, MA: Harvard University Press, 2010.

———. *Critical Ethnography: Method, Ethics, and Performance.* Thousand Oaks, CA: Sage, 2005.

Mair, Aaron. "Today's Fight for Environmental Justice." March 9, 2016. *Seven on Seven.* Podcast, 40:10. http://sevenscribes.com/s1e2-todays-fight-for-environmental-justice/.

Malatino, Hil. *Trans Care.* Minneapolis: University of Minnesota Press, 2020.

Manson, Gary. "The Witness Blanket at Vancouver Island University." November 10, 2016. YouTube video. https://www.youtube.com/watch?v=-bGokznnqgc.

Marshall, Daniel, Kevin P. Murphy, and Zeb Tortorici. "Queering Archives: Historical Unravelings." *Radical History Review* 120 (Fall 2014): 1–11

Marx, Leo. *The Machine in the Garden: Technology and the Pastoral Ideal in America.* Oxford: Oxford University Press, 1964.

Massey, Doreen. *For Space.* Thousand Oaks, CA: Sage, 2005.

McCammack, Brian. *Landscapes of Hope: Nature and the Great Migration in Chicago.* Cambridge, MA: Harvard University Press, 2017.

McKay, Susan. "Gender Justice and Reconciliation." *Women's Studies International Forum* 23 (2000): 561–70.

McKinnon, Sara Lynn, Robert Asen, Karma R. Chávez, and Robert Glenn Howard, eds. *Text + Field: Innovations in Rhetorical Method.* State College: Pennsylvania State University Press, 2016.

Meger, Amy Lowe. *Minidoka Internment National Monument: Historic Resource Study.* Seattle: National Park Service, U.S. Department of the Interior, 2005.

Michelet, Maren. *Agnes Mathilde Wergeland: Glimpses.* Minneapolis: Folkebladet, 1916.

Middleton, Michael, Aaron Hess, Danielle Endres, and Samantha Senda-Cook, eds. *Participatory Critical Rhetoric: Theoretical and Methodological Foundations for Studying Rhetoric in Situ.* Lanham, MD: Lexington Books, 2015.

Miller, J.R. *Shingwauk's Vision: A History of Native Residential Schools.* Toronto: University of Toronto Press, 1996.

Million, Dian. "Telling Secrets: Sex, Power and Narrative." *Canadian Woman Studies* 20, no. 2 (2000): 92–104.

Milloy, John S. *A National Crime: The Canadian Government and the Residential School System, 1879–1986.* Winnipeg: University of Manitoba Press, 1999.

Mitchell, Silas Weir. *Nurse and Patient, and Camp Cure.* Philadelphia: Lippincott, 1877.

———. *Wear and Tear, or Hints for the Overworked.* Philadelphia: Lippincott, 1871.

Moore, Jason. W. *Capitalism in the Web of Life: Ecology and the Accumulation of Capital.* London: Verso, 2015.

Morgensen, Scott Lauria. "The Biopolitics of Settler Colonialism: Right Here, Right Now." *Settler Colonial Studies* 1 (2011): 52–76.

———. *Spaces between Us: Queer Settler Colonialism and Indigenous Decolonization.* Minneapolis: University of Minnesota Press, 2011.

———. "Theorising Gender, Sexuality, and Settler Colonialism: An Introduction." *Settler Colonial Studies* 2 (2012): 2–22.

Morris, Charles E., III. "Archival Queer." *Rhetoric and Public Affairs* 9 (2006): 145–51.

———. "The Archival Turn in Rhetorical Studies, or The Archive's Rhetorical (Re)turn." *Rhetoric and Public Affairs* 9 (2006): 113–15.

———. "Hard Evidence: The Vexations of Lincoln's Queer Corpus." In *Rhetoric, Materiality, and Politics,* edited by Barbara A. Biesecker and John Louis Lucaites, 185–213. New York: Lang, 2009.

———, ed. *Queering Public Address: Sexualities in American Historical Discourse.* Columbia: University of South Carolina Press, 2007.

Muñoz, José Esteban. *Cruising Utopia: The Then and There of Queer Futurity.* New York: New York University Press, 2009.

———. "Ephemera as Evidence: Introductory Notes to Queer Acts." *Women and Performance: A Journal of Feminist Theory* 8, no. 2 (1996): 5–16.

Murphy, Michelle. "Distributed Reproduction." In *Corpus: An Interdisciplinary Reader on Bodies and Knowledge,* edited by Monica J. Casper and Paisley Currah, 21–38. New York: Palgrave Macmillan, 2011.

Murray, Alice Yang. *Historical Memories of the Japanese American Internment and the Struggle for Redress.* Stanford: Stanford University Press, 2007.

Nakanishi, Don T. "Surviving Democracy's 'Mistake': Japanese Americans and the Enduring Legacy of Executive Order 9066." *Amerasia Journal* 35 (2009): 52–84.

Na'puti, Tiara R. "Archipelagic Rhetoric: Remapping the Marianas and Challenging Militarization from 'A Stirring Place.'" *Communication and Critical/Cultural Studies* 16 (2019): 4–25.

Nash, Linda. *Inescapable Ecologies: A History of Environment, Disease, and Knowledge.* Berkeley: University of California Press, 2006.

Nash, Roderick. *Wilderness and the American Mind.* New Haven: Yale University Press, 2001.

Newman, Carey, and Kirstie Hudson. *Picking Up the Pieces: Residential School Memories and the Making of the Witness Blanket.* Vancouver, BC: Orca Books, 2019.

Newman, Louise Michelle. *White Women's Rights: The Racial Origins of Feminism in the United States.* New York: Oxford University Press, 1999.

Ngai, Mae M. *Impossible Subjects: Illegal Aliens and the Making of Modern America.* Princeton: Princeton University Press, 2004.

Niblett, Michael. "Energy Regimes." In Szeman, Wenzel, and Yaeger, *Fueling Culture,* 136–39.

Nishime, LeiLani, and Kim Hester Williams. "Introduction: Why Racial Ecologies?" In *Racial Ecologies,* edited by LeiLani Nishime and Kim Hester Williams, 3–18. Seattle: University of Washington Press, 2018.

Nixon, Rob. *Slow Violence and the Environmentalism of the Poor.* Cambridge, MA: Harvard University Press, 2011.

North, Irene. "Museum Exhibit Depicts the Life of Empire, a Once Thriving African-American Community in Wyoming." *Scottsbluff Star-Herald,* April 8, 2018.

O'Brien, Jean. *Firsting and Lasting: Writing Indians Out of Existence in New England.* Minneapolis: University of Minnesota Press, 2010.

Okamura, Raymond Y. "The American Concentration Camps: A Cover-Up through Euphemistic Terminology." *Journal of Ethnic Studies* 10 (1982): 95–109.

Ono, Kent A. "Re/Membering Spectators: Meditations on Japanese American Cinema." In *Countervisions: Asian American Film Criticism,* edited by Darrel Hamamoto and Sandra Liu, 129–49. Philadelphia: Temple University Press, 2000.

Oravec, Christine. "John Muir, Yosemite, and the Sublime Response: A Study in the Rhetoric of Preservation." *Quarterly Journal of Speech* 67 (1981): 245–58.

Orland, Barbara. "Turbo-Cows: Producing a Competitive Animal in the Nineteenth and Early Twentieth Centuries." In *Industrializing Organisms: Introducing Evolutionary History,* edited by Susan Schrepfer and Philip Scranton, 167–90. New York: Routledge, 2004.

Packer, Jeremy, and Craig Robertson, eds. *Thinking with James Carey: Essay on Communications, Transportation, History.* New York: Lang, 2006.

Park, Lisa Sun-Hee, and David Naguib Pellow. *The Slums of Aspen: Immigrants vs. the Environment in America's Eden.* New York: New York University Press, 2011.

Parrika, Jussi. *Geology of Media.* Minneapolis: University of Minnesota Press, 2015.

Pascoe, Peggy. *What Comes Naturally: Miscegenation Law and the Making of Race in America.* Oxford: Oxford University Press, 2009.

Pezzullo, Phaedra C. "Environment." *Oxford Research Encyclopedia of Communication.* October 26, 2017. https://doi.org/10.1093/acrefore/9780190228613.013.575.

———. "Introduction: Environmental Communication in China and Beyond." In *Green Communication and China: On Crisis, Care, and Global Futures,* edited by Jingfang Liu and Phaedra C. Pezzullo, xiii–xliv. East Lansing: Michigan State University Press, 2020.

———. "Overture: The Most Complicated Word." *Cultural Studies* 22 (2008): 361–68.

———. "'There Is No Planet B': Questions during a Power Shift." *Communication and Critical/Cultural Studies* 2 (2013): 301–5.

———. *Toxic Tourism: Rhetorics of Pollution, Travel, and Environmental Justice.* Tuscaloosa: University of Alabama Press, 2007.

Pezzullo, Phaedra C., and Robert Cox. *Environmental Communication and the Public Sphere.* 6th ed. Newbury Park, CA: Sage, 2021.

Pezzullo, Phaedra C., and Catalina de Onís. "Rethinking Rhetorical Field Methods on a Precarious Planet." *Communication Monographs* 85 (2017): 103–22.

Pezzullo, Phaedra C., and Kathleen P. Hunt. "Agribusiness Futurism and Food Atmospheres: Reimagining Corn, Pigs, and Transnational Negotiations on Khrushchev's 1959 U.S. Tour." *Quarterly Journal of Speech* 106, no. 4 (2020): 399–426.

Pezzullo, Phaedra C., and Ronald Sandler. "Conclusion: Working Together and Working Apart." In *Environmental Justice and Environmentalism: The Social Justice Challenge to the Environmental Movement,* edited by Ronald Sandler and Phaedra C. Pezzullo, 309–20. Cambridge, MA: MIT Press, 2007.

Phillips, Kendall R. *Framing Public Memory.* Tuscaloosa: University of Alabama Press, 2004.

Podobnik, Bruce. "Toward a Sustainable Energy Regime: A Long-Wave Interpretation of Global Energy Shifts." *Technological Forecasting and Social Change* 62 (1999): 155–57.

Powell, Miles A. *Vanishing America: Species Extinction, Racial Peril, and the Origins of Conservation.* Cambridge, MA: Harvard University Press, 2016.

Predock, Antoine. "American Heritage Center and Art Museum." Antoine Predock Architect. Accessed October 20, 2020. http://www.predock.com/Wyoming/wyo.html.

———. "Canadian Museum for Human Rights." Antoine Predock Architect. Accessed October 27, 2020. http://www.predock.com/CMHR/CMHR.html.

Puar, Jasbir. *The Right to Maim: Debility, Capacity, Disability.* Durham: Duke University Press, 2017.

"Queer Nature." Queer Nature. Accessed August 1, 2020 https://www.queer-nature.org.

Rand, Erin J. *Reclaiming Queer: Activist and Academic Rhetorics of Resistance.* Tuscaloosa: University of Alabama Press, 2014.

Rawson, K.J. "Accessing Transgender//Desiring Queer(er?) Archival Logics." *Archivaria* 68 (2010): 123–40.

———. "The Rhetorical Power of Archival Description: Classifying Images of Gender Transgression." *Rhetoric Society Quarterly* 48 (2018): 327–51.

Razack, Sherene H. *Dying from Improvement: Inquests and Inquiries into Indigenous Deaths in Custody.* Toronto: University of Toronto Press, 2015.

Regan, Paulette. *Unsettling the Settler Within: Indian Residential Schools, Truth Telling, and Reconciliation in Canada.* Vancouver: University of British Columbia Press, 2011.

Rifkin, Mark. "'Geo into Bio and Back Again,' or Tracing the Politics of Place and Sovereignty." *American Quarterly* 71 (2019): 871–79.

———. "Indigenizing Agamben: Rethinking Sovereignty in Light of the 'Peculiar' Status of Native Peoples." *Cultural Critique* 73 (2009): 88–124.

———. *When Did Indians Become Straight: Kinship, the History of Sexuality, and Native Sovereignty.* Oxford: Oxford University Press, 2011.

Rifkin, Mark, Daniel H. Justice, and Bethany Schneider, eds. "Sexuality, Nationality, Indigeneity." Special issue, *GLQ* 16, nos. 1–2 (2010).

Rockwell, Alphonso David. *The Medical and Surgical Uses of Electricity.* New York: Treat, 1903.

Roediger, David R., and Elizabeth D. Esch. *The Production of Difference: Race and the Management of Labor in U.S. History.* Oxford: Oxford University Press, 2012.

Rollo, Toby. "Feral Children: Settler Colonialism, Progress, and the Figure of the Child." *Settler Colonial Studies* 8 (2018): 60–79.

Rosenberg, Gabriel N. *The 4-H Harvest: Sexuality and the State in Rural America.* Philadelphia: University of Pennsylvania Press, 2016.

———. "How Meat Changed Sex: The Law of Interspecies Intimacy after Industrial Reproduction." *GLQ* 23 (2017): 473–507.

———. "Youth as Infrastructure: 4-H and the Intimate State in the 1920s Rural United States." In *Boundaries of the State in U.S. History,* edited by James T. Sparrow, William J. Novak, and Stephen W. Sawyer, 183–208. Chicago: University of Chicago Press, 2015.

Ross, Anne, Katherine Pickering Sherman, Jeffrey G. Snodgrass, Henry D. Delcore, and Richard Sherman. *Indigenous Peoples and the Collaborative Stewardship of Nature: Knowledge Binds and Institutional Conflicts.* Walnut Creek, CA: Left Coast, 2011.

Rowe, Aimee Carrillo, and Eve Tuck. "Settler Colonialism and Cultural Studies: Ongoing Settlement, Cultural Production, and Resistance." *Cultural Studies ↔ Critical Methodologies* 17 (2017) 3–13.

Rubin, Gayle. *Deviations: A Gayle Rubin Reader.* Durham: Duke University Press, 2011.

Ruffin, Kimberly N. *Black on Earth: African American Ecoliterary Traditions.* Athens: University of Georgia Press, 2010.

Ruppel, Kristin T. *Unearthing Indian Land: Living with the Legacies of Allotment.* Tucson: University of Arizona Press, 2008.

Russo, Joey. "Time Gets Strange: Texan Hard Luck Strategies." In Engle and Wong, *Feelings of Structure,* 106–15.

Rydell, Robert W. *All the World's a Fair: Visions of Empire at American International Expositions, 1876–1916.* Chicago: University of Chicago Press, 1984.

Ryerson, Egerton. *Report on Industrial Schools.* Indian Residential School. 1847. https://collections.irshdc.ubc.ca/index.php/Detail/objects/9435.

Rymhs, Deena. *From the Iron House: Imprisonment in First Nations Writing.* Waterloo: Wilfrid Laurier University Press, 2008.

Sandilands, Catriona. "'Queer Life': Ecocriticism after the Fire." In *The Oxford Handbook of Ecocriticism,* edited by Greg Garrard, 305–19. Oxford: Oxford University Press, 2014.

———. "Some 'F' Words for the Environmental Humanities: Feralities, Feminisms, Futurities." In Heise, Christensen, and Niemann, *Routledge Companion,* 443–51.

Sandilands, Catriona, and Bruce Erickson. "Introduction: A Genealogy of Queer Ecologies." In *Queer Ecologies: Sex, Nature, Politics, Desire,* edited by Catriona Sandilands and Bruce Erickson, 1–50. Bloomington: University of Indiana Press, 2010.

"Sanitarium and Hospital Exhibits at the Columbian Exposition." *National Popular Review.* Accessed December 13, 2021. https://babel.hathitrust.org/cgi/pt?id=mdp.39015071513348&view=2up&seq=2.

Scharff, Virginia. "The Independent and Feminine Life of Grace Raymond Hebard: 1861–1936." In Clifford, *Lone Voyagers*, 127–45.

———. *Twenty Thousand Roads: Women, Movement, and the West*. Berkeley: University of California Press, 2003.

Schneider, Bethany. "A Modest Proposal: Laura Ingalls Wilder Ate Zitkala-Ša." *GLQ* 21 (2015): 65–93.

Schneider, Jen, and Jennifer Peeples. "The Energy Covenant: Energy Dominance and the Rhetoric of the Aggrieved." *Frontiers in Communication* 3 (2018): 1–12.

Schneider, Jen, Steve Schwarze, Peter K. Bsumek, and Jennifer Peeples. *Under Pressure: Coal Industry Rhetoric and Neoliberalism*. London: Palgrave Macmillian, 2016.

Schuller, Kyla. *The Biopolitics of Feeling: Race, Sex, and Science in the Nineteenth Century*. Durham: Duke University Press, 2018.

Schuster, David. *Neurasthenic Nation: America's Search for Health, Happiness, and Comfort, 1869–1920*. New Brunswick, NJ: Rutgers University Press, 2011.

———. "Personalizing Illness and Modernity: S. Weir Mitchell, Literary Women, and Neurasthenia, 1870–1914." *Bulletin of the History of Medicine* 79 (2005): 695–722.

Schwartz, Richard W. "Dr. John Harvey Kellogg as a Social Gospel Practitioner." *Journal of the Illinois State Historical Society (1908–1984)* 54 (1964): 5–22.

Schweighofer, Katherine. "A Land of One's Own: Whiteness and Indigeneity on Lesbian Land." *Settler Colonial Studies* 8 (2018): 489–506.

———. "Rethinking the Closet: Queer Life in Rural Geographies." In Gray, Johnson, and Gilley, *Queering the Countryside*, 223–43.

Scott, Joan W. "Gender: A Useful Category of Historical Analysis." *American Historical Review* 91 (1986): 1053–75.

"Secretary Haaland Announces Federal Indian Boarding School Initiative." U.S. Department of the Interior. June 22, 2021. https://www.doi.gov/pressreleases/secretary-haaland-announces-federal-indian-boarding-school-initiative.

Sedgwick, Eve. *Tendencies*. Durham: Duke University Press, 1993.

Seitler, Dana. "Unnatural Selection: Mothers, Eugenic Feminism, and Charlotte Perkins Gilman's Regeneration Narratives." *American Quarterly* 55 (2003): 61–88.

Seymour, Nicole. *Strange Natures: Futurity, Empathy, and the Queer Ecological Imagination*. Urbana: University of Illinois Press, 2013.

Shah, Nyan. "Between 'Oriental Depravity' and 'Natural Degenerates': Spatial Borderlands and the Making of Ordinary Americans." *American Quarterly* 57 (2005): 703–25.

———. *Contagious Divides: Epidemics and Race in San Francisco's Chinatown*. Berkeley: University of California Press, 2001.

———. *Stranger Intimacy: Contesting Race, Sexuality, and the Law in the North American West*. Berkeley: University of California Press, 2011.

Sheller, Mimi. "The New Mobilities Paradigm for a Live Sociology." *Current Sociology Review* 62 (2014): 1–23.

Shome, Raka. "Space Matters: The Power and Practice of Space." *Communication Theory* 13, no. 1 (2003): 39–56.

Simpson, Audra. "Settlement's Secret." *Cultural Anthropology* 26 (2011): 205–17.

———. "Whither Settler Colonialism." *Settler Colonial Studies* 6 (2016): 438–45.

Simpson, Leanne Betasamosake. *As We Have Always Done: Indigenous Freedom through Radical Resistance.* Minneapolis: University of Minnesota Press, 2017.

———. *Dancing on Our Turtle's Back: Stories of Nishnaabeg Re-creation, Resurgence, and a New Emergence.* Winnipeg: Arp Books, 2011.

Singh, Julietta. *No Archive Will Restore You.* Lexington, KY: Punctum Books, 2018.

Slotkin, Richard. *Gunfighter Nation: The Myth of the Frontier in Twentieth-Century America.* Norman: University of Oklahoma Press, 1998.

Smith, Henry Nash. *Virgin Land: The West as Symbol and Myth.* Cambridge, MA: Harvard University Press, 1950.

Smith, Neil. *Uneven Development: Nature, Capital, and the Production of Space.* Athens: University of Georgia Press, 1990.

Snorton, Riley C. *Black on Both Sides: A Racial History of Trans Identity.* Minneapolis: University of Minnesota Press, 2017.

Solly, S.E. "The Principles of Medical Climatology." *Journal of the American Medical Association* 25 (1895): 129–31.

Solnit, Rebecca. *A Field Guide to Getting Lost.* New York: Penguin Books, 2006.

———. *Savage Dreams: A Journey into the Hidden Wars of the American West.* Berkeley: University of California Press, 1994.

Somerville, Siobhan B. *Queering the Color Line: Race and the Invention of Homosexuality in American Modernity.* Durham: Duke University Press, 2000.

Spence, Mark David. *Dispossessing the Wilderness: Indian Removal and the Making of the National Parks.* Oxford: Oxford University Press, 1999.

Spillers, Hortense J. "Mama's Baby, Papa's Maybe: An American Grammar Book." *Diacritics* 17, no. 2 (1987): 64–81.

Steedman, Carolyn. *Dust: The Archive and Cultural History.* New Brunswick: Rutgers University Press, 2001.

Stern, Alexandra. *Eugenic Nations: Faults and Frontiers of Better Breeding in Modern America.* Berkeley: University of California Press, 2016.

Steubner, Stephen. "Raising a Stink: Factory Dairies Catch Idaho's Magic Valley by Surprise." *High Country News*, April 15, 2002.

Stewart, Kathleen. "Atmospheric Attunements." *Environment and Planning D: Society and Space* 29 (2011): 445–53.

Stockton, Kathryn Bond. *The Queer Child, or Growing Up Sideways in the Twentieth Century.* Durham: Duke University Press, 2009.

Stoler, Ann Laura. *Carnal Knowledge and Imperial Power: Race and the Intimate in Colonial Rule.* Berkeley: University of California Press, 2002.

———, ed. *Haunted by Empire: Geographies of Intimacy in North American History.* Durham: Duke University Press, 2006.

————. *Race and the Education of Desire: Foucault's History of Sexuality and the Colonial Order of Things.* Durham: Duke University Press, 1995.

Stuckey, Mary E. "Presidential Secrecy: Keeping Archives Open." *Rhetoric and Public Affairs* 9 (2006): 138–44.

Supp-Montgomerie, Jenna. *When the Medium Was the Mission: The Atlantic Telegraph and the Religious Origins of Network Culture.* New York: New York University Press, 2021.

Sze, Julie. *Environmental Justice in a Moment of Danger.* Berkeley: University of California Press, 2020.

Szeman, Imre. "Conclusion: On Energopolitics." *Anthropological Quarterly* 87 (2014): 453–64.

————. "Conjunctures on World Energy Literature, or What Is a Petroculture?" *Journal of Postcolonial Writing* 53 (2017): 277–88.

————. "Literature and Energy Futures." *PMLA* 126 (2011): 323–25.

Szeman, Imre, and Dominic Boyer, eds. *Energy Humanities: An Anthology.* Baltimore: Johns Hopkins University Press, 2017.

Szeman, Imre, and Jennifer Wenzel. "What Do We Talk about When We Talk about Extractivism?" *Textual Practice* 35 (2021): 505–23.

Szeman, Imre, Jennifer Wenzel, and Patricia Yaeger, eds. *Fueling Culture: 101 Words for Energy and the Environment.* New York: Fordham University Press, 2017.

Takemoto, Tina. "Looking for Jiro Onuma: A Queer Meditation on the Incarceration of Japanese Americans during World War II." *GLQ* 20, no. 3 (2014): 241–75.

Takezawa, Yasuko. *Breaking the Silence: Redress and Japanese American Ethnicity.* Ithaca: Cornell University Press, 1995.

TallBear, Kim. "Making Love and Relations beyond Settler Sex and Family." In *Making Kin Not Population,* edited by Adele E. Clarke and Donna Haraway, 145–64. Chicago: Prickly Paradigm, 2018.

————. *Native American DNA: Tribal Belonging and the False Promise of Genetic Science.* Minneapolis: University of Minnesota Press, 2013.

Taylor, Diana. *The Archive and the Repertoire: Performing Cultural Memory in the Americas.* Durham: Duke University Press, 2003.

Taylor, Sunaura. *Beasts of Burden: Animal and Disability Liberation.* New York: New Press, 2017.

Terry, Jennifer. *An American Obsession: Science, Medicine, and Homosexuality in Modern Society.* Chicago: University of Chicago, 1999.

Teves, Stephanie Nohelani, Andrea Smith, and Michelle H. Raheja, eds. *Native Studies Keywords.* Tucson: University of Arizona Press, 2015.

"'They Need to Know': Graphic Content and the Canadian Museum for Human Rights." *CBC News,* October 20, 2016.

Threlfall, John. "Indigenous Oral Ceremony Finalizes Historic Witness Blanket Agreement." University of Victoria Fine Arts. October 17, 2019. https://finearts.uvic.ca/research/blog/2019/10/17/indigenous-oral-ceremony-finalizes-historic-witness-blanket-agreement/.

Todd, Zoe. "From Classroom to River's Edge: Tending to Reciprocal Duties beyond the Academy." *Aboriginal Policy Studies* 6 (2016): 90–97.

Tomiak, Julie, Tyler McCreary, David Hugill, Robert Henry, and Heather Dorries. "Introduction: Settler City Limits." In Dorries et al., *Settler City Limits,* 1–24.

Tongson, Karen. *Relocations: Queer Suburban Imaginaries.* New York: New York University Press, 2011.

Towns, Armond R. "Geographies of Pain: #SayHerName and the Fear of Black Women's Mobility." *Women's Studies in Communication* 39 (2016): 122–26.

———. "Toward a Black Media Philosophy." *Cultural Studies* 34 (2020): 851–73.

Trachtenberg, Alan. *The Incorporation of America: Culture and Society in the Gilded Age.* New York: Hill and Wang, 1982.

"A Tribe Called Red Cancels Performance at Human Rights Museum." *CBC News,* September 18, 2014.

Troian, Marth. "Indian Residential Schools: 5,300 Alleged Abusers Located by Ottawa." *CBC News,* February 2, 2016.

Tuck, Eve. "Suspending Damage: A Letter to Communities." *Harvard Educational Review* 79 (2009): 409–27.

Tuck, Eve, and K. Wayne Yang. "Decolonization Is Not a Metaphor." *Decolonization: Indigeneity, Education and Society* 1 (2012): 1–40.

Turner, Frederick Jackson. *The Frontier in American History.* New York: Holt, 1921.

Tyburczy, Jennifer. *Sex Museums: The Politics of Performance and Display.* Chicago: University of Chicago Press, 2015.

Uhrbrock, Richard Stephen. "June Etta Downey." *Journal of General Psychology* 9 (1933): 361–84.

Ujiiye, Tiffany. "Potential Buyout to Save Minidoka Camp from Farm Waste and Stench." *Pacific Citizen* 30. Accessed July 5, 2021. https://www.pacific-citizen.org/potential-buyout-to-save-minidoka-camp-from-farm-waste-and-stench/.

Urry, John. "Inhabiting the Car." In *Against Automobility,* edited by Steffan Böhm, Campbell Jones, Chris Land, and Matthew Paterson, 17–31. Oxford: Blackwell, 2006.

———. "The 'System' of Automobility." In *Automobilities,* edited by Mike Featherstone, Nigel Thrift, and John Urry, 25–50. London: Sage, 2005.

VanHaitsma, Pamela. "Between Archival Absence and Informational Abundance: Reconstructing Sallie Holley's Abolitionist Rhetoric through Digital Surrogates and Metadata." *Quarterly Journal of Speech* 106 (2020): 24–47.

———. *Queering Romantic Engagement in the Postal Age: A Rhetorical Education.* Columbia: University of South Carolina Press, 2019.

Van Nuys, Frank. *Americanizing the West: Race, Immigrants, and Citizenship, 1890–1903.* Lawrence: University of Kansas Press, 2002.

Vats, Anjali. *The Color of Creatorship: Intellectual Property, Race, and the Making of Americans.* Stanford: Stanford University Press, 2020.

Voyles, Traci Brynne. *Wastelanding: Legacies of Uranium Mining in Navajo Country.* Minneapolis: University of Minnesota Press, 2015.

Wanzer-Serrano, Darrel. *The New Young Lords and the Struggle for Liberation.* Philadelphia: Temple University Press, 2015.

Watts, Sarah. *Rough Rider in the White House: Theodore Roosevelt and the Politics of Desire.* Chicago: University of Chicago Press, 2003.

Weaver, Scott. "Cow Country: The Rise of CAFO in Idaho." *Boise Weekly,* September 1, 2010.

Wells, Christopher W. *Car Country: An Environmental History.* Seattle: University of Washington Press, 2013.

Wenzel, Jennifer. "How to Read for Oil." *Resilience: A Journal of the Environmental Humanities* 1, no. 3 (2014): 156–61.

West, Isaac. *Transforming Citizenships: Transgender Articulations of the Law.* New York: New York University Press, 2014.

Weston, Kath. "Get Thee to a Big City: Sexual Imaginary and the Great Gay Migration." *GLQ* 2 (1995): 253–77.

"What We Do." Minidoka Pilgrimage. Accessed 5 July 2021. https://www.minidokapilgrimage.org/what-we-do.

White, James Boyd. "Law as Rhetoric, Rhetoric as Law: The Arts of Cultural and Communal Life." *University of Chicago Law Review* 52 (1985): 684–702.

White, Richard. *Railroaded: The Transcontinentals and the Making of Modern America.* New York: Norton, 2011.

Whyte, Kyle Powys. "Our Ancestor's Dystopia Now: Indigenous Conservation and the Anthropocene." In Heise, Christensen, and Niemann, *Routledge Companion,* 206–15.

Will, Barbara. "Nervous Origins of the American Western." *American Literature* 70 (1998): 293–316.

Williams, Raymond. *Border Country.* Cardigan: Parthian Books, 1960.

———. *The Country and the City.* Oxford: Oxford University Press, 1973.

———. *Keywords: A Vocabulary of Culture and Society.* New York: Oxford University Press, 1983.

———. *The Long Revolution.* Cardigan: Parthian Books, 2011.

———. *Marxism and Literature.* Oxford: Oxford University Press, 1977.

———. *Politics and Letters: Interviews with the New Left Review.* London: Verso, 2015.

Wilson, Ara. "The Infrastructure of Intimacy." *Signs: Journal of Women in Culture and Society* 41 (Winter 2016): 247–80.

———. "Intimacy: A Useful Category of Transnational Analysis." In *The Global and the Intimate: Feminism in Our Time,* edited by Geraldine Pratt and Victoria Rosner, 31–56. New York: Columbia University Press, 2012.

Wilson, Brian C. *Dr. John Harvey Kellogg and the Religion of Biologic Living.* Bloomington: Indiana University Press, 2014.

Wilson, Sheena, Adam Carlson, and Imre Szeman, eds. *Petrocultures: Oil, Politics, Culture.* Montreal: McGill-Queen's University Press, 2017.

Wolfe, Patrick. "Settler Colonialism and the Elimination of the Native." *Journal of Genocide Research* 8 (2006): 387–409.

Woolford, Andrew. *The Benevolent Experiment: Indigenous Boarding Schools, Genocide, and Redress in Canada and the United States.* Lincoln: University of Nebraska Press, 2015.

Woolford, Andrew, Jeff Benvenuto, and Alexander Laban Hinton, eds. *Colonial*

Genocide in Indigenous North America. Durham: Duke University Press, 2014.

Worster, Donald. *Under Western Skies: Nature and History in the American West.* Oxford: Oxford University Press, 1992.

"Wyoming State Profile and Energy Estimates." U.S. Energy Information Administration. Accessed July 3, 2012. https://www.eia.gov/state/?sid=WY#tabs-5.

Yep, Gus A. "Toward Thick(er) Intersectionalities: Theorizing, Researching, and Activating the Complexities of Communication and Identities." In *Globalizing Intercultural Communication: A Reader*, ed. Kathryn Sorrells and Sachi Sekimoto, 85–102. Thousand Oaks, CA: Sage, 2016.

Index

Founded in 1893,
UNIVERSITY OF CALIFORNIA PRESS
publishes bold, progressive books and journals
on topics in the arts, humanities, social sciences,
and natural sciences—with a focus on social
justice issues—that inspire thought and action
among readers worldwide.

The UC PRESS FOUNDATION
raises funds to uphold the press's vital role
as an independent, nonprofit publisher, and
receives philanthropic support from a wide
range of individuals and institutions—and from
committed readers like you. To learn more, visit
ucpress.edu/supportus.

www.ingramcontent.com/pod-product-compliance
Lightning Source LLC
Chambersburg PA
CBHW020512270326
41926CB00008B/840